Identifying Consumption

Identifying Consumption

Subjects and Objects in Consumer Society

Robert G. Dunn

TEMPLE UNIVERSITY PRESS
Philadelphia

Temple University Press
1601 North Broad Street
Philadelphia PA 19122
www.temple.edu/tempress

⊛ The paper used in this publication meets the requirements of the
American National Standard for Information Sciences—Permanence of
Paper for Printed Library Materials, ANSI Z39.48-1992

Library of Congress Cataloging-in-Publication Data
Dunn, Robert G., 1940–
    Identifying consumption : subjects and objects in consumer society /
Robert G. Dunn.
        p.   cm.
    Includes bibliographical references and index.
    ISBN-13: 978-1-59213-869-2 (cloth : alk. paper)
    ISBN-13: 978-1-59213-870-8 (pbk. : alk. paper)
    ISBN-10: 1-59213-869-1 (cloth : alk. paper)
    ISBN-10: 1-59213-870-5 (pbk. : alk. paper)   1. Consumption
(Economics)—Social aspects.   2. Identity (Psychology)   I. Title.
    HB801.D86 2008
    306.3—dc22   2007050271

2   4   6   8   9   7   5   3   1

In Memory of Peter Lyman
(1940–2007)
Friend, mentor, collector

Contents

Acknowledgements

Book authors are always indebted to an array of influences, privileges, experiences, and people. Confining myself to only the latter, I wish to express my debts to the following people. For their support, guidance, friendship, and helpful criticisms, I thank Fred Block, Jon Cruz, Elliott Currie, and Jim Stockinger, all of whom read parts or all of the manuscript. Their thoughtful and challenging comments broadened and sharpened my work. Conversations over the years with Maxine Craig, Gary Cross, Karla Hackstaff, Pierrette Hondagneu-Sotelo, Phyllis Larimore, Ron Lembo, Paul Lichterman, Paul Lopes, Mike Messner, and Ken Tucker have made a difference in how I've thought about the topic of consumption and identity. On a more personal note, my friendships with Tom Caruso, Peter Lyman, Rupert Smith, and Barrie Thorne have been especially important in sustaining my energies. Each contributed in special and perhaps unintended ways to my understanding of the objects, meanings, and tribulations of consumption, in particular that intriguing variety known as collecting. Finally, my thanks to the anonymous reviewers who made this book possible and especially to my always supportive and encouraging editor, Micah Kleit.

Introduction

What is "Consumption"?

Broadly understood, "consumption" defies simple definition, encompassing a vast range of human practices and mental and feeling states (shopping, buying, acquiring, using, possessing, displaying, maintaining, collecting, wasting, desiring, daydreaming, fantasizing), all of which involve complex relations and attachments to an infinite variety of objects and experiences. Material expansion and the proliferation of new forms of consumption have rendered mainstream economic ideas about consumption obsolete. Images and information are now consumed in greater quantities than goods and services, a result of tremendous growth in those sectors of the culture industry specializing in signifying processes designed to entertain and sell. This new category includes the packaged experiences of mass media, amusement parks, shopping malls, tourism, and other forms of commodified entertainment and distraction (Gottdeiner 2000; Rifkin 2000). Of special importance more recently is the burgeoning field of information technology, which is transforming older forms of media and amusement.

A subject matter of this scope lacks disciplinary boundaries and analytic center. In the past, mainstream economics, which viewed the consumer as a rational decision-maker creating "aggregate demand," held a monopoly on consumption studies. However, other social sciences entering the field have introduced new kinds of studies and discourses dealing with the noneconomic dimensions and "nonrational" factors involved in consumption practices. Despite long-standing alliances between psychology and economics in the areas of advertising, marketing, and retailing, there have also been psychological and psychoanalytic *critiques* of consumption, beginning most notably with the Frankfurt School of critical theory. Additionally, historians and anthropologists have illuminated the broader social and cultural origins of modern consumption.

Ironically, the discipline of sociology has been a latecomer to the field. And oddly enough, sociologists in the United States—the apex of modern consumerism—have lagged far behind consumption scholars in other countries, most notably the United Kingdom, a genuine paradox given the unprecedented material prosperity among the rich and affluent in the United States in the last twenty years or so and the mass media's unabashed celebration of leisured wealth.

Thoroughly interwoven with the fabric of everyday life in developed societies, and given a dramatic expansion in cultural production, consumption is now an interdisciplinary topic focused on culture. Incorporating perspectives and interpretive methods from anthropology, history, sociology, and the humanities, the burgeoning field of cultural studies has thoroughly reoriented the study of consumption. The widespread popularity of cultural studies is in large measure a consequence of the societal penetration of new cultural forms and apparatuses designed specifically for selling commodities. Growing numbers of social theorists and sociologists, especially those of a "postmodern" persuasion, have recognized in this transition newly forged links between culture and consumption. While the "cultural turn" in sociology was pioneered primarily by those promoting a productivist paradigm (the "sociology of culture"), a discernible shift toward a "cultural sociology" of a more interpretive and ethnographic persuasion has opened this field to the study of consumption practices.

Reading and Writing Consumption

Despite dramatic growth in the field of cultural studies, interdisciplinary work still too often is slow to develop. This is certainly true of consumption studies, too many of which pay small heed to the interconnections among economic, cultural, social, psychological, and social psychological processes constituting consumption practices. Moreover, theoretical imbalance weakens those varieties of cultural studies (chiefly in the United States) shaped by critiques of orthodox Marxism and the antieconomistic tendencies characterizing the discourses of numerous cultural and identity movements of the post-sixties era. Rejection of the crude Marxist model of economic base and cultural superstructure was a significant theoretical gain often purchased at the price of an equally flawed cultural determinism leaving little or no room for economic influences. In the rush to uncover the signifying processes of capitalism, linkages between production and consumption have often been obscured, discouraging more nuanced formulations of the persistent connections between economic and cultural forces. With the turn to interpretive methods, semiotic analysis and antitotalizing ethnographic approaches have enjoyed growing popularity. But despite their impressive contributions, these approaches have minimized or ignored the systemic economic foundations of cultural and social practices.

Consumption, like all social practices, is shaped and conditioned by a multitude of material and nonmaterial factors. But compared to other social practices, consumption now forms the most powerful link between the economic and sociocultural realms. Consumption links exchange value and the satisfaction of material need and want to the production of meaning, identity, and a sense of place and social membership.

The roots and nature of distinctly modern forms of consumption, as well as the evolution of consumer culture, are inseparable from the rise of a mature system of commodity exchange ushered in by industrial capitalism. Indeed, the theory of the commodity form, which posits the elevation of exchange over use value, laid much of the groundwork for the very idea of modernity as a new social and cultural formation based on an expanded and rationalized marketplace. These developments always presupposed an ethos of individualism linked to a cultural framework of personal achievement and recognition through the acquisition, display, and use of worldly possessions. Modern Western notions of the formation of an individual/social self therefore have always been strongly bound to a set of beliefs surrounding the satisfaction of economic need and ambition as well as personal desire. In this sense, modernity itself can be read as the systematic commodification of need and want, a highly rationalized and organized reduction of the full range of satisfactions to the exchange and use of commodities.

At the same time, Western modernity has always been met by countermovements attempting to alleviate or resist the dominant tendencies of a commodifying and rationalizing society. The rise of romanticism, workers' revolts, and the emergence of various utopian movements opposed to modern industrial capitalism are well-known examples of a large array of efforts to confront the worst ills of nineteenth-century modernity with alternative visions and ways of life. With the shift of emphasis in the twentieth century from production to consumption, consumer movements and an assortment of cultural avant-gardes have arisen as countertendencies to the increasing force of the corporation and oppressive bureaucratic institutions. The modern problems of alienation, dehumanization, and inequality have thus generated a continuing succession of responses aimed at restoring dignity, power, and a sense of meaning and identity to those most frustrated and harmed by the ascendancy of the modern economy.

Nonetheless, the wholesale inscription of subjectivity in the modern commodity is the source of a fundamental transformation in identity formation and the structure of the self. The culture of commodities and its modes of consumer involvement shape modern subjects' search for meaning, social membership, and self-definition. By examining the subjective properties of commodities, we can begin to grasp the underlying connections between a wealth-accumulating economy and the cultural positions and understandings of its social subjects.

Such a conceptualization, however, needs to maintain the analytical distinction between the exchange and use values of commodities. Whereas the former is the basis of the commodity form, the latter represents an appropriation of useful objects by social subjects acting as consumers. Consumption, therefore, needs to be considered as a complex, multivalent phenomenon, a manifestation of economic, social, cultural, historical, and psychological processes and effects. In this sense, consumption practices occupy a tension between commercially based commodification and subjectively based satisfactions and meanings.

Keeping these considerations in mind, the present study addresses the following questions: If consumption is now the major locus of cultural production—of meaning creation—how does this take place and with what effects? How do we theorize consumers as social subjects seeking meaning, pleasure, identity, and place? To what extent are the social and cultural practices underlying the formation of self and identity dependent on consumption as opposed to other factors, and on the commodity form as opposed to other kinds of relationships with objects? These questions will be addressed in a mode that departs from recent academic work. While striving to avoid reductionisms and determinisms, my approach explores consumption generically rather than interpretatively or ethnographically. In this theoretical mode, the particular, local, and subcultural are sacrificed for a *structural* and *processual* framework that views consumption as a "complex unity" but that nonetheless is understandable in terms of lived experience. This analysis is multidimensional in the sense that it takes into account (1) the underlying ("objective") structural conditions facilitating and constraining consumption practices, and (2) the desires, practicality, and creativity shaping the ("subjective") actions and meanings of social subjects in their positions as consumers. In other words, consumers will be read as social and individual subjects who are (1) agents acting out of largely unconscious forces shaped by the productive and reproductive needs of capitalism, and (2) as actors consciously seeking to satisfy needs and desires in meaningful ways.

Consumer Culture

An inevitable consequence of the ever-rising consumption requirements of a developing capitalist economy, consumer culture represents an unprecedented interpenetration of economic and cultural forces, an intertwining of the logic of growing markets with the new cultural logics of advanced communications, information technologies, and entertainment industries. Consumer culture is part of the modern takeoff of commodification and as such, presupposes and further develops a social/cultural framework of individualism and an ethos of democratized pleasure and self-fulfillment, all in a market setting. Consumption in advanced capitalist society thus has a dual nature in which the economic and cultural are both internally specialized but simultaneously fused.

Consumption constitutes the main link in the circuit of capital flow and accumulation (purchases/sales as the moment of profit realization) that is the source of profit. To this end, consumption has been increasingly rationalized in a Weberian sense (Weber 1958a, 1958b). But consumption also holds complex meanings for social subjects in terms both of the signifying codes and symbolisms governing the social exchange of commodities and the satisfactions and pleasures that consumption provides the self. In other words, commodity exchange is shaped and regulated both by (1) the systemic requirements of capitalist production, and (2) the search for status, power, pleasure, fulfillment, achievement, and other goals that consumption represents subjectively to consumers. The pursuit of these goals is, in turn, structured by the social relations of class, gender, race, ethnicity, sexuality, and other socially and culturally marked divisions and differences within the population. Mapping the subjectivity of consumption thus depends upon an economic *and* cultural contextualization of consumption practices.

The triumph of consumer culture means that, while every sale and purchase is at bottom an economic event, the object of consumption today is increasingly culture itself. The views of the controversial French theorist Jean Baudrillard (1981, 1988, 1998) serve as a point of departure for the now widely accepted notion that in technologically advanced and highly mediated cultural systems, the object of consumption is not so much tangible products as coded cultural meanings. This claim is true in a double sense frequently overlooked in discussions of Baudrillard. Beginning with the proposition that commodities acquire the status of signs, Baudrillard argued that the physical characteristics of commodities are less important than their social and cultural significance within a coded universe of objects. The circulation of goods and services gives rise to a semiotic system rooted in the commodity's inherent capacity to signify. In this view, acts of consumption have less to do with the satisfaction of need and want than with the construction of meaning within the social and cultural worlds in and through which commodities circulate and exchange with each other semiotically. But the consuming of culture is to be understood in yet another sense. Television shows, commercial film, videos, advertising in all its guises, theme and amusement parks, packaged tours, shopping malls, fast-food outlets, professional sporting events—all are examples of the consumption of meanings and pleasures packaged and sold as *discrete experiences and events*. Within this sphere, forms of amusement, entertainment, and even art are commodified and marketized. The first level of interpenetration represents a culturalization of the commodity, whereby goods and services are inscribed in calculated ways with significance and a set of rules. At the second level, commodity logic enters the realm of representation itself. Once commodified, culture acquires a new materiality in the form of (primarily) visual imagery that constitutes a realm of exchange *sui generis*.

The origins of the idea of a consumer culture can be traced to the tradition of critique prefigured in Marx's early comments on commodity fetishism. The view that culture was a system of power and domination embodied in the commodity form was pioneered by the Frankfurt School and later taken up by the Birmingham School of British cultural studies, in whose hands the argument for domination was tempered by the notion of "resistance." Eventually the discourse of the commodity form faded from view, only to be replaced by linguistic notions of culture as a system of constraint and control, a familiar theme in a variety of semiotic and structuralist scholarship. Claims about the vulnerability of cultural codes were soon introduced by poststructuralist theories, which emphasized the instabilities of language and meaning. The common thread in these theories was a linking of culture to power and a reading of the subject as both absorbed by and resisting systems of ideology, signs, and discourse.

From another angle, critical conceptions of consumer culture have drawn on suggestive comparisons between twentieth-century consumerism and the political economy of Marx in the nineteenth. Here, the modern consumer is likened to the factory worker lamented in Marx's classic texts on capitalism. While it is a mistake to think that Marx never addressed consumption, his economic writings, in fact, dwelt almost entirely on transformations in the sphere of production. While Marx saw labor ideally as the vehicle of expressive self-development and fulfillment, he found in the reality of the capitalist workplace a condition of alienation. Estranged from themselves and their own activity, individual producers confronted the products of their labor as alien things. Commodities represented the dispossession of the worker not only with regard to ownership and control, but also in terms of meaningful and satisfying work. Similarly, critics of consumption have made claims about the alienating and "falsifying" features of *consumerism*, which they see as a manipulation of the needs and wants of the consumer for the sake of profit. In this account, consumerism leads to a state of perpetual dissatisfaction while simultaneously bolstering class inequality and oppression. Further, just as the relations of production dehumanize workers, rendering them powerless before machine and product, the relations of consumption separate consumers in a fragmented, impersonal, and artificial landscape of materialistic excess. In both cases, the individual confronts a reification, a "thing-like" existence emanating from an impersonal system of commodity exchange.

Consumerism

While consumption as a social practice has always rested on cultural foundations, consumer culture is a uniquely modern (some would say postmodern) formation with its own distinctive characteristics. What is perhaps most momentous about consumer culture, however, is that its *raison d'être* extends far beyond a calculated and managed satisfaction of individual needs and wants. Consumer culture has been a breeding ground for the notion that we should embrace the pleasures of *consumption-for-its-own-sake*. Thus, the essence of consumer*ism* is the principle that consumption is an end-in-itself, its own justification. Deeply rooted in the profit motive, consumerism is now a widely shared ideology and worldview capable of creating strong attachments to consumption as a way of life, based on a belief in the enduring power of material possessions and commercial distractions to bring happiness and personal fulfillment. Through consumerism, the experience of self and other is increasingly framed by the idea that life's meaning is reducible to the purchase, ownership, and use of commodities and what these commodities signify about the person.

At the same time, though consumer culture is infused with consumerism, it is important to draw a distinction between the two. Consumer culture consists of a system of meanings, representations, and practices that organize consumption as a way of life. Consumerism, in contrast, is an ideology that seductively binds people to this system. By converting consumption from a means to an end, consumerism turns the mere *acquisition* of commodities into a basis of identity and selfhood. At its extreme, consumerism reduces consumption to a therapeutic program of compensation for life's ills, even a road to personal salvation. Consumerism thus deforms consumer culture, a system that, for all its faults, contains real possibilities for the satisfaction of human need and desire. Thus, given the distortions of consumerism, it is important to imagine a consumer culture that is uncorrupted by consumerist beliefs, attitudes, and drives. Such an imagining is a persistent presence throughout this book and is explicitly addressed in the Conclusion.

It nonetheless needs to be acknowledged that, at least since the decade of the seventies, consumerism has been in the ascendance, not only in the United States but throughout much of the world. Both driven by and driving "globalization," consumerism has spread rapidly from the United States to Europe and now to other regions of the globe undergoing rapid economic growth and westernization, most notably the countries of east and south Asia. Not only has global competition intensified consumerist policies and practices domestically in the United States, but consumerism is showing its face in aspiring economies everywhere. Domestically and globally, the push for greater economic affluence is supported by frequent appeals to the notion of "consumer sovereignty," an ideological slogan announcing a shift to a worldwide consumerist agenda. While the notion of "sovereignty" only *promises* power to consumers as it provides a smokescreen for corporate control, the part of this global ideology that is real is apparent in the growing internationalization of the consumer marketplace. Consumer products and styles cross borders with astonishing ease, increasingly in the form of eclectic amalgams of cultural traditions from all over the globe. Consumer goods are rapidly acquiring an international look, signifying the spread of consumption as a way of life even before there is a material basis for it in many regions of the developing world.

A theoretical study of consumption of the type I propose may seem far afield from these global developments and only indirectly related to fundamental questions of material existence and survival in societies outside the economically prosperous "first world." Yet casual observation of the growing modernity and Western-style commercialism of other countries points to the increasing dominance and universality of consumer culture and the potential seductions of consumerism among widely varying populations. Analyzing the cultural and ideological workings of consumption in advanced Western societies thus provides a template for grappling with the social, cultural, and psychological consequences of economic development on a global scale. Questions of identity are of utmost importance in this regard. The rise of a consumer culture in the twentieth-century West from the beginning depended upon the formation of identities organized around the attractions and social meanings of mass-produced commodities and a belief in goods possession as the bedrock of selfhood and status. The mobilization of desire around buying habits and material possessions was implicitly geared to the production of a consumer identity on a broad scale.

Yet the fruits of the consumer way of life have never been evenly distributed. In this respect, consumerism displays the familiar traits of all ideologies. It promises much and delivers little, it claims to represent the general interest while serving a set of particular interests, it strives to hide discrepancies between the ideal and the real, and it functions as a sometimes powerfully cohesive social force that obscures glaring inequalities. The gap between the rise of consumer identities and the ability of most people to successfully pursue a consumer way of life is an underlying contradiction of advanced capitalist societies and a major source of their chronic tensions. However, this gap also has implications for the future of developing countries as they rapidly adopt the consumerist agenda.

At the same time, the production of consumer identities has always been a flawed process. Much has yet to be learned about the degree to and ways in which people living in Western societies actually identify themselves through their consumption practices or with the idealizations and promises of consumerism. On the one hand, modern identity and selfhood are predicated on achievements of the consumer; on the other hand, it remains unclear the actual extent to which consumerism determines, shapes, or conditions personal and social identity and how this varies with class differences.

Hence, while the power of consumerism seems to grow unabated, there are persistent discrepancies between its claims and the everyday practices and conditions of consumer society. An analysis of the relationship between consumption and identity needs to consider the effects of social inequality in the impact of consumer culture on social relations and identity formation. Beyond this, the challenge in theorizing consumer identity is to determine the actual degrees and kinds of involvement of social subjects in consumption as a way of life, as well as to sort through the complexities and ambiguities of identity itself.

The Legacy of Critique

The common deficiency in critiques of consumerism stems from the theoretical conundrum plaguing social theory in general, if not all the social sciences: how to reconcile "actor" and "structure," "subject" and "object"? Despite their many strengths, classical theories of consumption have developed a critical understanding of consumer culture at the expense of an adequate theory of social and individual subjectivity. In the Marxist tradition, economic determinism and manipulation theory, which in their purer readings see the consumer respectively as slave and puppet, beg complicated questions about the nature of human need and desire; its real, imagined, or potential satisfaction under different historically specific conditions; and more generally, the consumer's search for meaning and place. In another vein, the status-seeking tradition, originating with Thorstein Veblen's classic *The Theory of the Leisure Class* (1934) and continuing through popular writers such as John Kenneth Galbraith (1958) and Vance Packard (1957), has narrowly read modern consumerism as little more than the machinations of a self-perpetuating game of status competition among members of different classes and their assorted strata. Yet another tradition, associated with authors such as Christopher Lasch (1979), Daniel Bell (1978), and others, sees in consumerism a major source of self-seeking hedonism breeding narcissism, social isolation, anomie, and an erosion of the work ethic. Finally, the tradition of cultural studies, while known for its serious engagement with the popular consciousness of consumers and various forms of "resistance" to domination, has tended to limit itself to textual and social readings of consumption practices at the sacrifice of fully comprehending the subjectivity of consumption and its locus in the self. Their enduring contributions notwithstanding, these critical perspectives overgeneralize their conclusions while ignoring important questions about the relationship between commodities and subjects. Not only are these theories overly pessimistic, but also by concentrating on the systemic roots of consumption and consumerism in capitalist society they fail to provide a balanced appreciation of the place of consumption in the search for self and identity.

The Problem of Subjectivity

It seems odd that, while a terminology of subjectivity is indispensable to discourses about consumption (consider "need," "want," "desire," "satisfaction," "pleasure"), these concepts seldom if ever get adequately defined or developed. We can begin by saying that needs are minimum shared requirements for survival and well-being, whether biological, material, social, cultural, or psychological. In contrast, wants are more subjective and personal in nature, implying choice. Desire is a more elusive but richer concept associated with appetite, drive, longing, yearning, passion, or other physical, mental, or emotional feeling-states.

While it is important to give these terms a formal definition, the bigger challenge is to delineate the states or conditions to which they refer. One of the key characteristics of high-consumption society is its attempt to *conflate* need, want, and desire, all of which tend to merge in a whole complex of subjective feelings and meanings surrounding the commodity. Related to this is the intriguing problem of insatiability. Given the nature of desire, manipulative advertising strategies, and the incessant novelty of a rapid turnover economy, consumer culture conspires to perpetuate a sense of restlessness and lack. The sources and ramifications of this state—what I call "chronic marginal dissatisfaction"—is the key to theorizing the nature of the system of consumption in our time.

In my view, the problem of subjectivity lies at the center of numerous unresolved controversies about consumer society. One such controversy concerns the fate of social relations. On one side are claims (from "modern" and "postmodern" thinkers alike) about consumption destroying social relationships, accompanied by images of fragmented selves and identities in a world rendered impersonal, rootless, privatized, rapidly changing, and overly differentiated by an ever-expanding marketplace (or "cash nexus"). On the other side are arguments claiming that consumption brings people together in new modes of association in which family and friends spend time together in the enjoyments of shopping and entertainment. To clarify this kind of debate, it is necessary to closely examine the subjective and social dimensions of the consumer experience.

Finally, how are we to think about the self in the face of critiques of consumerism? Given the implications of self-negation or distortion in the writings of the Frankfurt School, is there any room in theories of consumption and consumerism for notions of genuine self-realization? More generally, how are we to think about the relationships among self, other, and the world of objects? Exploring the realm of subjectivity provides an opening for these questions and a window onto the possibility of alternatives to the prevailing system.

Social Subjects, Consumption, and Identity Formation

To examine the relationship between consumption and identity, one must locate consumption practices in the subjective spaces between the following: (1) the economic and signifying apparatuses of consumer culture (production, advertising, marketing, public relations, entertainment), which constitute consumers as *agents* of a profit-driven system and massive culture industry (the commodity form); and (2) a quest for pleasure, self-definition, fulfillment, social acceptance, place, and a sense of belonging, all of which constitute consumers as *actors* in a world of goods (the object world). In developed societies, the latter are increasingly unrealizable except within a context of commodity exchange. Market-based individualism and bureaucracy assign these functions to a commercialized realm of "leisure pursuits." At the same time, subjects find ways to appropriate commodities as objects of satisfaction and meaning both within the structure of the commodity form and often outside its coded definitions and rules.

To situate consumption in this fashion, it is necessary to consider identity formation from the standpoint of (1) the social dynamics of consumption, and (2) consumption as a set of cultural processes. From both perspectives, identity inheres in consumption practices as a function of (1) system-based codes imposed on agents, and (2) subjects' ability as actors to appropriate a range of objects for purposes of self-definition and expression within *and* outside the codes. Identity formation through consumption is often linked to traditional or conventional social roles and loyalties (kinship, occupation, ethnicity) but can extend beyond these to the creation of new kinds of identities circumscribed entirely by the appropriation of commodities. In both cases, identity formation occurs at the conjunctures of status, lifestyle, and self-processes—the major nodes around which consumption produces its meanings and effects.

Conventional sociological studies focus largely on the structural or positional features of consumption, the conceptual underpinnings of which are class and status. Consumer subjectivity has always been closely articulated with the social and cultural dimensions of class, which correspond approximately to the concepts of status and lifestyle. However, class has lost much of its significance, and with the growth of consumer culture, the sociology of consumption has turned to questions of status and more importantly, lifestyle. Although it can also describe a living pattern outside the orbit of consumer culture, for most researchers, lifestyle refers to the expressive aspects of consumer spending, the practices that identify and differentiate consumers within the marketplace of goods, services, and entertainments. Analysis of the connections between consumption and identity, therefore, revolves primarily around the meaning of lifestyle phenomena and their impact on definitions of self and other.

Modern/Postmodern

Although consumer culture has been theorized as both cause and symptom of a postmodern condition, consumption and consumerism are quintessentially modern themes. But it is important to recognize that these assume different shapes in the critiques of modernity and postmodernity, respectively.

In the context of modernity, critiques of consumption have struck recurring themes of privatization and social withdrawal. The main dynamic of modernity, the argument goes, has been a mutually reinforcing relationship between market growth and privatization within evolving structures of consumption. Thus, self projects and identity formation have been intertwined with a *private* appropriation of cultural goods, with implications of withdrawal from the structures of public and community life in favor of individualized, interpersonal, and often isolated modes of consumption. At the same time, claims abound that modernity has evolved new social forms of consumption centered on lifestyle practices. But modernity also differentiates and sorts people in unpredictable ways. Moreover, in the realm of technology (today, television, video, wireless, the Internet) modernity, it is argued, leads to an erosion of Enlightenment values of autonomy and reason insofar as it creates dependencies on ever more complicated and mysterious gadgets, even though these technologies in many respects reinforce and extend democratic modes of participation. In these and other ways, modernity thus displays its own dialectics (Adorno and Horkheimer 1972), providing a basis for the distinction between "modern" and "postmodern."

From the standpoint of the subject, the commodity form leads to an increasing fragmentation of experience and meaning. Inherent in the logic of the modern marketplace, this fragmentation occurs concomitantly with an intensification of difference, also promoted by the market. While many postmodernists' comments about a "de-centered" subject and fluid, fragmented identities seem overstated, it seems undeniable that in post-sixties Western society, identity has been made more complicated and precarious by an eruption of difference. Conceptually, of course, identity and difference are two sides of the same coin, each existing through and by means of the other. Yet it seems today that identity is overwhelmed by difference. To a large extent, this has taken the form of a relativizing "otherness" that undermines a coherent sense of self and other.

Postmodernity, however, poses the problems of fragmentation and incoherence in yet another sense. Social subjects are disoriented by an accumulated excess (or which is the same thing, deficit) of meaning brought on by the material and visual overabundance of commodity society. In a vast, eclectic, and changing landscape of competing objects and images, identity formation can only be problematic at best and hazardous at worst.

Understanding and appraising consumer culture calls for an examination of these conditions in both their celebratory and critical implications. Postmodernity needs to be understood as a series of mutations in modernity that emerge from its internal contradictions and that develop alongside modernity without entirely replacing it. Hence the two conditions coexist. While in seeming opposition, modern and postmodern conceptions capture different aspects and levels of contemporary consumption. In focusing on the struggle for selfhood and identity, the modern discourses of individuality, impersonality, and isolation are no less indispensable than the postmodern discourses of fragmentation and difference.

Beyond Political Economy and Cultural Studies

Despite the abiding presence in this study of the tradition of commodity critique, especially the Frankfurt School version, my goal is to construct a theoretical framework and methodology that move beyond overly simple claims of domination to a more balanced and nuanced account of the dynamics of contemporary consumption. The semiotic, poststructuralist, and anthropological strains of cultural studies have played a significant role in modifying, developing, or repudiating certain themes of this earlier tradition, offering a counterweight to one-dimensional readings of consumption. While there is room for skepticism about the textual paradigm's ultimate usefulness for social analysis, to the extent that theory necessarily reflects the sociohistorical circumstances of its production, an emphasis on textuality and language is consistent with the reassertion of culture and particularly the rise of semiotics in the commercialism of advanced capitalist societies.

However, I propose moving beyond both existing critical *and* cultural theory to a position that occupies key tensions between them, attempting to synthesize elements of both. But this is a position that moves the analysis to an entirely different level insofar as it reads consumption practices from the vantage point of consumers as individual and social subjects with everyday conscious and unconscious desires and motivations. In place of the domination/resistance paradigm of cultural studies but not completely unrelated, I propose a less political and more analytical series of distinctions for an accounting of self and identity in commodity society. Such distinctions as "semiotic"/"symbolic" and "actor"/"system" are, I believe, more illuminating of the discursive, social, and psychological dimensions of consumption and more effective in grasping the experiential dimensions of consumer society than conflict models. Threading through this analysis is the question to what extent the meanings of consumption are controlled by the commodity form as opposed to consuming subjects. At the same time, while attempting to maintain a nonpartisan stance, my analysis attempts not to lose sight of the distortions, deformations, and pathologies characterizing consumer culture and society.

Chapter Schema

This study is divided into two parts. Part One outlines the theoretical terrain of consumption, beginning with the major traditions of commodity critique and cultural theory and concluding with a new mode of analysis focused on the subjectivity of consumption.

Chapter One examines the relationship between commodities and subjects, identifying theoretical lineages in the critique of commodity society, including the Marxist critique of commodity fetishism, the Veblen tradition of status seeking, and portrayals of consumerism as a form of hedonism. This chapter ends by framing consumption in terms of a historical/theoretical transition from need to desire.

Chapter Two outlines culturalist approaches to consumption, selectively retracing the contributions of semiotics, anthropology, and cultural studies, including important figures such as Baudrillard and Pierre Bourdieu. This chapter concludes by proposing that consumption as a cultural process be read critically in terms of an historical transition from symbolizing to signifying processes.

Chapter Three again examines the relationship between self and commodity. Using the traditions of commodity fetishism and cultural theory as a backdrop, the commodity is "deconstructed" in terms of its internal relations with the consuming subject, disclosing the important psychological and social dimensions of consumption. This chapter examines the meaning dimensions of consumption in terms of signs and symbols. Emphasis is placed on the phenomenon of consumer insatiability and its structural and social psychological dynamics. Finally, consumer culture is situated in relation to the modern ethos of self-fulfillment and its hedonistic strains.

Part Two explores the social relations of identity, with emphasis on the phenomena of status and lifestyle as sociocultural manifestations of commodity exchange and object appropriation. Theories of status and lifestyle are explored and critiqued from the standpoint of consumption as a basis of identity formation and social membership.

Chapter Four addresses the dynamics of status and lifestyle and their bearing on identity. The focus of this chapter is the workings of the consumer marketplace in a "post-Fordist" economy, where rapid goods turnover and product differentiation accelerate the fashion cycle and the production of lifestyles, blurring and redrawing status boundaries. The major issue will be the extent to which consumption practices are an expression of status-seeking behavior as opposed to a search for social membership and belonging without regard to hierarchy.

Chapter Five attempts an overall theoretical assessment of the relationship between consumption and identity, including challenges to prevailing assumptions about this topic. Following a comparison of "modern" and "postmodern" conceptions of identity and identity formation, the theory of social constructionism is critiqued and applied to the task of analyzing identity formation through consumption. The chapter concludes with an analytical typology structured around a distinction between "codified" and "individuated" modes of identity formation.

Commodities,
Objects,
the Subject

I The Triumph of the Commodity: Theoretical Lineages

n many respects, the contemporary world of commodities is no different from the object world of premodern societies (Appadurai 1988, Douglas and Isherwood 1996). In both cases, objects perform indispensable material and cultural functions for members of the group. Modern society, however, has created a vast and dynamic *system* of objects whose main purpose is economic.

The cultural foundations of modern consumption would be unthinkable without the gigantic economic system created by modern markets and technologies. The objects of modern society have been absorbed into a complex system of commodity exchange within which they circulate and that imparts to them a peculiar status and power. While many of the basic functions of objects today remain unchanged from earlier periods, in contemporary capitalism objects are taken over by the *commodity form* (Marx 1906, Lukacs 1971), which has come to serve as a dominant structuring principle of everyday life (Goldman 1983/1984). It is not so much the historically phenomenal growth in both quantity and variety of products as it is the commodity's ability to impose a *general form* on social and cultural relations that distinguishes the contemporary world of objects from that of the past.

A simple definition of consumption might be "the utilization of economic resources for the satisfaction of human need and want through the purchase and use of goods and services."[1] While this definition suffices for classical economics and common usage, it falls short of describing the complexities of consumption disclosed by behavioral research and a huge literature on the social and cultural aspects of modern consumption practices. And yet both standard economic conceptions *and* behavioral and cultural interpretations tend to neglect important features of the inner dynamics between commodities on the one hand and consumers as *individual and social subjects* on the other.

Explaining the rise of consumption as a way of life directs our attention to a major historical shift from issues of survival (need) to questions of want, specifically the planned, systematic arousal of consumer desire. But to talk usefully about the sources and effects of desire in capitalist society, it is necessary to examine the objective and subjective aspects of desire in direct relation to the commodity form. Since the rise of cultural studies, most theorists and researchers have focused almost exclusively on consumption as a set of meanings and practices rather than on the larger system of commodities shaping present-day modes of consumption.[2] It is the complex nature and function of commodities themselves as objects having exchange, use, and other values that give form and meaning to our individual and collective lives as consumers.

The process of commodification powerfully shapes and conditions the self and the interactional dynamics of consumers as social actors. This calls for an analysis that identifies (1) the manifold ways in which individuals and groups are positioned by commodity relations in a whole system of economic, social, and cultural processes and divisions, and (2) how consumers themselves develop varying but often predictable kinds of relationships to commodities within a process of self-construction carried out in specific fields of social interaction and cultural signification.

As a prologue to a fuller discussion of the place of consumption in the search for meaning, selfhood, and identity, this chapter presents summaries of major theories of the commodity form. Three traditions will be briefly identified, in roughly historical order. First of all, the work of Marx initiated an extensive body of theory based on his revealing insights into capitalism as a system of commodity production, as found especially in his commentaries on alienation and commodity fetishism. Marx began a critique of capitalist modernity later extended by Georg Lukacs, Max Weber, Georg Simmel, and the Frankfurt School of critical theory. Second, a "Veblenesque" tradition is apparent in the intellectual heirs of the controversial author who studied the leisure class in the United States and whose famous notion of "conspicuous consumption" influenced generations of writers who have seen commodities as status-seeking objects. A third but less clearly defined tradition views commodities and consumption in relation to themes of desire and pleasure. This approach has both affirmative and critical tendencies, seeing consumerism variously as a manifestation of a culture of hedonistic self-fulfillment or as a type of narcissism exhibiting excessive and even pathological drives towards immediate gratification.

These theoretical lineages provide initial points of departure for a consideration of the social, cultural, and psychological significance of consumption today. My presentation of these traditions will be abbreviated and focused on questions of the relationship between commodities and subjects, drawing attention to the place of self in the social world of objects.

Capitalist Modernity: Commodities, Subjects, Objectification, Domination

The theoretical legacy of the nineteenth century is foundational for a consideration of the problem of commodities and subjects in market society. Rapid expansion in the world of material goods during the rise of industrial capitalism was accompanied by movements of thought that raised fundamental questions about the nature of the subject-object relationship. Within these movements, the path-breaking ideas of Georg Wilhelm Friedrich Hegel, Marx and their heirs wielded major influence as responses to the disintegration of traditional ways of life in the material and intellectual ferment of capitalist modernity.

Issues of consumption can be located at the epicenter of these modernizing developments. Interestingly enough, contrary to customary claims that consumer society was an outgrowth of the industrial revolution, research has shown that cultures of consumption among both the nobility and ascendant middle classes of Europe emerged prior to and alongside the growth of industrial capitalism (Campbell 1987; McCracken 1990; McKendrick et al. 1982; Mukerji 1983; Williams 1982). According to this view, newly developing desires for consumer goods served to *drive* the industrial revolution by creating types and quantities of demand far exceeding the supply available in preindustrial markets. The implication of these studies is that the term "industrial revolution" is something of a misnomer for what was in many respects a consumer revolution based upon innovations in the tastes and preferences of comfortable and increasingly demanding classes. The evidence thus seems to support what theory itself would suggest. Notwithstanding its dependence on a revolution in the means of production, the rapid expansion of capitalist industry was very much a direct response to newly rising cultural and social expectations for consumer goods and a real increase in consumer demand among new classes. Aside from its implications for theories of the independent influence of culture on economic development, this historical interpretation serves to highlight difficult questions about the relationship between production and consumption, and specifically the social crisis precipitated by their structural separation in the capitalist mode of production.

Commodification: Marx and Lukacs

It was Marx who provided the groundwork for an ontology of consumer society and culture by laying bare the fundamental material and social dynamics of this structural transformation. Positing the disconnection between the spheres of production and consumption as a generalized problem of human alienation, which he conceived as the commodification and alienation of labor, Marx set out to examine, in both abstract and concrete terms, the consequences of this split for the fulfillment of practical human need. Marx underscored the conceptual inseparability of production and consumption as interrelated *processes*. In the Introduction to the *Grundrisse* (Marx 1973, 83–111), he sketches in quasi-Hegelian fashion the close "identities" between production and consumption, elaborating their relationship as phases in a material dialectic of object and subject. In these notes, Marx initially separates production and consumption analytically, defining them as the beginning and end points, respectively, of the product as it passes to the consumer by way of distribution and exchange. Importantly, Marx implicitly recognizes the noneconomic moments of consumption, alluding to its biological, sociocultural, and even psychological elements. "In consumption," he states, "the product steps outside this social movement (of production, distribution, and exchange) and becomes a direct object and servant of individual need." Consumption is thus a separate and distinct phase in the total circuit of capital, whereby goods become "objects of gratification" for the individual. While conceptualizing all four phases as belonging to a general system of production, Marx nonetheless singles out consumption as occupying a special place in the circuit. As an activity standing both inside and outside the productive system, he argues for conceiving consumption "not only as a terminal point but also as an end-in-itself" that "actually belongs outside economics except in so far as it reacts in turn upon the point of departure and initiates the whole process anew" (ibid., 89). But in the section that follows, Marx moves to another level of analysis, talking about consumption and production in a decidedly dialectical manner, saying that each is "immediately" present in the other as "opposite(s)." He makes the mundane point that production and consumption are the two poles of economic life and that neither could exist without the other. For Marx, however, production is the dominant economic moment. After introducing refinements, referring to how production mediates consumption and vice versa (for instance, consumption "creates for the products the subject for whom they are products," it "reproduces the need" upon which production is based [ibid., 91, 92]), Marx concludes with a productivist emphasis, arguing that the mediations of production are the stronger ones, since production produces not only the "object" but the "manner" and "motive" of consumption (ibid., 92).

These passages suggest that Marx's understanding of consumption was far from simple and that he perhaps neglected the topic not merely out of his preoccupations with a theory of production, but because of the analytical challenge the topic posed in the larger scheme of things. Indeed, he seemed unable (or unwilling) to move beyond such abstruse formulations as "the person objectifies himself in production, the thing subjectifies itself in the person" (in another text, "consumption" is substituted for "the person"[3]) (ibid.). His discussion is confined to the most general, abstract, and self-evident observations about the mutually indispensable relationship between production and consumption. Nonetheless, the logical power of these formulations serves as an important reminder of the inner connections between consumption and production in the shaping of consumer culture. At the same time, it is the *structural detachment* of production from consumption that informs the main theme of estrangement running through Marx's work. In this respect, the forces of commodification provide the key to understanding the generalized condition of alienation in capitalist society. The famous passages in Part I, Chapter 1, "Commodities," of the first volume of *Capital* outline Marx's theory of the commodity form, which is the fundamental expression of the alienation of labor occurring in the split between production and consumption. In his view, the commodity is the unconditional starting point for investigating not only capitalism, but also the transformed character of production, labor, work, consumption, and the satisfaction of need accompanying growth in the capitalist mode of production. Objects produced for immediate consumption are defined by their use value, whereas products sold in the marketplace acquire exchange value through a system of monetary equivalence defining products in terms of their quantitative values. As an object of exchange, the commodity represents the separation of consumption from production and the simultaneous alienation of social relations in a depersonalized market setting.

But Marx sees the commodity under modern capitalism not only as an object of exchange but as representing a new and mystifying force. Not only does the commodity transform the character and structure of social intercourse, but also it alters society's mode of existence in ways that distort our very perception and experience of the world and others. The commodity constitutes a second order of existence: it is an object marked by alienation of the consciousness and social relations of individual producers, relations for which the commodity becomes a substitute and therefore a means of concealment. In short, commodities acquire their own ontological status and power, concealing their origins in the labor process. In Marx's words, "A definite social relation between men . . . assumes, in their eyes, the fantastic form of a relation between things" (Marx 1906, 83). Marx calls this phenomenon "commodity fetishism," suggesting a parallel to the phenomenon of religion as portrayed by thinkers like Ludwig Andreas Feuerbach

(1957) and, in a different register, Emile Durkheim (1961), whereby human powers and values are projected onto external objects of worship (Slater 1997, 112). By displacing the social relations of labor onto material objects, the products of labor, individuals come to experience the world of commodities as an independent and transcendent reality, detached from their lives as producers, leading Marx to characterize the commodity as a "mysterious thing."

Through the mediating influences of Weber and Simmel,[4] Marx's critique of commodity fetishism was elaborated and expanded upon by Georg Lukacs under the concept of reification. Literally meaning "to regard an abstraction as a thing," in social analysis this concept has generally been applied to the process whereby humanly created social forms are treated as immutable objects. By extending the idea of commodification from the labor process to the entire society, where it became a general structuring principle of social relations, Lukacs developed a focus on the whole system of commodity exchange. In his words, "The commodity can only be understood in its undistorted essence when it becomes the universal category of society as a whole" (Lukacs 1971, 86). Learning from Weber only to critique him, Lukacs developed the notion of reification through reference to Weber's "rationalization," arguing that the calculating and controlling features of this process are rooted in economic exchange and therefore capitalist social relations. Since the commodity form is universalized in a system of exchange relations, "reification" effectively replaces "rationalization" as the central explanatory principle of modern development (Plotke 1975, 200).[5] For Lukacs, the systematizations of rationalization are fundamentally economic in character, but extend beyond the realm of production to the sphere of consumption:

> . . . [T]his implies that the principle of rational mechanization and calculability must embrace every aspect of life. Consumer articles . . . now appear, on the one hand, as abstract members of a species identical by definition with its other members and, on the other hand, as isolated objects the possession or nonpossession of which depends on rational calculations. (ibid., 91)

Commodities come to occupy a place in a whole system of consumer goods, constituting a widespread objectification of life experience.

Additionally, commodities mark the transition from labor as the source of human fulfillment and identity (Marx's early writings) to the *possession* of things as the basis of social identity (Slater 1997, 119), but a possession only among isolated individuals. For Lukacs, then, the commodity form is the defining and determinative principle of capitalist social organization, representing a fundamental transformation to a social condition of calculated exchange and acquisition as the basic framework for all human transactions and practices.

The Marxian theme of alienation as commodification refers less to the proliferation of objects as an experiential or developmental issue for the individual than as a problem of recognition (Slater 1997, 111). Commodity fetishism points to a mode of representation in which the circulation of commodities constitutes a set of appearances that distort or falsify the "real" social relations of production and the "true" character of labor as the source of all value and as a vehicle of self-activity and expression. Commodity fetishism thus invites criticism of the whole sphere of consumption, but only at the level of representation (Miller 1991, 44). But whereas Marx's reading of commodification was limited to a forcible separation of workers from themselves as human beings in a thing-like realm of exchangeable objects, Lukacs sees the commodity as the basic structuring principle of the rationalization of society as a whole. The commodity imparts a facticity to the sociocultural system and even more importantly, to the character and structure of consciousness. In the experience and cognition of the individual, social reality thus acquires the character of unchanging and unchangeable objecthood. Commodities, thus, are the fundamental source of the false consciousness of workers, who are able to perceive and define themselves only through a possessive relationship to finished goods. Lukacs' concept of reification therefore extends the concept of alienation from the sphere of production to the sphere of consumption, pointing to the growing pervasiveness and systematicity of commodity culture.

The Consumption World: Simmel

In the work of Georg Simmel, whose account of modernity stands in an ambiguous and complicated relationship to both Marx and Lukacs, we find closer scrutiny of the relation between commodities and subjects. While echoing Marxian themes, Simmel effectively substitutes "modernity" for "capitalism," conducting a philosophically and psychologically oriented investigation of its particular cultural forms and dynamics. As Lukacs' teacher, Simmel surely influenced the former's widening of the notion of commodity fetishism within a critical theory of the tendencies of capitalist culture. It is also apparent that Simmel exercised influence on other heirs of the Marxian thematics of commodification and reification.

For Simmel, the condition of alienation is not specifically a product of capitalism but rather inherent in modernity. Paralleling Weber's stance toward Marx's alienated worker, Simmel states that the fetishism of commodities "represents only a special case" of the "general fate" of modern culture (Simmel 1968, 42). It is further apparent that Simmel can be properly read and appreciated only in the context of his wider effort to articulate a general theory of culture that, while derivative of Hegel's theory of objectification (Miller 1991), presents a unique version of the subject/object problem. Simmel was arguably a brilliant dialectician of culture, whose relevance to the topic of consumption still goes relatively unnoticed and whose reflections on culture and commodification, and their impact on the self, deserve greater appreciation and development.

Nonetheless, intense interest in the topic of modernity has drawn new attention to Simmel and especially his major work, *The Philosophy of Money* (1990). Simmel sees the development of a money economy as the basis for the rise of a modern social order organized around a maturely developed system of exchange (Frisby 1988, 87). For him, modern culture presupposes a fully developed framework of exchange value, a view that necessarily shifts attention to the sphere of consumption. While Simmel could be faulted for minimizing and dehistoricizing the economic sources of alienation, he can be credited for referring, if only tacitly, to key features of capitalism in explaining the constriction of subjects characterizing the reifications of consumer culture. And Simmel in a broad way does outline the historical dimensions of alienation in his account of the enlargement of what he calls "objective culture."

The tensions between Simmel and the Marxian tradition find expression in his theoretical ambivalence toward modernity and its psychological consequences. In *The Philosophy of Money*, Simmel reflects upon the impact of the money economy on social relations and the intellect, arguing that money introduces the impersonal qualities of abstraction and calculation into the full range of social and cultural life. On the more critical side, in an account rivaling the commentaries of Marx and Lukacs, Simmel draws a decidedly negative picture of alienating social conditions, alluding to the "processes of fragmentation, atomization, objectification, reification, and standardization brought about by the division of labor" (Frisby 1990, 27). But more affirmatively, Simmel offers provocative suggestions for the liberating potentials of exchange relations. The separation of producer and product is accompanied by enlarged opportunities for the consumption of a vast array of new products and experiences inherent in an expanding marketplace. Although monetary relations manifest and promote a reification of social relations, they also create a new realm of "objective" value constituted in the exchange and use of cultural goods. Simmel regards objects, not labor, as the vehicle of self-realization and therefore turns to commodities' potentials for fulfilling the needs and desires of the individual. The characteristics of commodity culture address the needs both of "variety and change" and "familiarity"; these dual needs are articulated in a "specific form that the value of objects requires, . . . differentiation and particularity . . . (and) . . . a certain comprehensiveness, frequency and permanence" (Simmel 1990, 72–73). The exchange economy is thus characterized as providing the conditions under which objects acquire meaning and significance ("value") *because* of their status as exchangeable and need-satisfying commodities. The emergence of a separate sphere of consumption gives rise to a new order of value and human satisfaction. Exchange relations create a widened realm of choice in which commodities provide the self a means of development and expressive enhancement. Broadly optimistic in this respect, Simmel suggests that the principle of exchange itself, and a corresponding growth in the powers of abstraction represented and reinforced by money, promote novel possibilities for individual freedom and equality (Miller 1991, 76).

Despite the modernist insights of *The Philosophy of Money*, however, this work offers only the barest outline of what is perhaps Simmel's most provocative contribution to an understanding of commodities and the individual: a tragic theory of culture. The main outline of this theory appears in "The Conflict in Modern Culture" and "On the Concept and Tragedy of Culture" (Simmel 1968), two essays offering an illuminating but sober assessment of the predicament of the self in commodity culture. What Simmel means by "culture" is itself partially definitive of the problem of the modern commodity. Following Hegel, Simmel regards the growth of "objective spirit," which is for him the totality of life forms and objects (what we conventionally think of as "culture"), as the original cause of the alienation of subject and object. But for Simmel, culture is not equatable to the realm of human creations *per se*, but designates a particular kind of *relation* between the individual and the objective spirit, "between subjective life, which is restless but finite in time, and its contents, which, once they are created, are fixed but timelessly valid" (Simmel 1968, 27). In Simmel's words, we encounter culture only when "the subject becomes objective and the object becomes subjective. This is the specific attribute of the process of culture" (ibid., 31). The birth of culture depends upon a unity between human objectifications (art, institutions, material goods, social forms) and the subject's meaningful inward appropriation of these objectifications ("internalization"/"interiorization" of objects). The production of meaning, the very core of culture, originates in the overcoming of the subject/object dualism ("culture asserts its unity by interpenetrating both" [ibid., 34]). Meaning depends upon and resides in a mutually constitutive interaction between these opposing moments. The object enters into the experience of the subject in a consciously chosen and personally meaningful way, and the subject attaches significance and sense of purpose to the object as a vehicle of its own development and self-expression.

Always preoccupied with form rather than content, Simmel sees culture as expressing itself through the cultivation of the individual, whereby the latter passes from a "natural" to a "cultured" state. Reflective of the romantic tradition, this conception of culture points to a process of individuation arising from the creative potentials of the person, "an inner, original nucleus" seeking realization. Culture thus emerges in a closing of the gap between the individualized potentiality of the subject and the objects of the external world. For Simmel, culture assumes not a collective but an individual form, manifesting itself in the unfolding of personal capacities and drives (Weingartner 1962, 69–78). What makes something a part of culture for Simmel is not its formal or substantive properties alone, but rather the subjective value it has acquired in its "reassimilation" (ibid., 72). In principle, anything in the "objective spirit" is capable of acquiring cultural meaning insofar as it is a human product, but this can happen only if the product *returns* to the subject as part of meaningful experience. Simmel addresses three kinds of obstacles to this return. First, by assuming a particular *form* in the world, objects separate themselves from their creators and potential receivers, taking on a life and logic of their own as things (Simmel 1968, 11–15). As such, objects come to be recognized and judged according to the formal norms of a particular field of objective value (art, technology, law, philosophy). Second, the products of the world are often (and increasingly through time) those of *others* living in different contexts of time, place, and circumstance and thus incapable of speaking to our own expressive needs. Both of these difficulties exemplify a disjuncture between an object's value *as an object* and its subjective relevance for and appropriation by individuals. Running through Simmel's account is thus a basic distinction between objective and cultural values (Weingartner 1962, 79–82). Finally, with the passage to modernity, an increase in the sheer quantity of goods leads to a massive accumulation of material culture. Simmel's reflections on the impact of industrial mass production anticipate subsequent critiques of commodity culture: "Thus vast supplies of products come into existence which call forth an artificial demand that is senseless from the perspective of the subject's culture" (Simmel 1968, 43). In the face of excess, the self attempts to "select . . . from among the contents (of culture) which offer themselves as means for its individual development" (ibid., 44). But this strategy often fails because "the infinitely growing supply of objectified spirit places demands before the subject, creates desires in him, hits him with feelings of individual inadequacy and helplessness, throws him into total relationships from whose impact he cannot withdraw, although he cannot master their particular contents" (ibid.).

This philosophical scenario directs our attention to the problem of how consumers are to recognize themselves in the vastly expanded world of modern cultural goods and how they are to construct a personally meaningful and active relationship to it (Miller 1991, 76–78). Recuperating the notion of "sublation" (*Aufhebung*), whereby the subject appropriates its own objective creations, Simmel, in a dismissal of the Marxian thematic of human fulfillment through labor, reconfigures the Hegelian problematic around mass consumption, but sees in the latter only a difficult and encumbered path to self-realization. The inherent disparity between the logic of individual development and that of the object world only grows worse under modernity, turning culture, inhabiting both worlds, into a "tragedy."

The Totally Administered Society: The Frankfurt School

Situated ambiguously alongside the Marxian narrative of capitalist modernity, Simmel's fertile contributions to a theory of commodity culture and the self were ultimately to be overshadowed by the work of the Frankfurt School, whose celebrated statements on the culture of advanced capitalism influenced generations of critics of consumerism and mass culture in the twentieth century.[6] The work of the school's leading figure, Theodor Adorno, is known for its rich and provocative insights into the nature and effects of commodification and its place in the creation of what he pessimistically saw as a new mode of social domination inhering in the cultural, technological, and bureaucratic apparatuses of industrial capitalism. For Adorno, consumerism was the core of a "totally administered society" constituted in commodity relations and technologies of entertainment, a system whose impact he saw as ensnaring the individual in conformist patterns of thought and behavior. Through a provocative alliance of Marx and Sigmund Freud, the reflections of Adorno and other members of the school sought to reveal how economic and technological forces penetrated the psyche of an increasingly isolated and atomized individual.

In "The Culture Industry: Enlightenment as Mass Deception," Adorno and Max Horkheimer (1972) put forth the main lines of a trenchant critique of consumer culture. To facilitate the culture industry's goals of entertainment and amusement, mass culture assumes a formulaic form marked by homogeneity and predictability. The manufacture and marketing of culture on a mass scale induces spectator passivity, creating dependency on a system whose main goal is social domination for profits. Under the spell of technology and material "progress," reason, the imagination, and similar values are thereby eclipsed by technique and "effect." Now a prolongation of the workday, leisure is organized and routinized by a cultural system that by means of imitation and repetition reduces everything to a matter of "style." The commodity form, more than a mere cause and symptom of alienation and source of false consciousness, invades the realm of everyday life, structuring and regulating the individual's every response and movement. For Adorno and Horkheimer, the "fusion" of culture and entertainment creates a system of seemingly total and inescapable social control. "The triumph of advertising in the culture industry is that consumers feel compelled to buy and use its products even though they see through them" (ibid., 167). Likening the repetitious character of mass cultural products to the "propaganda slogan" (ibid., 163), of which advertising is a potent embodiment, the authors see in mass culture the essential features of fascism. "The culture industry tends to make itself the embodiment of authoritative pronouncements, and thus the irrefutable prophet of the prevailing order" (ibid., 147). This gloomy and ominous evocation of Weberian and Lukacsian images of modernist rationalization frames the character of consumer culture, and the fate of the self, in a singularly negative fashion.

Adorno attempted to spell out in more detail the consequences of commodification in a series of essays on "serious" and "popular" music.[7] As commodity form, radio and other mass media transform works of "autonomous art," such as symphonies, into mere entertainment. The processes of standardization inherent in mass culture transform popular music into a series of formulas characterized by repetition and stereotyping (Adorno 1941a, 1941b, 1945, 1976, 1978). With the extension of commodity relations to both "high" and "low" realms of culture, individuals are turned into passive consumers of predetermined and packaged experiences. As a consequence, art loses it capacity for transcendence, insight, and redemption, and popular entertainment reproduces the experience of factory labor, providing easily digestible but ultimately regimented, superficial, and boring amusements.

The commodification of culture, however, provides only the basic conditions for what Adorno considers to be the salient danger of mass culture: its psychic intrusions. The packaged and programmed products of the culture industry constitute a pervasive system of psychological manipulation. In his essay "Television and the Patterns of Mass Culture" (1957), Adorno pursues an analysis of the psychological functions of mass culture on two distinct but interrelated levels. First, the formulaic structure of the mass media, through their "repetitiveness," "self-sameness," and "ubiquity," condition the spectator to a set of predetermined expectations and responses. Within this structure of automatic responses, mass entertainment is scripted for predictable and conformist outcomes: conflict resolution depends upon submission to the rules of society, thus affirming the status quo. Repeated exposure to media is thus a form of operant conditioning. Second, Adorno finds a pattern of psychological manipulation in the *content* of mass culture. Television entertainment relies heavily on the mythology of individualism to deflect attention from the systemic social sources of life problems. More significantly, the workings of mass culture presuppose a multilayered personality, whereby the latent meanings and messages of a commodity, by escaping the "controls of consciousness," can have more impact than its manifest content. Leo Lowenthal's term "psychoanalysis in reverse" thus came to characterize mass culture's strategy of reaching into the unconscious to exercise "hidden" control over spectator/consumer response (ibid.). In a later essay, Adorno underscored what he regarded as a more voluntary but still spurious and futile search for fulfillment through mass entertainment. As a way of life, capitalism generates feelings of insecurity, anxiety, and dependency, causing individuals to seek relief and compensation in the sphere of consumption through its "substitute gratifications" (Adorno 1975). Wanting to be deceived, people turn to mass culture through a cynical and reluctant search for refuge. Addressing the deprivations created by a mechanized market society, mass culture thus speaks to us in a predominantly psychological idiom.

Supporting this bleak and totalizing analysis is a claim that the system itself creates the needs it purports to fulfill. Adorno and Horkheimer argue unequivocally that the definition and satisfaction of consumer need come to be strictly identified with what the culture industry itself produces. The conception that need is created within a closed universe of commodity exchange and technological control is articulated most forcefully in Herbert Marcuse's *One-Dimensional Man* (1964). In an influential provocation, Marcuse claims that the capitalist system leads to a distinction between "false" and "true" needs. "'False' (needs) are those which are superimposed upon the individual by particular social interests in his repression: the needs which perpetuate toil, aggressiveness, misery, and injustice. . . . Most of the prevailing needs to relax, to have fun, to behave and consume in accordance with advertisements . . . belong to this category" (ibid., 4–5). In other words, "false" needs are artificially imposed on subjects for the purpose of selling products. In contrast, individuals' "true" needs are those essential to survival and basic well-being. For Marcuse, "true" needs are repressed by consumer society; for him, "products indoctrinate and manipulate" (ibid., 12). Therefore, the needs prevailing in industrial capitalism are not "true" needs but the systemically determined "false" needs to acquire and possess consumer goods.

Summary

The foregoing accounts offer predominantly economic explanations of the structure and character of consumer society. In these versions of capitalist modernity, the commodity form is an increasingly universal structure of exchangeability and rationality. The circulation of goods and services in a market society creates a social framework within which objectification, calculation, manipulation, and control become the operative principles of a system driven by economic interests. Under capitalism, social relations are increasingly shaped by the economic exchange of objects. This constitutes an estranged and objectified world whose parts function independently of the human needs and desires they determine. In this theoretical construction, the commodity form is the major figure of modern rationality, as exemplified by the features of calculability and manipulability permeating everyday life. The commodity form in this sense is cause and symptom of a basic alienation at the root of consumer society.

A distinctive and unifying theme in the tradition of commodity fetishism, most apparent among the Frankfurt thinkers, is the notion of need creation. Capitalist modernity engenders a culture in which human need is redefined by the goal of production for profit. Commodification is the main dynamic of an economic system dependent on the structuring and containment of culture and social relations for instrumental purposes. The inevitable consequence is a deep penetration of economic forms and interests into all sectors and domains of society.

Consumption as Status Seeking: Veblen and His Heirs

Material objects universally serve as indicators of social location, assigning and expressing one's place and role in society. With the rise of market individualism and a weakening of tradition, objects have assumed even greater importance as markers of social identity and difference. In a context of weakened communal ties and the accumulation of private wealth, commodities establish, rationalize, and regulate a social order built mainly around exchange relations. Indeed, there appears to be an inverse relationship between the decline of religious, familial, and community ties and the ascendance of commodities as objects full of social meanings.

The coming of industrial society with its ethos of economic achievement dramatically enlarged the social function of commodities. Differential spending on consumer goods came to serve as the main index of relative monetary success in what was becoming an increasingly complex class system. The status-differentiating functions of commodities meant that modern consumption was from the beginning comparative and competitive (Schor 1998, 7 passim), turning the commodification process into the basis of a new and evolving class structure.

The notion that consumption practices are expressions of class position has been a major premise in the sociological study of stratification. According to this view, the primary social function of consumption is to define one's status within a hierarchically organized system of signifying goods. Consumption practices thus serve to support status claims in a modern, complex, and continually changing social structure.

Conspicuous Consumption: Veblen

The idea of "conspicuous consumption" originated in the classic and influential essay by Thorstein Veblen, *The Theory of the Leisure Class* (1934). A harsh and cynical critic of the American social order, Veblen (writing during the Gilded Age) was a masterful observer of the evolution of social-class behavior. According to Veblen, what distinguished the rich was their "conspicuous consumption," a form of wasteful and lavish spending intended as an expression of wealth and therefore social success. While recognizing the lengthy history of such practices among the privileged classes, Veblen believed that conspicuous consumption had become the only effective means of communicating membership in the higher echelons at a time when expressions of class identity, or more specifically "reputability," had become dependent upon the "display of goods" (ibid., 86). Veblen's remark, "Since consumption of . . . goods is an evidence of wealth, it becomes honorific" (ibid., 74), points to a phenomenon associated with Weber's concept of status group, a category designating *inter alia* the social and cultural dimensions of class, in this case the role of material possessions in determining one's social placement within a community (Weber 1958a).

Veblen's major contribution to a theory of consumption, however, was his argument about the social dynamics of conspicuous spending, specifically his claim that this form of behavior establishes a system of emulation. Given the centrality of this principle to our understanding of consumption, it is worth quoting Veblen at length:

> The leisure class stands at the head of the social structure in point of reputability; and its manner of life and its standards of worth therefore afford the norm of reputability for the community. The observance of these standards, in some degree of approximation, becomes incumbent upon all classes lower in the scale. In modern civilized communities the lines of demarcation between social classes have grown vague and transient, and wherever this happens the norm of reputability imposed by the upper class extends it coercive influence with but slight hindrance down through the social structure to the lowest strata. The result is that the members of each stratum accept as their ideal of decency the scheme of life in vogue in the next higher stratum, and bend their energies to live up to that ideal. On pain of forfeiting their good name and their self-respect in case of failure, they must conform to the accepted code, at least in appearance. (ibid., 84)

In a society of blurred class lines, norms established by the highest class tend to sink toward the lower levels. By implication, traditional class cultures face extinction while the culture of the privileged and powerful comes to provide a standard or at least an ideal for everyone. More importantly, Veblen is arguing a felt need for reputability and acceptance among *all* classes, a need to show "good repute," a condition now dependent on "pecuniary strength" (ibid.). A need for good repute based on monetary success tends to breed emulative behavior in relation to those within close reach, specifically the next highest stratum. For all practical purposes, this is Veblen's version of the American ethos of achievement, of the inner drive to climb the ladder in search of an acceptable class identity. The achievement ethos finds its direct expression in the accumulation of possessions, and this takes the form of comparative consumption practices in relation to those immediately above one's present position. According to Veblen, the public display of possessions serves the dual purpose of satisfying the psychic need for social acceptance and providing much-needed signposts of class distinction.

This is a powerful-enough argument, but Veblen anticipates yet another social dynamic perhaps even more consequential for the class system and its unequally positioned members. Once one achieves a higher standard through acquisition, this new standard fails to provide any more satisfaction than the previous one, becoming a "point of departure for a fresh increase of wealth," thereby setting off a whole new round of acquisition. Since the goal of accumulation is to rank higher than others, this dooms the individual to a state of "chronic dissatisfaction" (ibid., 31). Veblen thus puts forth a comparative theory of the insatiability of desire, arguing that since the search for reputability is based on "invidious comparison," it is virtually impossible to attain complete and permanent satisfaction by this means (ibid., 32). Unless one occupies the very top of the class ladder, there will always be another rung to climb. The satisfaction of desire through comparative status attainment degenerates into an unwinnable game. The futile attempt at self-satisfaction through the deployment of commodities as competitive status markers is a manifestation of a social contradiction built into "open" stratification systems.

Affluence and Status Seeking: Galbraith and Packard

Veblen's theory of emulative spending was later taken up and modified by a number of economists and other social scientists during the economic expansion of the highly affluent post-World War II era. A dramatic increase in mass-produced consumer goods during this period created strong pressures toward conformity. As a result, the pattern of emulating the higher ranks was replaced by a tendency to "fit in" or "keep up" with members of one's *own* class or stratum (Schor 1998, 8). In actuality, fitting in and keeping up were two sides of a single tendency reflecting a major change in the dynamics of consumer spending (the purchase of "positional goods" [Frank and Cook 1995; Hirsch 1976]) and the overall class structure.

One aspect of this change was a burgeoning middle class and the emergence of its lifestyle as the dominant American norm. The other aspect, in an ironic reversion to the Marxian view of consumption, involved the effects of rising production levels. Recognizing the variability of material standards, James Duesenberry argued that since "one of the principal social goals [of our society] is a higher standard of living . . . the desire to get superior goods takes on a life of its own" (1949, 28). But in assessing this statement in his famous *The Affluent Society*, John Kenneth Galbraith argued that the push toward higher levels of consumption had to be traced directly to output. In his words, "The more that is produced the more that must be owned in order to maintain the appropriate prestige" (1958, 126). As a liberal economist, Galbraith understood the continued importance of the goals of producers to the rate and shape of aggregate consumption. Significantly, Galbraith couched his argument as a theory of need creation, stating that Duesenberry's view suggested that "the production of goods creates the wants that the goods are presumed to satisfy," a "direct link between production and wants" that is evident in the rise of advertising and salesmanship (ibid.). In effect, Galbraith explained competitive spending as a function of production rather than pressures towards social distinction. "As a society becomes increasingly affluent, wants are increasingly created by the process by which they are satisfied," a process Galbraith called "the dependence effect" (ibid., 128–9). In a tacit endorsement of the critical theory of need creation, Galbraith's view of the consumption process in the fifties extended the status-seeking tradition to include a consideration of the role of production on perceptions of self and other in the effort to fulfill socially derived expectations of class membership. Contrary to Veblen, however, who located the frustration of desire in the process of social comparison, Galbraith saw status competition as self-defeating because rising production levels meant a continual transformation in the material *standards* of status.

The best-known popular work on status seeking from this period was, of course, Vance Packard's *The Status Seekers*. Packard's accomplishment was to chronicle the social and cultural changes defining new forms of status behavior in the United States. Significantly, his discussion was no less than Galbraith's a product of growing material abundance. But more in the spirit of Veblen, Packard saw economic affluence as leading to a "crumbling of visible class lines" (1959, 5). It was precisely this disintegration of class that Packard believed generated a preoccupation with status, the "scrambling to find new ways to draw lines that will separate the elect from the non-elect" (ibid., 6). For Packard, the ironic result of spreading affluence in the fifties was increased anxiety about one's place in the class hierarchy and a fervent drive to consume in ways that re-established a sense of pecking order.

Summary

The status-seeking model of consumption is important in a number of ways. First, it draws attention to what might be called the "paradox of affluence."[8] The very forces generating emulative behavior—a monetized economy and expanding marketplace—undermine the goals to which this behavior is directed. Economic affluence raises commodities to an iconic status, especially in a context of weakening class distinctions. But with economic growth and a continually changing landscape of goods, these commodities become indicators of only *relative* success. In other words, no possibility exists for an endpoint to emulative spending. Second, status seeking is inseparable from an incessant redrawing of class lines. The blurred boundaries of class induce a perpetual search for new status symbols, the main effect of which is increasing *confusion* of class differences and identities. Status seeking therefore creates an odd kind of democracy in the expressive marketplace, erasing the very social distinctions that are its *raison d'être*. Finally, since all of these processes ultimately are driven by the goals of expanded production and higher living standards (and profits), a theoretical link is thereby established between status-seeking behavior and the notion of artificial need creation originally formulated by Marcuse. Following Galbraith, status competition can be theorized as an effect of production, traceable in principle to the enormous demand-creating apparatuses of advertising and other motivational systems upon which profitable production depends.

Desire and Pleasure: Consumerism and the Ethos of Hedonism

An emergence of the themes of desire and pleasure among a more recent generation of scholars dramatically shifts the terms of debate about the nature and impact of commodity relations, preparing the ground for the notion of *consumer culture*. New and deeper understandings of modern consumption have arisen in studies of the historical roots of consumer culture in the changing landscape of urban, industrial society and the rise of an ideology of *consumerism*. Just as an expanding sphere of consumption had for years guaranteed persistent growth in production, at the cultural level the rise of *consumerism* served to provide a moral endorsement of pleasure seeking as a basis of social and personal relations and lifestyles (Gabriel and Lang 1995, 100). While preexisting consumer demand drove industrial expansion, expanding consumer *culture* not only counteracted the Protestant work ethic's moral strictures against immediate gratification, but even more succeeded in overcoming the prohibitive regulations of late nineteenth-century Victorianism. A full-blown consumer culture eventually took shape in the manufacture and democratization of desire by commercial advertising, mass marketing, and new forms of merchandising. Predicated on a need to escape the drudgeries of work and production, this culture represented and nourished a new ethic of hedonistic self-gratification (Ewen 1976; Leach 1993; Fox and Lears 1983). In its manifestations as entertainment, this ethic promised compensation for economic insecurity and industrial boredom. In the form of goods consumption, consumer culture meant an aestheticization of everyday life in which the pleasurable fantasies and sensations surrounding the leisured acquisition, possession, and use of stylized products became the rewards of economic effort and achievement.

Today, the idea of consumption as the pursuit of pleasure is axiomatic. Ever since C. Wright Mills (1956) observed that white-collar work had become merely a means (income) to an end ("the good life"), many writers have situated consumption within a new moral order of self-gratification seen as compensating the downside of industrialism and bureaucracy. The controversial implications of this transition and its manifestations in what many regard as an excessive American materialism have kept social and cultural critics busy from World War II to the present, a period characterized by famous debates about the impact on both individual and society of a hedonistic and increasingly self-centered mass culture.

Hedonistic Capitalist Culture: Bell

A familiar reference point in discussions of consumer hedonism is Daniel Bell's thesis in *The Cultural Contradictions of Capitalism* (1978) that the historical shift from production to consumption has created a hedonistic ethos undermining the moral underpinnings of the modern capitalist economy and polity. In his words, "The cultural, if not moral, justification of capitalism has become hedonism, the idea of pleasure as a way of life" (ibid., 23). In Bell's (first) argument, the rise of consumerism generates within the cultural sphere contradictions between the goals of hedonistic self-satisfaction on the one hand and productive hard work and efficiency (necessary for a healthy economy) on the other. In his (second) broader argument, where Marx saw developing economic forces contradicting and weakening an outmoded bourgeois "superstructure," Bell seems to see a rapidly forming culture of self-gratification running ahead of the evolution of productive forces in the economy. For Bell, culture today reigns "supreme" (ibid., 33) and its dynamism outpaces that of the productive, political, and even technological spheres of society.

By highlighting the hedonistic element, Bell makes a compelling case for the ascendance of a consumer culture whose priorities represent a major shift in economic and social life. At the same time, his claims about the new primacy of culture help lay the groundwork for a conceptual shift toward culture as an explanatory framework of social change. To rephrase his argument, consumer culture was now in the "driver's seat." One certainly hears in Bell's analysis a conservative voice lamenting the erosion of the moral value system of Western capitalism. He sees in contemporary culture a hollowed-out modernity subverted by a "postmodernist" agenda of constant experimentation for its own sake, in his view a situation calling for a cautionary framework of limits. It would be a mistake, however, to allow Bell's tone or slant to detract from his analysis of the institutional developments elevating culture to a new position of power. Bell's thesis attempts to establish the hegemony of culture in the context of an ascendant sensibility and psychology of pleasure.

Pleasure Seeking as Social Control: Bauman

While Bell expresses concern for the threat hedonism poses to the capitalist order, some theorists make just the opposite argument, seeing the hedonistic orientation as *serving* capitalism, solidifying existing social arrangements through an organized system of mass consumption and entertainment. This line of argument is an extension of the Frankfurt critique of the gratificatory mechanisms of the culture industry. A notable spokesman for this view is Zygmunt Bauman: in his words, "The capitalist system deploys the *pleasure principle* for its own perpetuation"; "Seduction is the paramount tool of integration (of the reproduction of domination) in a consumer society" (1992, 50, 97–98, original italics). Bauman's critique of consumption is representative of the prevailing critical view, appearing perhaps most forcefully in Adorno, that commodities offer compensatory pleasure as an antidote and alibi to the disciplining and alienating conditions of capitalist society. In this view, the pleasure principle functions as a means of social control, the goal of which is preservation of the status quo. In contrast to Adorno, however, who in the name of a theory of the weakened ego claims that mass culture is destructive of self and identity—the autonomous individual—Bauman narrowly argues that instant and manipulated gratification is a simple mechanism of system integration. By harnessing the pleasure principle in an organized and targeted fashion, consumer culture functions as a tool of social, economic, and political reproduction.

A Culture of Narcissism: Lasch

The era of cultural rebellion in the decades of the sixties and seventies came to an abrupt end when at the start of the eighties newly elected Republican President Ronald Reagan announced that "America is back." In the meantime, however, the value of self-fulfillment had already established itself as a celebrated theme in U.S. life.

To the extent that self-fulfillment has served as tacit justification for pleasure seeking, this cultural movement has changed and complicated the terms of debate about modern consumption by introducing deeper questions about the self and its relation to society. As against those who have welcomed hedonism as a necessary ingredient of self-nurturance as against the impersonal forces of market and bureaucracy, influential critics have blamed hedonism for undermining and even pathologizing the self. Chrisopher Lasch sees gratificatory consumption not as a mechanism of social control but as symptomatic of psychological distress and dysfunction (1979, 1984). Lasch sees in consumerism "a larger pattern of dependence, disorientation, and loss of control" promoting the passivity and spectatorship inherent in the capitalist system of mass production and consumption (1984, 27). What Lasch originally characterized as a culture of narcissism and later reformulated as a problem of psychic self-survival involves a deepening connection between consumer culture and the formation of a self-absorbed personality inextricably bound to the immediate gratifications of consumer hedonism. But for Lasch, hedonism per se is not the problem so much as a *dependence* on mass consumption as a systematic source of need fulfillment and ego gratification. Echoing Adorno in a psychological register, Lasch posits commodity culture as a root of ego weakness. This is the major consequence of the hedonistic features of consumerism as a vehicle of self-identification and gratification.[9]

Hedonism and the Romantic Ethic: Campbell

A more recent historically inflected subgenre of cultural studies represents a major departure from the tradition of critical theory. Among an array of works on the historical and social sources of consumerism is Colin Campbell's *Romantic Ethic and the Spirit of Modern Consumerism* (1987). Suspending critical judgment, this study seeks a deeper cultural understanding of hedonistic consumption, one it finds traceable to the Romantic movement and its impact on the formation of the modern self.

Defining pleasure as a "quality of experience" as opposed to a "state of being" (ibid., 60), Campbell distinguishes between "traditional" and "modern" hedonism. The latter emerges with a relocation of emotion and agency within a self both liberated from oppressive external influences and capable of self-consciousness. According to Romanticism, through the power of imagination, modern individuals are capable of exercising control over the meaning of the objects and experiences composing their worlds, thereby maximizing an internal experience of pleasure. The modern capacity for imagination thus becomes the source of a new kind of "self-illusory hedonism" (ibid., 76). In Campbell's view, the pleasures of consumption are rooted in the imaginative processes of the self, whose internal emotions generate a sense of pleasure surrounding the meanings and anticipations associated with various objects and experiences. Pleasures produced through the imagination occur in the form of daydreaming, a state of mind Campbell takes as typifying a hedonistic consumer mentality.[10] The hedonism of modern consumption, then, is not in the immediate sensations imparted by the act of consumption but in the imaginative and illusory feelings produced *in relation* to such acts, both anticipated and completed. Desire and pleasure thus are constituted in a subjective imagining of consumption's *meanings* for the self.

In Campbell's interpretation, the pleasure-seeking character of modern consumption is derived from an early modern "ethic of feeling" that eventually evolved into a Romantic ethic legitimating the idea of pleasure for its own sake. In a provocative analysis, Campbell joins his reconstruction of a Romantic ethic to a reinterpretation of Weber's thesis of the Protestant work ethic. Where Weber seemed to find only rationalization of the harshest kind, Campbell sees the presence of an ethic of consuming pleasure emerging *alongside* the imperative to produce through hard work, frugality, and discipline. By implication, both production and consumption emerge in their modern guises under an ideal of rationalized ethical conduct. Further, it seems according to other authors that Romanticism brought together hedonism and "an aesthetic attitude toward life" (Gabriel and Lang 1995, 107), providing new forms of sensibility that could serve as a foundation for an aestheticization of the world of commodities. Far from formless pleasure seeking for its own sake, on this view consumer culture, by drawing on the Romantic outlook, provided a sense of substance and coherent purpose to the pleasurable consumption of commodities. For Campbell, the powerful impulse toward the pursuit of pleasure in modern consumerism, based on a separation of individual desire from collective need, resides in both the freed subjectivity and the ethical persuasions of the Romantic movement.

Summary

With the exception of Adorno, the psychological dimensions of consumption remained only implicit in theories focused on the commodity form and its impact on subjectivity. Thinking of consumption as a form of pleasure fundamentally changes the terms of analysis and shifts attention from identificatory to gratificatory functions. These functions are not entirely separable to the extent that what it means to satisfy desire or experience pleasure is incorporated into our definition and sense of self. However, the hedonism theorists raise specific questions about the deeper psychological dynamics and effects of consumption, often reiterating and extending Freudian categories into commercial terrain. From this perspective, the "pleasure principle" is an indispensable premise in explanations of consumer motivation and efforts to capture the conscious and even more importantly, the unconscious meanings of consumption from the standpoint of the subject.[11] Relatedly, hedonistic readings point to the historical separation of want from need, the potential insatiability of want, and the cultural, social, and theoretical construction of want as narratives of desire and pleasure.

Conclusion: From Need to Desire

Beginning with Marx and culminating in the Frankfurt School and their followers, the concept of the commodity form and related themes of alienation, rationalization, objectification, and manipulation have provided intellectual tools for exploring the dominating and exploitative features of capitalist culture and social relations. It is worth emphasizing three characteristics of this tradition. First, it establishes determinative and ever-tightening systemic connections between economic production and sociocultural life. The commodity form is seen as the dominant structural relation of advanced capitalism, determining the social relations and cultural forms of consumer behavior and self-formation. Second, especially in the work of Lukacs, this tradition establishes linkages between new modes of economic production and the rationalizing forces of modernity. Between Simmel and Lukacs, we find an emergent social psychology describing (1) the rise of new forms of consciousness and mental structures based on exchange relations, and (2) an imagery of rationalization evoking an oppressiveness associated with the reification of objects and social relations. Both of these thinkers posit a close relationship between the principle of market exchange and the rationalization of culture. Relatedly, commenting on the cultural impact of the commodity form, some members of the Frankfurt School focus on the privatizing and manipulative effects of mass consumption as a form of domination, thereby putting forth the notion of an "administered culture." Third, by demystifying the structural separation of consumption and production, this theoretical tradition lays claim to the notion of "artificial needs." In this view, a major imperative of a profit-driven economic system is to push consumption beyond the level of basic or "true" needs to the creation of novel or conditioned needs, which in turn become the basis of new and expanding markets.

By contrast, status-seeking theory seeks to address the social functions of the commodity as object, viewing consumption as a terrain for the expression of social hierarchy. Veblen's interest in the consumption side of class behavior has much in common with Weber's inquiry into the status group as a manifestation of "economically related" social and cultural action patterns. The notion of conspicuous consumption evokes an analytical distinction between economic and social class inherent in Weber's model of inequality but often overshadowed by the attention given Weber's concept of status group. In Veblen's view, consumption serves to differentiate social class structure through a system of significatory markings. Despite its specific relevance for class inequality, this view of consumption can be applied more generally to the expressive processes differentiating modern social groupings. But in observing the social dynamics of consumer society, the status-seeking tradition uncovers some of the inherent contradictions of status systems, for example the unavoidable cyclical weakening and redrawing of hierarchical boundaries. By addressing the social meanings and effects of real-life consumption practices, the status-seeking tradition imparts an important empirical dimension to the study of consumer relations, enabling social critics to raise questions about the alleged injurious effects of emulative spending. Ironically, while rooted in Veblen's sardonic attitude toward the spending habits of the monied classes, this tradition became popular among mainstream social scientists during a period of consumer democratization in the fifties and sixties, who accordingly critiqued *middle*-class affluence. As against the theory of commodity fetishism, most writers in the status-seeking tradition (with the exception of Galbraith) ignore the interests of producers, adopting instead a critical view of *consumer* motives. But insofar as these critics scrutinize the connections between goods possession and invidious social distinction, they develop their own limited kind of commodity critique in the form of an everyday, practical sociology of status-based consumption.

Finally, authors reading consumption as a form of hedonism re-raise a number of psychological issues shaping the Frankfurt critique, especially that of Adorno. Freudian constructions of the subject of mass culture reflect an historical shift toward an economy in need of rising levels of consumer desire and a cultural apparatus capable of stimulating and controlling consumption on a mass basis. While the Freudian categories explicit in Adorno's work remain only implicit in writers such as Bell, Lasch, Bauman, and Campbell, these categories continue to inflect responses to a culture whose commercial success depends upon a psychoanalytically oriented view of consumers.

The trajectory from Marxian political economy to hedonism theories—the shift from a discourse of need to one of desire—reflects underlying changes in the imperatives of capitalist production. While in its early stages geared mainly to basic needs of the population, an expanding capitalism depends upon the enlargement of want beyond the daily requirements of food, clothing, shelter, and other necessities. The concept of need thus serves as a normative foundation for the critique of commodity fetishism and for the theory of false need creation.[12] Terminology, however, has been an obstacle to precise thinking about the character and importance of the transition to a consumption system based on the stimulation of desire. Terms such as "conditioned needs" or "false needs" point to the manipulations and deceits of commercial pleasure-based consumption, but obscure important distinctions between need and want.

Deploying the notion of manipulation, Marxian-inspired critiques rightly focus on the systematic and sophisticated links between the profit motive and modern-day consumption, thereby underscoring the relevance of production for the functioning and shape of consumer culture. But these critiques reach their limit in failing to take into account the viewpoint and experience of the consumer. For the consuming subject, pleasure seeking contains an inherently positive moment, a gratification and compensation that needs to be taken seriously as representing an important counterweight to claims of manipulation. The thematization of pleasure therefore is double-sided, projecting both the specter of domination and control and a more optimistic but neglected line of questioning about the subjective and social functions and meanings of consumption at the point of gratification.

A foundation of consumer culture from its beginnings, pleasure seeking has become a salient theme in contemporary theoretical and historical treatments of consumption. Campbell's provocative work illustrates how pleasure as a cultural and psychological phenomenon is subjectively and actively constituted within the experience of self. The theme of pleasure thus invites numerous possibilities for a theory of consumption capable of balancing the one-sidedly negative diagnoses of an Adorno or Lasch.

Against the backdrop of commodity fetishism but emerging from the insights of the status-seeking and hedonism lineages, the constitution of self and identity in consumer culture can be read in terms of both its identificatory and gratificatory functions and their interrelationships. But before pursuing the place of identity and pleasure in consumption, we need to explore some varieties of post-Marxian theories of consumption and culture and their relationships to the three major perspectives discussed in this chapter.

2 Culturalizing Consumption

I n recent decades, "culture" has become uncommonly popular in academic studies.[1] To provide a brief background, a growing formalistic concern with the problem of meaning—culture's *élan vital*—first emerged in the twentieth-century linguistic turn,[2] a development in which philosophers took up a variety of problems associated with language and its uses. This led eventually to the formation of three distinct but overlapping bodies of theory: semiotics, structuralism, and poststructuralism.[3] Despite important differences, the unifying thread of these theories has been a claim for the primacy of language and discourse as the irreducible ground of meaning. The main popular impact of these developments has been the notion, embraced by many in the U.S. cultural-studies tradition, that everything (both material and nonmaterial objects) can be "read" as a "text." In their later phases, these developments gave rise to a sense of epistemological and representational crisis, as conveyed in the poststructuralist emphasis on the instabilities of language and as associated specifically with the movement called "deconstruction" (Derrida 1976, 1978). Some regard this crisis as the defining moment of "postmodernism," broadly understood as a problematization of meaning, a position or sentiment endorsed by the Nietzschean dictum that "everything is interpretation." In this view, what we take to be knowledge or truth is contained (or imprisoned) in unstable cultural constructs that are as contingent, particularistic, variable, and relative as "lived culture" itself. In a strong version of this argument, even purportedly objective, universal, scientifically based views of nature are cultural constructs conditioned and shaped by the social and formal structures of language and discourse and therefore as susceptible to instability as any discursive system.

Associated mainly with French theory, the textual metaphor has had a significant impact, encouraging the idea that cultural phenomena in general are comparable to the workings of language and discourse in particular. But what began as a linguistic turn was succeeded by a "cultural turn," as manifested in the widespread growth of the loosely defined, interdisciplinary field of cultural studies. While notions of textuality remained, cultural studies was driven more by new social and historical understandings of culture and a sense of its ascendant importance in the twentieth century. While recognition of the rise of new and powerful apparatuses of culture has remained mostly implicit, the popularity of cultural studies refracts the impact on human consciousness of a commercialized consumer culture and specifically the expansion of new technologies of communication.

This chapter provides an account of how the semiotic perspective in particular has shaped the study of consumption and consumer culture, along with an appraisal of cultural studies and its contributions to this enterprise. While semiotics and cultural studies provide powerful insights and tools, I argue that lacking in both is a conception of individual and social subjects adequate to the task of understanding the workings of consumption and consumer culture.

Given its growing significance, the concept of culture needs to be put into theoretical context. In the "omnibus" anthropological conception of culture derived from the study of preindustrial life, everything in organized human society is "cultural" by definition.[4] Theories of modernity, by contrast, have assigned culture to a specialized and autonomous realm of aesthetic creativity and formalization (Dunn 1998; Habermas 1983, 1984; Lash 1990; Weber 1958b). Importantly, theories of postmodernity imply a *return* to an anthropological state of cultural omnipresence. However, if everything is again now cultural, this is so in the novel sense that society is saturated with images and information and therefore in a general state of semiosis.[5] In this argument, media-based postmodern society reverses the differentiating tendencies of modernity, leading to a process of "de-differentiation," a dissolution of the boundaries of cultural specialization (Lash 1990), or what Fredric Jameson referred to as "an explosion: a prodigious expansion of culture throughout the social realm" (1984, 86). In this respect, commodity society represents a massive interpenetration of the economic and cultural spheres.[6] Within the consumer marketplace, the main effect of these tendencies is a collapse of formerly distinct forms and genres, resulting in a generalized cultural eclecticism (Dunn 1998; Jameson 1984). Thus, the earlier compartmentalization of culture, involving segregation of the aesthetic dimension, is followed by a reabsorption of the aesthetic by the objects and images of everyday life. This reaestheticization marks the birth of the consumer-culture industry.

The source of aesthetic reabsorption can be traced to the two faces of the commodity. Initially an object of use and exchange, the commodity simultaneously bears its own unique powers of visual representation. As discussed in Chapter One, Marx saw the commodity as a new mode of representation, constituting a novel world of appearances in which, as Lukacs observed, perception and consciousness undergo radical transformation. For Marx, commodity exchange substituted for the unmediated, direct encounters of precapitalist social relations a new and reified world of objects. As "relations among things" displaced "relations among people," the commodity disclosed its true essence as an entirely new form of cultural experience and meaning. It was implicit in Marx's theory of fetishization that in the capitalist mode of production objects acquire an ontological and social significance exceeding their use and exchange value. As Lukacs made explicit, the commodity imparts to human consciousness an ideological structure. For Simmel, commodification shapes social and cultural experience-in-general. Finally, the Frankfurt School explored the deeper psychological, cultural, and political effects of commodification in the context of twentieth-century technology and mass culture. But despite these early attempts to uncover the noneconomic meanings and effects of the commodity, it was left to later thinkers to situate the commodity in a *cultural system* of objects and to characterize its aesthetic functions (Chapter Three).

The Signing of Consumer Culture

The Commodity/Sign Form: Baudrillard

The provocative French theorist Jean Baudrillard is a pivotal figure in post-Marxist cultural analysis. Baudrillard began as a Marxist analyst of consumer culture but later became a harsh critic of the Marxist paradigm of political economy.[7] In his critique of Marxist productivism, Baudrillard laid much of the groundwork for subsequent theoretical reconstructions of capitalist culture.

Baudrillard's breakthrough consisted of adapting a structuralist semiotics to the idea of commodity fetishism, thereby combining economic and cultural models of commodification. The result was his famous concept of the "commodity/sign form." In this concept the commodity is an object not only of economic but more importantly of *semiotic* exchange, an object that signifies within a *socially meaningful system* of objects. In this model, commodities resemble "texts" that operate as constituent elements of the overall "text" of commodity culture. Commodities are constituent elements of a *sign system*, their meaning determined by their coded relations with all other commodities. Importantly, as commodities acquire a semiotic character, signs simultaneously acquire the status and character of commodities. In this interpenetration of culture and economy, the commodity is transformed in favor of the cultural side of its now-double existence. The rise of a "political economy of the sign" therefore implies that "the cultural" has in some sense come to subsume the economic and social dimensions of consumption while at the same time itself being absorbed into the commodity form. Thus,

> Today consumption . . . defines precisely the stage where the commodity is immediately produced as a sign, as sign value, and where signs (culture) are produced as commodities. . . . Nothing produced or exchanged today (objects, services, bodies, sex, culture, knowledge, etc.) can be decoded exclusively as a sign, nor solely measured as a commodity; . . . everything appears in the context of a generalized political economy. . . . The object of this political economy . . . is no longer today properly either commodity or sign, but indissolubly both. (Baudrillard 1981, 147–48)

Baudrillard thus understands aestheticization as the saturation of society in signs, or more precisely images that *contain* or *function* as signs. Consumer culture is thus constituted as a system of signification. Commodities become signifying objects, vehicles of semiotic meaning, in short, "signs."[8] The commodity form thereby gives rise to a system of cultural representation operating independently of the commodity's economic and practical functions (ibid., Baudrillard 1988; Kellner 1989). Signification, which according to Baudrillard now structures the entire capitalist order, inheres in both the commodity and the underlying logic of political economy. Simultaneously, this implies a commodification of culture since nothing escapes the logic of political economy.

In a Veblenesque reading, the commodity/sign form governs a system of difference in terms of which commodities as signifying objects differentiate social positions and memberships. Baudrillard, like Veblen, sees the commodity as a marker of social standing. As commodities/signs, goods (say, automobiles) are positioned in the consumer marketplace according to a system of encoded differences (make, model, price) that communicate messages about the status of their owners. Although Baudrillard himself pays scant attention to class inequalities, his semiotizing of the commodity in principle lends itself to a more systematic and detailed analysis of Veblen's class-based conspicuous consumption.

But Baudrillard's main contribution is a theory of the commodity form, a theory that extends the Frankfurt critique to an image-based cultural system, drawing attention to that aspect of the world of commodities that is pure signification and image, what Guy Debord calls "the spectacle" (1977). Since in their function as relational markers commodities exchange among themselves as signifiers, the circulation of commodities comprises a semiotic system, whereby "things" in the marketplace function like "words" in a language. Further, commodities become self-referential; as signifiers they acquire meaning within the system's own structurally defined and predetermined boundaries (again, just as in language), in what Baudrillard refers to as "the law of the code" (1981, 147). Echoing the Frankfurt theme of domination, Baudrillard sees the system of commodities as constituting a closed universe of discourse equivalent to a system of social control. Whereas the Frankfurt thinkers found social control in the effects of administrative/technological rationalization and psychological manipulation, Baudrillard locates social control in the effects of signifiers, which collapse meaning and experience into pre-established and self-legitimating rules. In this view, consumption practices are less an outcome of the requirements of economic production than an effect of the coded messages of its sign system.

Baudrillard is a seminal theorist in the reconstruction of the commodity fetishism tradition. On the one hand, his critiques undermine the Marxist base/superstructure model supporting the theory of ideology. The signification model of society invalidates the very notion of ideology by effacing distinctions between thought and its underlying material conditions, and between "truth" and "falsehood." By repudiating Marxist political economy, Baudrillard casts his lot with semiotics. But on the other hand, Baudrillard seems to retain a special concept of ideology. His model of the commodity/sign form implies a total autonomization of signification and therefore the elimination of a place for "real" social relations and practices outside the code. In the semiosis of commodities, Baudrillard then sees "need," "purpose," and "function" as no longer real but as having entered into the realm of ideology in the form of "alibis" (Slater 1997, 146–47).

Widely regarded as a postmodern thinker, Baudrillard himself rejects the label, and it is clear from *For a Critique of the Political Economy of the Sign* and his subsequent work that Baudrillard is critical of "actually existing" postmodernism. In fact, he violates one of its cardinal principles by measuring the semiosis of contemporary culture against a normative construct, which he calls "symbolic exchange" (Baudrillard 1993). This notion anchors his critique of commodity culture: the semiotic code leads to and depends upon the destruction of symbolic exchange, an event that Baudrillard considers a loss. What is meant by symbolic exchange, what might be meant generally by a distinction between "signs" and "symbols," and how such a distinction furthers our understanding of the cultural consequences of commodification are questions that are addressed later in this and subsequent chapters.

Notwithstanding his gesture to what he sees as a lost state of affairs involving a richness and authenticity of meaning and experience among "primitive" peoples, Baudrillard's version of consumer culture is in its way as reductionist and deterministic as the productivist Marxism he disavows. His mistakes are informative. Baudrillard's account suffers the inherent weakness of structuralist semiotics in general. In his model, consumer culture is a totalizing system of signification where meanings are fixed by pre-existing codes. It is doubtful that alternative or oppositional forces can emerge when culture is reduced to a seamless web of sign systems. Baudrillard's analysis excludes the gaps and fissures in the sign system itself as well as the potential for modifying or abolishing the sign system by active social subjects. Baudrillard effectively eliminates subjectivity and the field of social relations. Consumers are only systemic agents and not individual and social subjects who think, feel, judge, decide, and act upon their various needs and desires. Finally, it is clear that in his writings on consumption Baudrillard embraces a one-sided cultural or semiotic determinism that for all its penetrating insight is ultimately as misplaced as the economic determinism it replaces. While rightly retaining an emphasis on the commodity form, he fails to escape its limitations by adhering to a structural model of signification. Baudrillard thus projects a pessimism that is comparable to that of the Frankfurt School, which also failed to consider ways in which the system of domination precipitates its own openings or is confronted by either the possibility or reality of social resistance and opposition.

Meanings and Social Practices: Anthropological Functionalism

The contributions of anthropology to a culturalizing of the commodity have already been implied. This field always has regarded culture not only as a system of meaning but more centrally as a whole way of life. By training and inclination, anthropologists contextualize consumption in the inherited daily practices of the group, whether routine or celebratory. Shaped by the study of tribal societies with relatively rudimentary economies, anthropology has seldom if ever recognized distinctions between expressive and utilitarian or "high" and "low" dimensions of culture. Interestingly enough, to the extent that postmodernism means a breakdown of hierarchy, given the historical trend toward an integration and democratization of aesthetic practices, anthropology finds itself in the somewhat ironic but theoretically logical position of being a postmodern discipline.

Theories of signification can be linked to anthropology in any number of ways. As Don Slater suggests (1997, 148–53), the systemic structure and stability implied by semiotics has its analogue in the Durkheimian tradition of social order. In Durkheim's model of "primitive" solidarity, a system of shared, encoded meanings forms the basis for the production and reproduction of collective life. Unlike Baudrillard's semiotics, however, in this model of order, shared meanings are rooted in concrete, everyday social practices. In his late studies of religion, Durkheim illustrated this model by investigating the relationship between collective representations and the ritual habits of the group. For him, the meanings and motivations attached to collective representations were embodied in group needs and practices. Patterns of ritual served to express and renew strongly held beliefs and values, shaping the daily round of material, social, and spiritual practices of group members. While Durkheim saw integration and order as the outcome of group ritual, he understood these processes not in terms of linguistic factors alone but also as the effect of sacralized patterns of collective action (Durkheim 1961, 1964).

Durkheim's sociological functionalism opened new doors to the study of group practices, and even his later anthropological or "culturalist" phase, focused on the study of religion (1961), retained strong functionalist elements. This is relevant to the highly regarded work of Mary Douglas and Baron Isherwood, *The World of Goods* (1979), which in important respects occupies a theoretical intersection between semiotics and anthropology. Although as consumption theorists these authors draw on several analytical sources, at bottom they work from a Durkheimian perspective by seeing goods consumption as a functional foundation of social order.

Aligning themselves with semiotics, Douglas and Isherwood begin by saying, "We start with the general idea that goods are coded for communication" (ibid., xxi). But the authors quickly move beyond semiotics to the "social character" of consumption, arguing that goods provide "marking services" and "consumption rituals," necessary elements of social organization and integration. Since they are not "active agents" but only "signals," goods must be understood in the context of *use*, in the larger arena of practical purposes fulfilled through social interaction. Significantly, Douglas and Isherwood see consumption practices as inseparable from the maintenance of group life in general.

In their words, "The theory of consumption has to be a theory of culture and a theory of social life." While acknowledging the source of cultural meaning in the *relations* among goods, Douglas and Isherwood rightly argue that the relational determinants of meaning cannot be seen as operating independently of the social purposes and practices through which these meanings arise and which they define and regulate. Meaning production is found not only in the *formal* relations making up a system of goods (Baudrillard) but more importantly in the *social* relations within which these goods are appropriated and used by group members. A system of goods, then, is instilled with social meanings through the group purposes and social interactions attached to them in the process of production and consumption. Meaning is infused with practice and vice versa.

Douglas and Isherwood recognize that goods can be regarded either from the standpoint of their meanings or their functions (Slater 1997, 150), but proceed to regard goods in the latter sense as objects that "are needed for making visible and stable the categories of culture" (Douglas and Isherwood 1979, 38). Since meaning "flows and drifts," (ibid., 43) the function of goods is to ritualistically fix meaning as part of the establishment and preservation of organized social life. "Rituals are conventions that set up visible public definitions" (ibid.). Hardly a mere adjunct of culture, consumption is a basic ritual and therefore a necessary *constituent* of culture. The function of goods, then, is to provide ritualistic reference points that publicly structure group practices and therefore hold the cultural system together.

In Douglas and Isherwood's account, goods consumption is readable as an explanation of social order. The very coherence of group life is traceable to patterned habits of goods consumption among group members. At the same time, the authors leave ample room for social change by acknowledging the creative dimension of meaning. First of all, by tying meaning systems to social practices, they infuse meaning with a sense of creativity. Second, the authors make a number of statements suggestive of the inherently unstable and fluid character of meaning. Humans create rituals to "fix" meaning but "consumption is an active process in which all the social categories are being continually redefined" (ibid., 45). In actuality, this is perhaps an unjustified characterization of tribal life and applies more to posttraditional societies. But more importantly, this statement represents a significant departure from the classic Durkheimian integrationist bias. By giving social context to the operation of meanings, Douglas and Isherwood shift from an emphasis on order toward the more realistic possibility that even ritualized meanings are in principle always susceptible to change.

Culture, Class, Power: Pierre Bourdieu

Many are indebted to the ambitious and sophisticated work of Pierre Bourdieu, whose dedication to synthesis of the central tenets of nineteenth-century social theory make him in certain respects a culminating figure in the lineages of capitalist modernity traced in Chapter One, particularly the status-seeking tradition of Veblen. More systematic and sociologically grounded than Baudrillard, Bourdieu distinguishes himself from the former by his persistent focus on social inequality and the effects of class domination.

Bourdieu's wide-ranging interests in language and expressive processes, and his insistence that culture and society are to be read as systems of relations, are obvious manifestations of the impact of semiotics in late twentieth-century French intellectual life. However, Bourdieu rejects the formal semiotics of Saussure, arguing for the sociohistorical nature of linguistic phenomena and for studying them in the context of the social and cultural practices they constitute and express (Bourdieu 1991, Editor's Introduction). Contrary to Baudrillard, Bourdieu denies the autonomy of signification systems, locating them in the social and cultural processes reproducing hierarchical class divisions. For him, the relational and binary character of semiotic difference betrays its embeddedness in class inequalities. Like Veblen, Baudrillard, and Douglas and Isherwood, Bourdieu conceptualizes culture as a system of markings encoding social difference. However, culture as a system of representation emanates from a need to express and establish distinct positions within a *social* system structured by classes and class fractions. Bourdieu's trademark method of contextualizing signification merges culture and class within a classificatory scheme of social distinction.

Attempting to integrate cultural and class analysis, Bourdieu effectively redefines class as the relations of consumption. A provocative extension of Douglas and Isherwood,[9] Bourdieu's analysis of cultural goods assigns them the function of objectifying and legitimizing class differences and representing shifting oppositional relations among classes. While material conditions form the basis of social inequality, "these material differences are experienced and represented *dispositionally* as cultural distinctions" (Swartz 1997, 179, emphasis added).[10] Implicitly adopting a functionalist perspective, Bourdieu focuses on the conservative features of culture: economic inequality is translated into social and cultural differences in the form of "symbolic power," which in turns serves to *reproduce* the class system.[11] But in contrast to Baudrillard's semiotic determinism, in Bourdieu's social subjective conception, goods comprise a signifying system only in relation to *perceptions* and *definitions* of class relations and practices. In *Distinction* Bourdieu writes,

> One only has to bear in mind that goods are converted into distinctive signs, which may be signs of distinction but also of vulgarity, as soon as they are perceived relationally, to see that the representation which individuals and groups inevitably project through practices and properties is an integral part of social reality. A class is defined as much by its *being-perceived* as by its *being*, by its consumption—which need not be conspicuous in order to be symbolic—as much by its position in the relations of production. (Bourdieu 1984, 483)

While attempting to reinstate an anthropological view of culture, Bourdieu simultaneously focuses his attention on the contours of the modern class system, especially the dominant classes. Here, he reconstructs the idea of class conflict, which in advanced societies takes the form of cultural and symbolic struggles for distinction within what he calls a "field" of struggle.[12] Contrary to Marxist class struggle, these struggles tend to be reproductive and integrative, perpetuating rather than undermining the system.

The logic of Bourdieu's redefinition of class as relations of consumption requires him to introduce the modern notion of "taste," which he strategically defines in terms of his model of cultural classification. But while he wishes to understand taste dispositionally, in practice it appears as a structural concept.[13] Taste is "the propensity and capacity to appropriate (materially and symbolically) a given class of classified, classifying objects of practices" (ibid., 173) but it is also "a system of classificatory schemes" (ibid., 174). Taste is the location of the active semiotic function of the system of cultural goods and practices; it is the transformative link between physical objects and their culturally signifying meanings. "Taste is the practical operator of the transmutation of things into distinct and distinctive signs" (ibid., 174). By emphasizing its structurally determined character, Bourdieu imparts to taste a sense of inevitability under a given set of material and social conditions. Inculcated through the socializing agencies of family and education, taste is a necessary product of one's social background and position. In his words, "Taste is a practical mastery of distributions which makes it possible to sense or intuit what is likely (or unlikely) to befall—and therefore to befit—an individual occupying a given position in social space" (ibid., 466).

Closely related, Bourdieu, echoing Weber's conception of status groups, defines "lifestyle" as the systematic expression of class agents' taste dispositions. Lifestyle is "a unitary set of distinctive preferences" generated by taste (ibid., 173). Lifestyle is the cultural differences among the classes coalescing as identifiable patterns of consumption. At first "concealed" from analysis, lifestyle is "the unity hidden under the diversity and multiplicity of the set of practices performed in fields governed by different logics and therefore inducing different forms of realization" (ibid., 101). Lifestyle, then, is the coherent form taken by the distinct cultural practices of the different classes and class fractions.

Yet, despite his gestures to hierarchy, Bourdieu is clearly more interested in class *identities* than inequalities. He pays much less attention to the material gaps supporting the class system than to the group identities of the agents whose tastes and lifestyles position and represent the different classes within the social order. These identities are formed through the processes of cultural classification that class agents actively construct in the struggle for social position.

Unlike Weber, Bourdieu tends to conflate economic class with its cultural correlates. Whereas Weber explicitly distinguishes class and status group, Bourdieu claims that class and status are aspects of the same phenomenon and therefore not separate groupings. Economic groups appear and function as status groups in everyday life, since the latter are the social and cultural *manifestations* of class membership and position. By privileging status over class, Bourdieu conflates what Weber saw as independently varying social formations.[14] Despite his own antireductionist stance, Bourdieu thus tends to ignore nonclass aspects of cultural expressions and projects, restricting consumption-based identity formation to the system of class differences (Miller 1991, 156).

Bourdieu's work on class represents a major contribution to a sociology of consumption, including suggestive implications for the study of identity. However, his approach suffers obvious limitations. First, his overtures to the subject notwithstanding, Bourdieu emphasizes the structural and classificatory divisions of society at the expense of the subjective dimensions of consumption and social actors. Indeed, in *Distinction* Bourdieu slips back into the very objectivism he had hoped to overcome. Second and relatedly, *Distinction* suffers from its ahistorical perspective, and Bourdieu's analysis generally misses the dynamic dimensions of modernity captured in the work of thinkers such as Marx, Weber, and Simmel (ibid.,155). Third, Bourdieu's penchant for mapping oppositionally structured classification schemes, though often capturing the conventional contours and feelings of class difference, leads to an overly simplified and rigid model of cultural consumption. While his schema might represent consumption relations in French society, its applicability to the range of advanced capitalist societies remains problematic. Not only do class systems vary considerably, but also his framework neglects the phenomena of mass consumption and target marketing, which often follow other than class lines. This makes his analysis especially controversial for advanced societies with blurred class boundaries, such as the United States.[15]

Ultimately, Bourdieu's work falls short of a theory of consumption.[16] By neglecting the subjectivity and actual practices of social actors, Bourdieu brackets the *processes* of consumption in favor of an analysis of its *effects*—the reproduction of the class system by means of classificatory taste strategies. Bourdieu unarguably provides a fuller and richer elaboration of the Veblenesque picture of spending as social positioning through display, demonstrating that it is the practice of taste, not production, that defines class difference and the overall shape of class structure and struggle. But in Bourdieuian sociology the *processes* of consumption themselves remain a shadow.

Summary and Critique

The semiotic model firmly establishes that the meaning of a commodity exceeds its use and exchange values, and on this premise consumption historically re-enters the realm of culture. The anthropological and Bourdieuian contributions elaborate the cultural underpinnings and functions of commodity exchange, showing how social order and hierarchy are created and maintained through patterns of goods consumption. Put differently, those places in society where commodities are most dramatically present in our lives—the shopping mall, the showroom, the advertisement—have become sites of *cultural* production in which economic goods are transformed into components of complex meaning systems, reversing the evolutionary separation of culture and economy.

These theories, however, share a strong conservative bias toward social integration, offering only limited insights into how cultural meanings originate, circulate, and change over time. In the formal semiotic model, meanings are entirely self-referential insofar as they arise and operate in a way that is determined by the internal codes (rules) of a sign system. Semiotics in the strict sense regards culture as organized like a language and as therefore exhibiting the structure and order we habitually associate with language as a relatively autonomous and coherent system of meaning. Anthropological functionalism, as exemplified in Douglas and Isherwood's study, similarly centers our attention on the integrative and ordering effects of consumption practices. The authors' recognition of meaning change notwithstanding, Douglas and Isherwood argue that consumption constitutes an overall pattern of ritual, lending stability and predictability to society. Finally, Bourdieu's classification system highlights an ordered hierarchy of semiotically marked statuses, in which taste differences in cultural consumption indicate a person's position in the class system.

Yet, unlike semiotics, anthropological functionalism addresses the social relations and practices that constitute the context in which meanings are produced and consumed, the interactional and practical foundations upon which systems of meaning arise and which they reciprocally influence. Similarly but by very different means, Bourdieu connects the classification of taste differences to cultural and institutional practices, showing how systems of cultural meaning must be read in the context of the actual social relations and practices they define.

At the same time, neither semiotics nor anthropological functionalism offers an adequate account of the generative and creative dimensions of meaning, its unstable and changeful aspects as rooted either in language/discourse or the subjectivity of actors. Douglas and Isherwood, and Bourdieu, demonstrate the inseparability of meaning and practice, the ways of doing things and interrelating socially "on the ground" that give every culture its lived character and material embodiments. However, these authors fail to capture the fluidity and contestability of cultural meaning. Semiotics sees meaning as imprisoned in self-enclosed sign systems, while the anthropological reading offers a relatively conservative and undynamic picture of consumption practices reflecting the tightly knit character of premodern societies. Oddly, Bourdieu's concept of habitus, designed to link actors and social structures, is not an explicit part of his treatment of class consumption patterns.

To find a view of consumption practices as not only reproductive and orderly but also disruptive and oppositional, we turn to the field of cultural studies, a voluminous body of work that includes engaging and lively accounts of both the structures of domination in consumer culture and the forms of active resistance to these structures.

The Legacy of Cultural Studies

In its British version, the field of scholarship and research known as cultural studies can be thought of as a moving, shifting coalescence composed of the tradition of commodity fetishism discussed in Chapter One and certain strands of semiotics and anthropology. Cultural studies is less a coherent body of work than a large array of projects critically engaging major theoretical developments and tendencies emanating from Marxism in the twentieth century.[17] What most distinguish cultural studies are its multiple intellectual and theoretical tendencies, its interdisciplinarity, its innovative conceptualizations and readings of culture, and its political commitment.

Defining Cultural Studies

Considering its diverse forms and the changes following upon its Americanization, there can be no easy agreement on a definition of cultural studies. As Stuart Hall has commented, "Cultural studies is not one thing." . . . "It has never been one thing" (Hall 1990, 11, quoted in Grossberg et al. 1992, 3). Looking back over its life of fifty years or so, cultural studies appears unusually heterogeneous and broad in sweep. Encompassing theories ranging from Marxism (especially Louis Althusser and Antonio Gramsci) to semiotics, feminism, structuralism, poststructuralism, and postmodernism, cultural studies comprises a large corpus of empirical research and an assortment of methodologies spanning the social sciences and humanities. But it does not follow that cultural studies is without a definite theoretical orientation and sense of purpose. Perusing its history and seminal texts reveals an internal logic and direction, giving a discernible unity to an extraordinary diversity.

Cultural studies proceeds implicitly from the premise that all objects in the world can be regarded as "cultural" insofar as they are meaningful and part of a subject's "lived experience." We inhabit a world of culture, and so it is culture that is the ontological and epistemological ground of everything we know and experience. In this respect, cultural studies as a movement or field constitutes the identifiable core, especially in its institutional locations in the United States, of the "cultural turn" in academia. Its adherents have made strong, however nuanced, statements on such issues as textuality, the self-reflexivity of knowledge, the problem of identity and difference, and postmodern notions of contingency and provisionality. At the same time, from the beginning cultural studies has insisted on a close relationship between "culture" and "society" (Williams 1960), more specifically the interrelatedness of the economic, social, cultural, and historical moments of its objects of study, as well as the dynamic contradictoriness of all the social relations (class, race, ethnicity, gender, sexuality, age, nationality) embedded in cultural phenomena.

From the outset, cultural studies was closely allied to Marxism. Indeed, according to one commentary, "All the basic assumptions of cultural studies are Marxist" (Storey 1996, 3). While this might beg questions about the meaning of "Marxist," it is clear that British cultural studies has always placed strong emphasis on the sociohistorical context of cultural phenomena along with the view that modern industrial societies are unequally divided along class and other lines (ibid.). But an understanding of cultural studies begins with a recognition that it developed (like the Frankfurt School) largely as a critical response to the crises of twentieth-century Marxism, most notably the theoretical failures of the base/superstructure model but in some sense also the relative absence of class consciousness and revolution among the working classes in Western capitalism. However, it was primarily the base/superstructure problem that instigated the shift from notions of economic primacy to a more balanced view of the interrelatedness of the material and symbolic spheres that is the hallmark of key cultural-studies texts.

The political character of cultural studies is apparent in its early concern for disempowered populations, most notably youth cultures and working-class communities (Brake 1980; Hebdige 1979; Hoggart 1957; Thompson 1966; Williams 1960; Willis 1977, 1978, 1990). But cultural studies can be regarded as political more generally in its focus on (1) "the popular," or the everyday lived experiences of the underlying population, and on (2) the unequal divisions giving rise to contradictory and conflictual relations among social groups (Storey 1996). While drawing on interpretive and evaluative conceptions and methods (a trend most apparent in humanities-based U.S. examples), cultural studies is centered on an anthropological conception of culture and its ethnographic methods, which in the context of modern industrial society logically directs attention to popular culture.

What most distinguishes the approach of British cultural studies, however, is the claim that culture is to be viewed as relations of power. But popular culture is seen as contested terrain, to be viewed through the lens of structured relations of dominance *and* resistance involving struggles over the communication or construction of meaning. Gramsci's (1973) concept of hegemony, with its emphasis on the idea of consent as the foundation of the ruling powers' control, is used to conceptualize power relations as potentially unstable. From the standpoint of cultural studies, the source of this instability is to be found in the many meanings that necessarily enter into the "encoding/decoding" process shaping the production and consumption of popular cultural discourses. While formulated primarily with regard to how television audiences consume media messages (Fiske 1987, 1989a, 1989b; Hall 1980), the concept of the "polysemic text" is in principle applicable to all forms of popular culture. Hence, the power relations constituting the production and consumption of culture are seen as dependent on inherently contestable meanings. In contrast, as some have disapprovingly argued (Nelson 1996), U.S. cultural studies, less theoretical and political than its forebear, while retaining a focus on the popular meanings of cultural products and practices in their everyday contexts and situations, has largely lost any perspective on culture as a system of power and domination.

Given its interests in culture and power, defining cultural studies can benefit from a comparison to the Frankfurt School. Both interrogate the idea of "cultural domination," the earlier thinkers by examining the modern apparatuses of the state, economy, and culture industry, the British scholars by scrutinizing the ideological structures of cultural communication. In the more pessimistic views of the Frankfurt School, however, a way out of the system of total administration is apparently impossible, whereas in the approach of cultural studies there are discernible moments of "resistance" to the ideological messages of the ruling powers, whether in the schools (Willis 1977), the mass media (Fiske 1987, 1989a, 1989b; Morley 1980, 1986, 1992), or other sites of contestable meaning (Hall and Jefferson 1976). For Adorno, in the face of a controlling and manipulating cultural system there was only refuge in "autonomous" art. By contrast, cultural-studies scholars have turned to the potentially oppositional and emancipatory practices of specific subcultures, which they see as sources of autonomy and liberation. The overall difference in the leanings of the traditions is perhaps captured in the conceptual/discursive gap between "mass culture" (commercialized, imposed from above) and "popular culture" (authentic, arising from below), although most cultural-studies scholars would reject any fixed boundaries between the two, arguing for a tension between these opposing "moments." Nonetheless, we find in cultural studies a trajectory leading away from the discourse of commodity fetishism to notions of subcultural formation, reflecting a theoretical transition from political economy to a semiotic conception of material culture as actively constituted in particular discursive and social relations that are inherently unstable (the poststructuralist moment) and thus potentially emancipatory. In this transition, Althusser's revisions of Marx and specifically his reformulation of the concept of ideology facilitate a rethinking of notions of structural determination, while the Gramscian concept of hegemony is deployed to reveal the complex but dynamic and often indeterminate effects of power at the level of "common sense" located in the lived beliefs, representations, and everyday practices of individual and social subjects (Hall 1996).

Beginning with its initial engagements with the meanings of "culture," and specifically the modern rise of cultural division and hierarchy giving birth to the idea of "elite" vs. "popular" culture, early cultural-studies work effectively shifted attention from the production to the consumption side of capitalism. This shift was prefigured in the founding texts by Richard Hoggart (1957), E.P. Thompson (1966), and Raymond Williams (1960), all of whom wrote about the lived meanings and experiences of "ordinary" people—members of a common working population—who were the source of popular cultural formations. Eventually, the notion of culture as a "way of life" and specifically the concept of popular culture became identified with the consumption practices embodying the shared meanings and representations of particular groups. Cultural-studies researchers began to study how "ordinary" people consume the cultural objects constituting their worlds, whether in the form of television, movies, clothing, or other mass-produced products. In doing so, cultural studies effectively repositioned consumer culture, loosening its conceptual ties to political economy and formal semiotics, both of which retain strong elements of reductionism. Cultural studies has thus attempted to conceptualize consumer culture as occupying a tension between structural relations operating at an unconscious level *and* active subjects who unconsciously and consciously define the meanings of cultural products via their own social positions and experiences as workers, consumers, youth, and so forth (Hall 1996). For cultural studies, popular culture is consumer culture in the complex sense that *on the ground* consumption involves subjects producing their *own* cultural meanings through a range of individual and social practices, drawing on a multitude of discursive frameworks and social experiences that they bring to their experience of mass culture. Here, the concept of subculture links the idea of a consumer culture to the theme of resistance by showing how local and diverse communities of consumers resist the incursions of commercial culture by recontextualizing, redefining, and reappropriating it for their own pragmatic and creative purposes.

A Critique

Disputing the one-dimensional and totalizing conception of commodity-based views, cultural studies posits an active as opposed to passive subject along with a creative process of meaning-making on the part of consumers whose relationship to the hegemonic commercial system is only partial, fragmented, and unstable. By empirically exploring various subcultural worlds, cultural studies locates alternative spaces where subjects can be found producing their own cultural practices and meanings. Overcoming the integrationist bias of the functionalism of Douglas and Isherwood, and Bourdieu, cultural-studies scholars see these creative spaces as potential sources of change. Actual consumption *practices* thus contain a range of subversive possibilities.

Despite these advances over previous theories, however, cultural studies can be found wanting on a number of grounds. First, by focusing on subcultural formations, the field neglects the mainstream population. Ironically, the "common" or "ordinary" person celebrated in the founding texts is often missing from later works, which favor marginal and deviant groups who are somewhat romanticized as radicals subverting the established order (Clarke 1991, 103, 111). Hence, the political commitments of cultural studies have restricted attention to subordinated groups, thereby introducing unrepresentatively strong reactive elements into subjects' responses to commercial culture. The resulting picture is often one of subcultures as oppositional political projects. As a consequence, the reality of conventional and habitual consumption practices across population divisions is largely ignored. The axiom that cultural meanings are structured within a set of power relations mistakenly assumes that people always read or represent their experiences in "explicitly political or ideological" ways (Lembo and Tucker 1990, 99).

Second, cultural studies is vulnerable to charges of exaggerating the active as opposed to passive character of the consumer. A selective focus on youth and deviant subcultures tends to skew our view of consumption toward the practices of the most innovative and volatile segments of the population while ignoring the more conformist elements and the patterned routines cutting across the social divisions of class, age, and so forth. A focus on deviant subcultures runs a risk of misrepresenting the actual effects of consumption as well as the balance of hegemonic and resistant forces at any given historical moment. These criticisms point to a kind of "cultural optimism" that is in certain respects the mirror opposite of the "structural pessimism" of the theory of commodity fetishism (Clarke 1991, 86) and as equally problematic.

Third, by looking only at subcultural resistance, cultural studies excludes an analytical picture of the individual, missing a host of subjective processes related to self and occurring at different moments in the consumption process—daydreaming, shopping, purchasing, possessing, using. Consumption is subjectively complex, involving a range of thoughts and feelings in individual consumers who are continuously making judgments and choices based on practical interests, feelings, and emotions. The multiple dimensions of individual and social subjectivity, including not only pleasure and pain but specific feelings of envy, pride, insatiability, anxiety, longing, greed, temptation, and so forth go unaccounted for despite their important place in the continuum of satisfaction and dissatisfaction against which the meanings of consumption need to be measured. Despite the risk of positing an abstract consumer beyond the positioning of class, gender, race, and so forth, a theory of consumption needs to address its social psychological structure and human attributes.

Finally, while recognizing the differentiations of social power based on class, gender, age, race, ethnicity, and nationality, cultural studies fails to recognize important distinctions among (1) different *forms* of consumption (goods, services, entertainment) and their material *contents*, and (2) the different *subjectivities* associated with these forms and contents. In emphasizing the social divisions and processes of the consuming population, cultural studies neglects the structural variety of consumption practices and their corresponding subjective formations.

Summary

The virtue of cultural studies is its politically engaged efforts to deploy an assortment of theoretical ideas and research methods for the sake of developing a comprehensive account of consumption and consumer culture. By shifting attention to the meaning structures and social relations of capitalist society, it has moved beyond the one-dimensionality of commodity theory and formal semiotics. While falling short of real synthesis, cultural studies has demonstrated the advantages of a non-disciplinary approach to culture, of drawing on multiple theoretical and empirical sources, and of a close focus on the object of study. Paradoxically, however, from the standpoint of consumption studies, the limitations of this field follow largely from giving too much attention to the practices and representations of actual social groupings. Thus, its anthropological, ethnographic, and semiotic bent is both its strength and weakness. Relatedly, the political interests of cultural studies tend to link it too closely to identity politics, with all of its attendant problems. Overall, a concentration on the "particular" leaves cultural studies vulnerable to charges of avoiding the "general." The ethnographic impulse to articulate the position of marginal groups succeeds at the expense of an analysis of the larger system of commodity production and consumption and how this shapes the consciousness and emotional lives of contemporary consumers.

Conclusion: Signification and Symbolization

In an historical reversal of modernity's differentiation of society into specialized spheres, the aesthetic dimension—for years consigned to museums, concert halls, galleries, and other institutions of "high culture"—has aggressively reclaimed daily life in the form of a commercialized system of signs and images, concentrated in advertising and the mass media. In the contemporary consumer landscape, the aesthetic has undergone metamorphosis as a consequence of an unprecedented growth in advertising, packaging, and media images accompanying technological and economic innovation. This cultural "explosion" is part and parcel of the rise of consumption as a collective and individual way of life.

The theoretical shift from political economy to cultural studies reflects this transformation. In an odd return to the condition of preliterate and traditional societies, material modes of representation have come to pervade everyday life, shaping perceptions of self, others, and the world in general. As will be shown in Chapter Three, in bringing about this transformation, a special role has been assigned to sign systems and more generally the dimension of aesthetic perception. Far from being a mere academic fad, the popularity of semiotics is a response to the semiosis of everyday cultural life instigated by commercialism and the commodity form. The culturalist tradition has shown us how to deconstruct commodities and images as cultural objects, reading them as signs or texts. Not only do commodities and images convey social and cultural meanings of an ideological nature, both dominating and contested, but also they mark identity and difference among individuals and groups. Aesthetics has been mobilized to provide a form for these processes. Culturalist readings of consumption have drawn extensively on semiotics, and to a lesser extent on aesthetic theory, as a strategy for illuminating the character and workings of these processes.

This massive development, however, is in need of historical perspective and fresh theoretical arguments. A beginning can be made by drawing a fundamental distinction between sign systems, which have been enlisted to serve the process of commodification and the rise of consumer culture, and symbol systems, which while serving the interests of sign systems simultaneously sustain the possibility of meaning outside the commodity form. As alluded to in Baudrillard's notion of symbolic exchange, the triumph of the sign stands in direct relationship to a decline in processes of symbolization. In many respects, the decay of symbols (Lefebvre 1984, 39, 62) remains the unwritten story of the cultural transformations of modernity as well as the ghost haunting the image-saturated landscape of postmodernity.

The task of distinguishing between signs and symbols remains an unfinished project that promises a new understanding of consumer culture. Following Robert Bocock's observation that "There is a confusion in much of the existing literature between 'signs' and 'symbols'" (1993, 72–73), I argue that overcoming this confusion is a necessary step in rethinking and reformulating the central problems of a critical cultural theory. This has particular relevance for the dialectic of domination and resistance, since the sign/symbol distinction is fundamental in reading and assessing the impact of consumer culture and its oppressive and liberatory implications for social subjects.

The sign is a rather impoverished but instrumentally effective vehicle of meaning. A major component of consumer culture, the role of the sign has been enlarged by commodification and commercialization, increasingly serving these interests through the deliberate efforts of advertisers and marketers. As an instrument for selling commodities, the sign itself is manufactured for a specific purpose.

In contrast to the reductive and unidimensional character of the sign, symbols are characterized by depth and multidimensionality. A symbol bears value and significance bestowed on it by the collective experience and memory of social subjects. Accordingly, the meaning of a symbol is as potentially rich, complex, deep, and fluid as human subjectivity itself. Because they are constructed and elaborated through the shared experiences, responses, and aspirations of human subjects, symbols represent a world of potentiality. To take a common example, while on one level the epitome of the materially fixed form and meaning of signs, national flags are also powerful symbols to the extent that they become highly charged with subjectively mediated and contested meanings and feelings. Thus, the American flag is not only replete with evocations of patriotism and nationalism but subverted into an object of antiwar and anti-American sentiment. As such, it is a symbol not only of positive identifications and aspirations but of political hostility and opposition.

It is already established that the meanings attached to signs are fixed by the rules (or code) governing their operation, such as in advertising messages, whose goal is a predefined behavior (purchases). As Baudrillard suggests, what most defines systems of signification is their operationality and functionality (1981). By contrast, what most defines symbols is their openness and range. The difference between signs and symbols approximates the distinction in language between "denotation" and "connotation," the latter being what Barthes calls "second order" signs (1957, 1964). Also as in language, the two processes occur in different mixes and balances in different cultures under different conditions. In consumer culture, the differences between signs and symbols become salient and consequential, and their relationship has major practical and political significance.

One source of confusion between signs and symbols is their interchangeability, or better, their mutual vulnerability. Any material or nonmaterial object is susceptible to symbolization, including signs themselves (as when commercial images are transformed into art by Andy Warhol). By the same token, symbols can erode through time and commercialization into mere signs (as when Warhol's art becomes indicative of a certain type of stylistic sensibility denoting popular urban fashion or even becomes an icon of semiosis itself). The ease with which a sign can turn into a symbol and vice versa in a rapidly changing mass consumer society introduces a set of dynamics and perpetual ambiguities that are historically unprecedented.

By overprivileging signs at the expense of symbols, cultural theory has conflated these distinct but interrelated dimensions of meaning. One consequence has been an overly close and uncritical identification of theory with the structures of commercial culture whose existence now depends upon a highly rationalized process of signification. In the absence of a distinction between the semiotic and the symbolic, conceptual spaces for human creativity and action "from below" tend to disappear in what appears to be a closed and impermeable system of manufactured representation. While registering a real historical tendency toward a corporate-based universe of meaning, by excluding a conception of the symbolic, semiotics and other varieties of structural analysis inadvertently foreclose theoretical exploration of alternative or oppositional possibilities that could reshape society.

The widespread attenuation of symbolic processes and the corresponding rise of sign systems points to a diminished and superficial culture. This implies a need in cultural analysis for a theory of the differences between signification and symbolization and their interrelationship (Jaeger and Selznick 1964; White 1949). Such a theory would provide a more complex reading of hegemony and opposition by showing how signs function as instruments of manipulation, how symbols can be vehicles of human creativity, hope, and renewal, and how the two intermix in complicated ways in contemporary consumer culture.

As exemplified by Baudrillard and Bourdieu, semiotic theory offers a compelling and powerful picture only of the dominant tendencies of consumer society. By contrast, a distinction between the narrowing signifying and broadening symbolic dimensions of consumer culture offers a strategy for disclosing the double nature of

consumption—the systemic forces of commodification and commercialization on the one hand and the creativity and aspirations of
actors on the other. How these two dimensions enter into a critical
cultural analysis of consumption will be explored in Chapter
Three.

3 The Subjectivity of Consumption

"Men (*sic*) make their own history but they do not make it . . . under circumstances chosen by themselves, but under circumstances directly encountered, given, and transmitted from the past."[1] This familiar quotation from Marx remains a classic nineteenth-century expression of what is generally regarded as the central problem of modern social theory: the dualism of subject and object, or what has come to be known as the "agency/structure" problem. In most formulations, the term "agency" has been substituted for "making history" to introduce an analytical expression for the truism that people act, an axiom with implications of freedom, choice, and autonomy. Similarly, "structure" (definable in numerous ways, but in most dictionaries as an arrangement of interrelated parts constituting a whole) is often the preferred term for "unchosen circumstances," a set of "objective" limiting conditions of a determinative social or historical nature that constrain and facilitate action. In a pure version of the agency image, society is implicitly understood as "people doing things" and "making meanings." As structure, society is "thing-like," an already-existing entity inhibiting or propelling action in ways often beyond subjects' conscious control. Here, society is understood as a preestablished field of meanings, conditions, and relationships that antedate and are reproduced (unwittingly or otherwise) by the conduct of individuals.[2]

The widely discussed agency/structure problem[3] is of special importance to an inquiry into the subjective aspects of consumption and the consumer. Typically, "agency" has referred to the active and subjective dimensions of social life, serving as the key term in various action theories giving primacy to the intentional or voluntarist elements of social behavior.[4] While the popularity of these theories reflects a much-needed reaction to what Anthony Giddens has called the "orthodox consensus" in sociology (1984, xv), most notably structural-functionalism and other objectivistic and naturalistic theories, these alternate theories have been overly abstract and general, remaining in the realm of "metatheory." Moreover, the swing to the subjective side of social life often has been at the expense of the objective side, resulting in a simple inversion of the weaknesses of opposing paradigms. These are but symptoms of the chronic dilemmas and antinomies accompanying the voluntarist/determinist, subjectivist/objectivist, and micro/macro dichotomies in social theory.[5]

Much of the difficulty stems from the concept of agency itself. One problem is that agency has a double meaning, which includes both (1) the idea of activity or the exercise of power, and (2) a notion of instrumentality or a means by or through which activity or power is *manifested*. While the first definition implicitly links behavior to the subject, the second closely ties agency to structure. The difficulty is that if agency refers to the *means* of executing or realizing something else, by implication agency is simply the outward or "active" manifestation of structure or some other force or influence. If this is the case, agency carries the same implications of limitation, regulation, and control (normative, situational, material, or otherwise) as structure. Given this ambiguity, the agency/structure dichotomy begs the question of the source or ground of human action and the origin and nature of whatever power is manifested. Secondly, and another aspect of the same problem, the concept of agency is inherently instrumental. Despite suggestions of activity or movement in the first definition, it is difficult in practice to think of agency as anything but a medium or vehicle for something other than itself, a means or proxy, as in the notion of "agent." For these reasons, it has proven difficult to analytically disentangle agency from structure. Efforts to do so have tended to reproduce a recurrent bias toward structure, serving only to perpetuate deterministic and reductionistic positions.[6]

Given these problems, in lieu of the language of agency/structure, I propose a discourse of "actor" and "system."[7] This serves a number of purposes. First of all, an "actor" is not a mere agent of something or someone else, but rather a human subject who thinks, feels, and acts in self-motivated, self-interested, and self-reflexive ways. Despite objections that, given the social and material foundations of human action, this can only be a useful theoretical fiction, this concept of the actor has a sound theoretical and empirical basis in the idea of self and its *reflexive* capacities. Such a conception is a necessary basis for exploring the *subjectivity* of action. By this, I mean a reading of social and cultural practices from the standpoint of subjects who experience, reflect upon, and define their own actions in conscious and reflexive ways, notwithstanding the largely unconscious forces emanating from a system.[8] Second, I suggest that the real lesson to be learned from the Frankfurt School, Baudrillard, and their critics, is to focus on the enduring dialectical *tensions* between actors and the system. In addressing commodity critique, whether, to what extent, and in what ways consumers are or merely appear to be puppets or dupes need to be considered in terms of these tensions. Third, the notion of "system" refers to real tendencies toward domination and control inherent in a bureaucratized capitalist society and semiotized cultural environment, and these tendencies obviously need to be taken into account in portraying consumers as actors. The notion of system in particular resonates with Baudrillard's account of the commodity/sign form (1981), which, predicated on a homology between political economy and semiotics, can be read as an extension of the Frankfurt claims of manipulation and domination. Lastly, not only is the notion of system more appropriate for analyzing consumer culture and its effects, but also the term is more manageable than "structure," which over the years has acquired a variety of meanings and applications. The terminology of actor and system avoids the pitfalls of the agency/structure dualism by providing a window on consumer subjectivity and a more grounded description of how the self is shaped by, and shapes, commodity society.

Reprising but moving beyond major points from the discussions of Chapters One and Two, this chapter explores the subjectivity of consumption. In contrast to the method of cultural studies, which relies on ethnographic and semiotic readings, I attempt to construct a generic consuming subject. This subject will be analytically located in the spaces among the main theoretical traditions in the study of consumption. Emphasis will be placed on the themes of *meaning*, *pleasure*, and *identity*. The consuming subject will be interrogated primarily in terms of the production and satisfaction of desire and its associated meanings and secondarily in terms of the shaping of identity and self. The one-sided critique of commodity theory tends to reduce consumption to the effects of market-based mechanisms of manipulation and control in what Baran and Sweezy called "the sales effort" (1966, 114). As a counterbalance, I present a set of formulations that highlight the mediating subjectivity and self-interest of the consumers toward whom the sales effort is directed. As social subjects, consumers both enact codes and construct their own meanings and identities. This approach involves an effort to accommodate or reconcile contending views of the consumer by addressing at once the material, social, cultural, and psychological dimensions of consumer culture. I argue that most debates about commodity society have lacked basis in an adequate analysis and portrayal of the subjective side of consumption and that this entails moving beyond inherited, well-worn critiques.

In what follows, an attempt will be made to ground the concepts of system and culture in the *relationship* between commodity and consumer and the mediating factors in this relationship. This takes the form of a general outline of the dynamics of meaning, desire and gratification in commodity culture considered from the standpoint of both system and actor. Additionally, this chapter begins to situate the self in present-day consumer society in anticipation of a fuller discussion of identity formation presented in Part Two.

Deconstructing the Commodity:
Aesthetics as Promise and Deception

In theories of modernity, four themes stand out as especially pertinent to consumption. First, in the original versions of commodity critique found in Marx and subsequently elaborated and modified by Lukacs, Simmel, Adorno, and Baudrillard, we find a line of thinking pointing to a growth in the power of *objects* and a corresponding diminution of the subject. Second, the Frankfurt School critiques have provoked recurring controversies over questions of *manipulation* and *domination* of consumers by a "totalizing" system of strategies designed both to sell products and shape subjectivity in ways beneficial to capitalism. Third, running through Lukacs, Weber, and Henri Lefebvre (and more recently the popular work of George Ritzer[9]) is a perspective that would attribute to consumer society deepening patterns of *rationalization*. Finally, from a later generation of theorists (though linked to the concerns of earlier thinkers as diverse as Weber and John Dewey) there emerges a set of arguments about the *aestheticization* of society associated with the process of commodification. To illuminate the nature and underlying processes shaping consumer subjectivity, all four themes need further development. It is particularly important to elucidate the process of aestheticization and to connect this process to the distinction between the semiotic and symbolic functions of commodities.

The aforementioned themes point to major tendencies in the logic of the modern capitalist system. However, these themes, in conjunction with a focus on the idea of system, constitute a view of consumption as a behavior and way of life imposed unilaterally from the centers of socioeconomic power, absent an active and mediating subject. Correcting this lopsided picture means looking at consumer society in terms of its relationship to—and dependency on—social actors. The main link in this relationship is the commodity as an object of meaning, satisfaction, and identification. In what follows, I attempt to "deconstruct" the commodity in its contemporary form for the purpose of revising and extending past critiques, focusing on how commodities shape consumer subjectivity and behavior and how consumers find meaning in commodities.

As we saw in Chapter One, Marx and Lukacs saw this "mysterious" thing, the commodity, as the source of the alienating and consciousness distorting conditions of capitalist society. Creating an oppressive "objecthood," the commodity form was the underlying cause of reification. However, these thinkers effectively deferred analysis of the *internal relations* of the commodity itself, concentrating instead on its external structural features in the context of class divisions and ideological formations. As a consequence, their understanding of the impact of the commodity form on human subjects was limited to a theory of alienation and reification, a problem of the increasing *abstractness* of life inherent in the growth of exchange value. Indeed, for Lukacs commodification was the force behind what Weber had seen as an increasing rationalization of society. We find a similar deferral in the writings of Simmel, who turned his attention to the social and cultural structures of commodity exchange and consumption. Curiously, there is a significant difference between Simmel's mixed but often positive appraisal of the formation of exchange relations in *The Philosophy of Money* and his later more pessimistic "tragedy of culture" essays on the problematic subject/object relation, in which consumption becomes a form of psychological alienation precipitated by an excess of goods. In these essays, Simmel forged a deeper ontological understanding of modern subjectivity. But by delimiting the problem of identity and recognition to the widening *gulf* between the self and object world, Simmel, too, postpones a probing of the commodity on its own terms. For all these thinkers, the commodity was seen as constituting a *structural* problem rather than as a material thing with particular qualities and meanings bearing the power to shape consumer consciousness and conduct.

To be sure, Marx recognized the commodity as inaugurating a world of appearances in which "relations among things" transformed our perceptions and experience. But his theory never grasped the commodity beyond the elemental categories of exchange and use value, a thing whose circulation, despite its reifying consequences, served the purposes of wealth accumulation and practical use. As we have seen, Baudrillard's task was to reconceptualize the commodity as a *cultural* object functioning within a *system* of cultural objects. This he accomplished by recognizing the commodity as an object with the power to signify, an insight only latent in the writings of Marx, Lukacs, and the Frankfurt School. Baudrillard's notion of the commodity/sign form established the commodity as a representational object having an operational purpose transcending its exchange and use values. However, the weakness in Baudrillard's move was its structuralist presuppositions. Since the idea of semiosis depends upon another version of "system," by substituting linguistic exchange for economic exchange, Baudrillard's model of the commodity/sign form reproduced a structuralist bias. Repudiating political economy for semiotics, Baudrillard, too, neglects an ontology of the commodity and the subject. As a signifying object, Baudrillard's commodity acquires meaning only in systemic relation to *other* commodities, and as a sign it becomes the operative element in a system of social status. Nonetheless, by adding sign value to exchange and use value, Baudrillard developed a conception of the commodity as a type of image. The commodity/sign constitutes a double reality: a constituent of a system, the sign also operates within the imaginary mental space of the consumer. But Baudrillard begs the question of what it is about the commodity/sign itself that makes it a meaningful and pleasurable object, why it holds an attraction for consumers in the first place. As Campbell (1995, 120) points out, there is an important difference between the *meaning* of an object (its significatory or denotative aspects) and its *meaningfulness* (its significance or import for the individual in terms of feelings, hopes, and desires as embodied in beliefs and values, involving connotation). Baudrillard failed to examine the latter, ignoring its important place in daydreaming, shopping, purchasing, possessing, and using. What he neglects in particular are the very real sensuous qualities built into the commodity—its *physical* attributes as constituted by the image-making processes of design, styling, and packaging—as well as how consumers *respond* to these qualities, whether in ways manufacturers and sellers intend or not. These aspects of the commodity, while intimately shaping its significatory effects, exceed semiotic or linguistic logic. In other words, commodities need to be defined also in terms of their meaningful characteristics, as symbolic objects.

While commodities can be meaningful also in other terms, including their functional value, I argue that commodities acquire meaningfulness most immediately and primarily as aesthetic objects, that is, by occupying our consciousness in their *materiality or sensuousness as objects.* Hence, explaining the attractions, motivations, and effects of consumption depends foremost on showing how commodities function as desirable aesthetic objects in the perception and imagination of consumers. Unlike conventional usage in the world of art, "aesthetic" here is defined not as having to do with beauty but more broadly as referring to "sensual experience." Jameson's comments on the aestheticization of commodity society implied that the expansion of consumer culture intensified our sense of the materiality of the world, reducing culture to a phenomenon of the physical and primarily visual senses: commodification produces culture as material image. Signification is only *one* aspect of this process, the other being the *sensual attributes and effects* of commodities as things. An inherent feature of manufactured goods and entertainments, the aesthetic, following a period of compartmentalization in a specialized realm of "autonomous art" (Dunn 1998; Lash 1990), has been reintegrated into daily life on a massive scale. This underappreciated aspect of the commodity is thus the starting point for examining the subjective dimensions of consumption.

In exploring how the commodity enters the everyday subjective experience of the consumer, a fruitful beginning is W.F. Haug's work on "commodity aesthetics" (1986, 1987). In place of Marx's twofold conceptualization of exchange and use value and Baudrillard's threefold scheme of exchange, use, and sign value, Haug introduces a psychologically fertile set of distinctions among exchange, use, and use *promise* value. Haug starts by saying that the fulfillment of exchange value—that is, product sales—requires that the commodity be a desirable and therefore attractive object. In Haug's formulation, this is accomplished by creating the *appearance* of use value (1986, 16). In this sense, "appearance" equals "promise." In the hands of designers and stylists, the commodity becomes a product of extensive aesthetic labor intended to appeal visually in order to motivate behaviorally. In his words, "The basic law of commodity aesthetics is the condition that not use-value but rather use-value promise triggers the act of exchange or purchase" (1987, 147).

Here, Haug claims for the commodity a different kind of double existence from that characterizing Baudrillard's duality of object and sign, namely, its *actual* use value and its *imagined* use value as embodied in its aesthetic construction. In turn, Haug's usage of "appearance" in connection with imagined or promised use value also carries a double meaning reflecting a broad conception of the aesthetic as something separate from the object: "The aesthetics of the commodity in its widest meaning—the sensual appearance and the conception of its use-value—become detached from the object itself" (1986, 16–17). Commodities function at the level of appearance both in the sense of having surface qualities *and* as "having the appearance of" a useful object. As such, they become imaginary objects.

Paralleling Baudrillard's break with Marxian economics, this ontology is premised on the commodity's inherent capacity for representational elaboration. However, if the commodity's sensuous appearance is a bearer of a "promise," this immediately introduces a subjective and specifically psychological dimension to the relationship between commodities and consumers. The commodity's sign functions in Baudrillard's theory are strictly sociocultural in character (see Chapter Four) whereas Haug, by approaching the commodity as physical object, additionally provides a basis for insights into the links between its material characteristics, cultural processes, and consumer psychology. A connection is established between the constructed characteristics of the commodity on the one hand and the subject's needs and desires on the other. For Haug, the elaborated surface appearances of the commodity create a space into which subjects are coaxed (or seduced), constituting what might be called an "imaginary of use." Within these imaginary spaces, the commodity becomes a vehicle of identity formation. In his words,

> The commodities are surrounded by imaginary spaces which individuals are supposed to enter and to fill in with certain acts. If an individual acts within them, these spaces organize his/her way of experiencing these acts and personal identity. These spaces organize the imaginations of those who enter them. The use of these imaginations is the social identity of the individuals. How do they 'see' themselves, their bodies, with the eyes of the unspecified others? (1987, 123)

This is a fundamental departure from thinking of commodities in system terms. These formulations place the actor in a cognitive/emotional paradigm that frames consumption as an "interior" act shaped by both conscious and unconscious processes within the realm of imagination. This has important ramifications. First of all, here consumption is not merely an outcome of systemic forces but an *encounter*, or series of encounters, between the subject and a world of commodified objects. Second, by implication consumption is to be read in its *temporal* dimensions. As a series of encounters, consumption is not a discrete act(s) of shopping, purchase, and so forth, but rather a continuous, ongoing process of subjective work based upon an exchange of meanings between consumers and commodities: commodities promise identity and recognition in return for consumers' psychic (and monetary) investment. In this scheme, the functioning of the commodity is defined by the consumer's subjective and behavioral trajectory as an actor in search of meaning and pleasure. Third, this view breaks with the determinisms of semiotic theory by positing an imaginary psychic space containing transformative possibilities for commodities and consumers alike. Unlike the closed universe of the sign system, this space contains potential for a negotiation of meanings and satisfactions, enabling multiple uses of commodities as well as metamorphoses in commodities themselves.

In acknowledging the commodity as an aesthetic object attempting to speak to an active subject or self, Haug places consumption in a social-psychological register. Haug points not only to the highly seductive appeal of the aestheticized product but also to the still essentially *social* character of its pull on the self. In his famously concise reflections in *Ways of Seeing* (1972), the essayist John Berger comments on "publicity images" (or advertisements) as comprising a language that presupposes a consumer in need of self-transformation and therefore potentially commodity dependent. According to Berger, advertisements, always speaking "of the future" (ibid., 130), begin by "working on a natural appetite for pleasure" (132) but only as a means for addressing our social anxieties. By urging us to transform ourselves through buying, the advertisement sends forth a powerful social message. "Publicity" offers the consumer "an image of himself made glamorous by the product . . . it is trying to sell. The image then makes him envious of himself as he might be." But this in turn stems from the "envy of others. Publicity is about social relations, not objects. Its promise is not of pleasure, but of happiness: happiness as judged from the outside by others." While neglecting the aesthetic work of the object in this process, Berger recognizes that in doing the bidding for the commodity, the advertisement plays on the pleasures of consumption only as an alibi for manipulating a deeper emotional need to be envied. The question of the veracity of this claim notwithstanding, Berger's reading of the commodity as promising self-transformation toward the goal of social acceptance converges with Haug's argument that the purchased commodity gives expression to how we think others will see us. In both authors, the commodity presupposes a *lack* in the consumer: an emptiness, anxiety, or discontent, the overcoming of which the commodity immodestly claims for itself. Psychologically speaking, then, what is promised by commodity aesthetics is a pleasurable recognition or fulfillment of self in the purchased object. Alongside demographically based sales and marketing techniques for addressing material needs, the sensuous appeals of the commodity project the possibility of self-gratification and enhancement within a world of others.[10]

This approach to the commodity also invites comparison of Haug and Adorno. Whereas Adorno was concerned with the psychodynamics of the relationship between mass culture and what he regarded as an isolated and atomized individual, Haug insists that a sociality effect is always operating in the commodity's promise of self-recognition. In fact, social research long ago revealed the limitations of Adorno's model of an isolated consumer of mass entertainment.[11] Adorno's arguments were also restricted by their almost exclusive focus on entertainment as opposed to store-bought goods or mass-market advertising. Further, Adorno employed an almost exclusively psychoanalytic conception of the subject. From this viewpoint, he critiqued the formulaic content of broadcast entertainment, where he found patterns of manipulation and conformity reaching into the unconscious recesses of already vulnerable and divided psyches. Of perhaps most consequence, while rightly attending to certain societally generated needs and psychological mechanisms of control, Adorno failed to grasp the profound impact and inherent ambiguities of the *image*. By contrast, Haug, beginning with an exegesis of the commodity as aesthetic object, links its psychodynamic aspects to both the image *and* social relations, grounding the problem of consumption in a search for identity. This raises a subsidiary issue of distinguishing among types of commodities and forms of consumption, for instance, between packaged entertainment (Adorno's commodity) and goods that are acquired and possessed (Haug's commodity). But more importantly, Haug's contribution moves us beyond Adorno's restrictive psychoanalytic picture of the self, highlighting the potentials of the cultural turn in critical theory initiated by Baudrillard while at the same time reinstating an active and motivated social self.

The search for identity in consumption is, of course, perilous. Actual use value seldom corresponds to promised use value. In the present context, this is less critical as a practical matter than as a set of perplexing psychological issues. Since appearance is not reality, Haug, in concert with familiar criticisms of the ploys of the marketplace, comments on the gap between use promise and genuine satisfaction. In a reiteration of Adorno, he regards the appeals of commodity culture as mass deception. "Appearance always promises more . . . than it can ever deliver. In this way illusion deceives" (1986, 50). The claims commodities make for self-fulfillment and social acceptance are ultimately fraudulent. However, Haug finds in this fraud a diagnostic tool, we might say a compensation for the deception, in what the illusion of the commodity tells us about our condition. The illusion—the "semblance" of the commodity—refracts real absences, wishes, and longings, sustaining a sense of utopian possibilities (Haug 1987, 116–117; Jameson 1979; Willis 1991).

> The illusion one falls for is like a mirror in which one sees one's desires and believes them to be real. . . . Despite the outrageous deception, something very strange occurs, the dynamics of which are greatly underestimated. . . . In these images, people are continually shown the unfulfilled aspects of their existence. (1986, 52)

Disclosing the illusion this way, however, leads in two possible directions, one pessimistic and the other perhaps less so. On the one hand, the illusion provides people, in Haug's formulation, "with a language to interpret their existence and the world" (ibid.) but "soon there is no other language than that supplied by the commodities" (1987, 117). This amounts to a closing of the discursive universe, a pre-emption of any possibilities other than those presented by the commodity system, a view echoing the Frankfurt thinkers and Baudrillard. On the other hand, Haug reiterates the familiar dialectical perspective, which postulates a number of possible openings and redemptions in opposition to commodity discourse. In a commotion of ideas, and in common with Leiss (1976, see below), he characterizes the commodity system as fundamentally "unstable," alluding both to the continual need for aesthetic innovation and the inevitable wearing out of the "imaginary wish fulfillment" effect on the consumer. Finally, in a repeat of British cultural studies, Haug resorts to the subcultural argument of "resistance," finding in subcultures "a moment of self-activity of individuals within the different social groups to which they belong," claiming for subcultures (especially youth) an inherent power of insubordination (1987, 125, 165). More broadly, Haug attempts to distinguish between the commodity system and a semiautonomous domain of "everyday life" (Lefebvre 1984; de Certeau 1984) or what Jurgen Habermas calls the "life-world" (Pusey 1987, 106). These are familiar terms designating the realm of lived experience in which social relations and human subjectivity serve as bulwarks against colonization by the system.

Further Deconstruction: The Sign/Symbol Matrix

Aesthetics is only one aspect of the meaning processes governing commodity production, and focusing exclusively on this dimension does not fully illuminate how commodities do their subjective work. Moreover, despite Haug's dialectical view, the theory of commodity aesthetics fails to provide a language that would redefine the problem of manipulation and domination and the possibilities of active "resistance."[12]

Understanding the complex and contradictory meaning processes of the commodity/sign, and recasting the domination versus resistance debate, points to yet another kind of duality inherent in the commodity. As argued in the Conclusion of Chapter Two, cultural analyses of consumption have failed to recognize the difference between signs and symbols, which are fundamentally different vehicles of social and cultural meaning. As indicated previously, signs serve an essentially instrumental purpose whereas symbols perform expressive functions. Importantly, while commodities have both semiotic and symbolic attributes, signs and symbols have divergent if not opposite representational effects.

This duality of the commodity, I argue, is key to understanding the cultural problem of commodity fetishism. We can begin by looking again at the commodity's values. On the one hand, the sign aligns itself with exchange value and is therefore a client of the commodity form. On the other hand, the symbolic properties of commodities give expression to the "meaningful" aspects of their use value, representing a range of possible psychic satisfactions sought by consumers in their capacities as social subjects. The interplay of semiotic and symbolic effects in the consumption of material goods thus parallels the ongoing tension in commodity society between exchange and use value, the contest between the monetary and narrowly class/status meanings of consumption as opposed to consumption's place in a search for a broader sense of meaningfulness connected to selfhood and identity. In the commodity system, these two categories stand in a complicated, unstable relationship. Recognizing the functional difference between the two, I suggest, enables us to formulate a more rigorous, grounded, and practical critique of consumer culture. This involves a closer look at how meaning gets structured into the commodity.

In a thoughtful contribution to work on material and specifically consumer culture, the anthropologist Grant McCracken (1988) has outlined a model of what he calls "meaning transfer." According to McCracken, in modern consumer society there are "three locations of meaning: the culturally constituted world, the consumer good, and the individual consumer" (72). Meaning, which is mobile, is "constantly flowing" (71) through these three locations. Meaning originates in "the culturally constituted world" and is subsequently transferred by the advertising and fashion industries to consumer goods and finally to consumers by means of a variety of "rituals" (possession, exchange, grooming, divestment) (72). In this manner, McCracken demonstrates how consumer culture is constituted by a triadic set of representational connections involving culture, goods, and consumers. By emphasizing that in modern culture meaning systems are materialized in concrete objects, he underscores the communicative power of commodities, their central role in meaning production, and our dependency on goods for self and collective definitions.

Of special importance is McCracken's assessment of material goods as a representational medium. He rightly points to the mistake of regarding clothing and other material goods as a "language," stressing that goods—as opposed to language—communicate in a fundamentally nondiscursive way, stating that "material culture undertakes expressive tasks that language does not or cannot perform" (68). While material culture is more limited in its "expressive range" than language, the former paradoxically gains advantages by its "inconspicuousness." In contrast to language, the messages conveyed by material goods are implicit, covert, insinuating, and propagandistic. This view attributes to material culture a special semiotic character of which language is incapable and that gives to material goods a more diffuse but powerful set of meanings and messages, stemming largely from their concreteness.

McCracken does not pursue a semiotic analysis of material goods, which would require an inquiry into their essentially visual nature, leaving open the question of how we are to characterize and interpret goods' representational capacities and the kinds of meanings they in fact produce. Yet his presentation provides a general framework for examining the play of signs and symbols and their relationship within consumer culture. In his argument, the commodity is contextualized in the cultural system—the commodity acquires its meaning from the extant structures of belief, value, and so forth in society at large. On the level of pragmatics, the meaning of the commodity depends on what advertisers, designers, and fashion experts do in transforming it into an object of significance for consumers.

What this argument leaves out, however, is the underlying rhetorical structure of this process. As signs, commodities signal highly instrumental meanings as part of a strategy of manipulating consumers to buy and enjoy status and pleasure. But this semiotic work depends on a vast repertoire of cultural symbols that comprise the deeper source of the commodity's appeal, its *meaningfulness*. What is transferred from culture to commodity, then, are *two* layers of representation: the semiotic codes serving the instrumental functions of commercial messages, and a pre-existing symbolic environment from which these codes are constructed and that resonates a larger system of social and cultural meaning. Serving its ultimate economic purpose, the commodity/sign converts socially shared symbolism ("culture") into codes and messages that stimulate consumer desire and give social form and meaning to particular purchases and spending patterns. The dynamics of desire and gratification, and the meanings of consumption generally, are thus located in a sign/symbol matrix in which an *already socially shared field of symbolic meanings* is appropriated and reconstituted by a commercially based sign system.

This view of the culturalization of the commodity explicitly raises normative considerations of quality and effect. While the semiosis of culture coincides with a decline in the efficacy of symbols, this development can never be complete so long as we are incapable of imagining the end of human culture altogether. Yet, the decline of symbolization—often thematized in modern social theory as a consequence of the rationalization of society[13]—does suggest an impoverishment of culture. The symbolic realm survives but in diminished form, both because of and despite the rise of commercially packaged culture. Symbols have been reduced to mere building blocks of the sign, standing ready to be recycled and reconstituted within the prevailing sign system. While the meanings conveyed by symbols are complex, expressive, and evocative, a sign communicates literally, by means of simple and direct messages. But to be communicative at all, signs need to speak a common language; symbols supply and animate the cultural reference points facilitating this communication. Moreover, signs are effective only to the extent that they are able to mobilize and reshape the power of shared symbols. Symbols thus supply signs with content—with metaphors, associations, evocations—while signs shape this content into easily accessible, commercially manufactured stereotypes and slogans for selling products.

This process can be illustrated by familiar examples from two major subsystems of the commodity/sign form. First, the subsystem of mass advertising relies on images of family, nature, adventure, individuality, and selfhood to generate positive symbolic associations with and thereby desires for products. For instance, the symbolism of happy nuclear families on camping trips or outdoor excursions is a powerful means of selling SUVs and other large motor vehicles. The symbolism of the professional working woman carrying a glossy briefcase to the high-rise office, connoting the pinnacle of feminine success and independence, is a compelling entree to the sale of expensive designer clothing. Second, the subsystem of commodities themselves takes on highly charged symbolic attributes in the aestheticization process. In the well-known case of automobile design and styling, manufacturers shape the curvaceous qualities of automobile "bodies" to produce erotic associations in the minds of prospective male buyers in an effort to symbolically link vehicle ownership with sexual pleasure.[14] In both instances, symbols and the symbolization process are extracted from their traditional or conventional contexts and transformed by signs into a stereotyped and formulaic order of meanings and desires constituted by advertising, commodities, entertainment, and the entire system of commercial images.

What happens to meaning as symbols are subsumed under signs? At first glance, given the way I have defined the differences between symbols and signs, it would seem that semiosis results in a constriction of meaning. Yet there is a special sense in which signs *enlarge* meaning. This occurs first of all through the skillful use of symbols and symbolization. Meaning is expanded by situating products symbolically in what producers believe are consumers' deepest longings and anxieties. This is accomplished by deploying familiar symbolic associations between the commodity on the one hand and the consumer's cultural storehouse of knowledge on the other. Feeding on symbolic material, the aesthetic work of the commodity *inflates* meaning by promising (see above) a range of uses or outcomes—pleasures, experiences, satisfactions—surpassing its actual use value. For instance, the aestheticized imaginary qualities of automobiles (basically only means of transportation) transform them into objects of pride, envy, selfhood, mastery, safety, power, fun, admiration, and so forth. In this sense, the proliferation of signs in consumer culture produces a meaning excess.

Interestingly, this replaces the old problem of "false" versus "real" needs with a more pertinent question: at what point and to what extent do the *imagined* use values embedded in commodity aesthetics become the *actual* use values of the object? Indeed, in practice many products are used, sensibly or not, on the basis of the consumer's imagination of their value or potency, such as when furniture is deployed in the home more for its appearance than for the sake of comfort or practicality. Commodification in the service of the senses and emotions thus has less to do with a confusion of need than a confounding of use value. In fact, casual observation suggests that utilitarian use value has been in decline and aesthetic use value on the rise, whether in terms of qualities promised by a given commodity or in terms of the actual number of commodities identifiable as either predominantly "utilitarian" or "aesthetic/sensuous" in character.[15]

While the sign system engulfs the consumer with surplus meaning, however, in another sense it simultaneously erodes meaning. Commodity aesthetics reduces symbolic associations to the status of a material image, relegating previously rich symbolic content evoking lived experience and often powerful meanings and feelings to a commercially fabricated sign system. In this respect, the ultimate effect of the sign is a constriction of meaning, its reduction to formula. The semiosis of symbols within the realm of commerce transforms the cultural process of symbolization into a series of instrumental psychological strategies and mechanisms whose aim is sales. The apparent contradiction between the enlargement of meaning and its diminution is more directly related to a basic distinction, however tenuous, between body and mind. The meaning of a sign is sensory in character (thus the importance of the aesthetic) while symbolic meaning is nonsensory—its locus is the mind (White 1949). The system of commodity/signs thus heightens meaning at the level of the physical senses while draining it from cognition and intellect. This is carried to its logical extreme once the sign is finally consumed by its own materiality, losing both concept and referent in the "floating signifiers" comprising the vast system of commercial images, as epitomized by the television ad. Finally, the sheer *volume* of signs in a high-consumption society paradoxically creates its own crisis of meaning as consumers are unable (or unwilling) to negotiate or absorb the excess.

Yet another difference between signs and symbols clarifies how the commodity/sign effects the production of meaning. Since it is constituted by a system or code, the meaning of a sign is always relatively fixed, it has a "structure" that limits its range. In contrast, symbols are constituted in and by human subjectivity. A function of the creative processes of mind, symbolization lends itself to an openness and fluidity of meaning. A dialectic of consumer culture would focus our attention on the intersection of these dimensions of meaning in the commodity/ sign, examining the relative effects of the sign structure and the symbolizing possibilities presented by commodified objects and images, especially their content.

It is the fate of the symbol to live a meager existence within the system of commodity/signs, even while it continues to reflect back to the consumer a realm of meanings and longings that transcends the system of commodity exchange. Although in a weakened state, symbols and symbolization remain the means by which the meanings of the commodity are enlarged and mediated by producers and consumers alike. Yet importantly, the symbolic realm is the source of shared creativity and therefore of potentialities for change and transformation initiated by social actors. In these terms, formations of alternative or oppositional culture are the reverse of the semiotic process of instrumentalization. One manifestation of this is the insubordination that occurs whenever manufactured signs are transformed into symbolic expressions. An example would be Andy Warhol's subversive act of turning commercial signs into the subject matter of art. Another would be the youthful subversion of the design and stylistic standards of Detroit automobiles (lowering, chopping, channeling, souping up), a rebellious expression of subcultural autonomy and reappropriation of commodities. The sign system or code thus never entirely escapes the possibility of its subversion by symbolization, with its implications of authenticity, selfhood, and freedom. The subject's capacity for symbolization can thus either be used by the sign system or become a vehicle of subversion, as we have seen frequently in age, race, ethnic, gender, and sexual subcultures. This moment of symbolic reappropriation has been a major focus of cultural studies. However, despite the prominence given collective symbolic insubordinations in the cultural studies literature, since the sign system operates in and depends upon the larger cultural system it remains always vulnerable to symbolic reappropriations by individuals as well as groups and communities. Mainly, *there is no necessary correspondence* between the coded messages attached to a commodity and the commodity's import for the identities and lives of those who consume it.

The dialectics of the relationship between the commodity and the consuming subject ultimately reduces to a matter of what transpires in that "imaginary space" created by commodity aesthetics. *Commodity aesthetics operates within a tension between the sign and the symbol.* Whether or not we want to say that the consumer is manipulated by the system becomes a question of the degree to which that space is controlled by the producer—dominated by the sign—or generative of symbolic activity not contained or containable by the sign. The contradiction inherent in commodity aesthetics is that while the commodity must solicit hope and expectation, it can only perform this task by stirring the longings and aspirations of subjects whose identities are ultimately rooted in *symbolic* capacities.

Locating commodities and consumers within a framework of aesthetic work structured by a tension between signs and symbols suggests important insights into the dialectics of consumption. This strategy links a systems perspective (with implications of degrees of determinism) with a subjective ontology of commodity and actor (with implications of degrees of autonomy and choice). This post-Baudrillardian sketch recognizes the commodity dualistically as belonging to economic and semiotic systems of exchange while simultaneously (as *object*) constituting a social-psychological process of psychic gratifications and sociocultural identifications among individual consumers. This account places the commodity at the center of a dynamic relationship between structured systems on the one hand and consumer consciousness and aspirations on the other. Unlike McCracken's model, however, which sees only a one-way movement of meanings from culture to product to consumer, the sign/symbol distinction provides a possibility for cultural meaning that is produced by consumers themselves.

The system and its actors stand in a mutually constitutive relationship structured both objectively *and* subjectively, within a complex network of signs and symbols. Economic and semiotic exchange presupposes a commodity capable of promising satisfaction and pleasure to its user, but the commodity can perform this function only by means of a complex strategy of meaning production. This immediately opens the door to symbolization, whose logic contradicts the workings of the sign.

By implication, as subjects, consumers enter into *transactions with* and construct *relationships to* commodities, however consciously or unconsciously this is accomplished. These relationships are formed within the discursive and structural boundaries of the commodity system. But *as relationships*, they depend upon the symbolic processes out of which they are constituted as well as the needs and desires of the subjects who form them.

Dynamics of Insatiability

Marcuse's distinction between "false" and "true" needs (Chapter One) has been one of the more controversial legacies of the critique of commodity fetishism. While it is indisputable that capitalism artificially stimulates consumer demand, how or to what extent this involves the creation of "false needs" or distorts our sense of need in general remains problematic.[16] In fact, despite its importance to Marxist critique and select aspects of consumer society, the concept of need has lost much of its relevance to the study of consumer culture.[17]

A preferred approach derives from the distinction between "needs" and "wants." The separation of these concepts along with a set of strategic methods for stimulating *want* is the defining moment of consumer capitalism. While their relationship varies over time and space, we usually think of needs in contrast to wants as a socially shared set of "minimum requirements" (Leiss 1976, 61) necessary for survival (food, clothing, shelter). Whereas need carries an implication of something more or less universal and fixed, want is variable and elastic, bearing connotations of individual choice, self-interest, and desire (different tastes or preferences in food, clothing, shelter). It follows that the systematic production and shaping of want is the foundation of a consumerist economy. While capitalism confuses the boundary, seeming to convert want into need (either as a conscious sales strategy or a by-product of overabundance), want is the more applicable term and the variable component in consumer demand. Want is the chief factor in the economic expansion that is both cause and effect of the transformation of consumption into consumerism.

Yet, this concept, too, turns out to be inadequate to the task of exploring consumer subjectivity. "Want" discloses little of the psychology and social psychology of consumption, particularly regarding questions of meaning, gratification, and identity. At the inception of the twentieth century, many thinkers in the United States, especially merchants and public-relations experts, already had publicly recognized the centrality of *desire* and its management in the forging of a new consumer society (Cross 2000; Ewen and Ewen 1982; Fox and Lears 1983; Leach 1993). A great deal is known about the subjective and behavioral manifestations and consequences of desire as manipulated by the motivational apparatuses of capitalism. However, what should most intrigue us about consumer desire is its alternating exhaustion and reproduction over time. In fact, at first glance the endless ebb and flow of consumer desire presents something of a puzzle.

This raises the difficult notion of "insatiability," curious because its pervasiveness amidst material abundance seems counterintuitive and provocative because it is both perplexing and by all accounts a necessary condition for the survival of capitalist society. Indeed, the phenomenon of insatiability is both a mystery and "the most characteristic feature of modern consumption" (Campbell 1987, 37). It goes without saying that the problem of insatiability has its origins in the impact of consumer culture. It is common wisdom that advertising and the rest of the apparatus of consumer culture attempt to stimulate and perpetuate motivations to buy. But consumer desire is hardly reducible to the effects of these motivational apparatuses. As Veblen was the first to recognize (Chapter One), the social logic of emulative spending leads inevitably to a state of chronic dissatisfaction. But this state also has its sources in the underlying psychology and structural and cultural dynamics of consumer society.

Insatiability can be defined as a chronic state or feeling of unsatisfied or unfulfilled desire. Given this definition, consumer insatiability can be understood broadly in terms of a combination of two interrelated factors: (1) the nature of desire itself, and (2) the historically specific conditions of modern consumer capitalism, in particular its dynamic and changeful character. While it is important to acknowledge certain givens of human psychology and the human condition, emphasis clearly needs to be placed on the intended and unintended consequences of the capitalist economic and cultural systems. Since capitalist society as presently constituted depends upon a consumer chronically restless and dissatisfied and therefore predisposed always to buy, it is axiomatic that widespread insatiability is a prerequisite for the functioning and survival of this society.

The first place to seek the sources of insatiability is in the psychodynamics of desire itself. By nature seemingly infinite and limitless, without predetermined boundaries or objects, desire takes the form of inner feelings variously of appetite, urge, craving, or longing. Desire has both bodily and mental components: it is part of our innermost physical and emotional drives, on the one hand, while fundamental to the realm of imagination (Belk et al. 2000, 99), and specifically fantasy, on the other.

Of all the psychological possibilities for explaining this force, the most relevant theoretical approaches are those of behaviorism and psychoanalysis. The production of desire can be examined, first of all, from the standpoint of the satisfaction of an organism's needs. In this model, desire is a complex function of the interplay of reward and punishment, satisfaction and deprivation. To take only one example, Scitovsky (1992) implicitly draws on this model in a psychological critique of the mainstream economic conception of consumer motivation, which, he argues, overlooks the relationship between motivation (here, another term for "desire") and levels of and changes in mental and physical arousal. Both underarousal and overarousal stimulate the organism to seek equilibrium. What the organism seeks, he claims, is satisfaction of need, which can take the form of an experience of either comfort or pleasure. Comfort is a "negative good," that is, an avoidance of discomfort, whereas pleasure is a "positive good" (59). Desire, therefore, can be located in this calculus of pain avoidance and pleasure seeking. Interestingly, in Scitovsky's view, comfort is associated with the *level* of arousal while pleasure is based on *changes* in the arousal level (61) and is therefore the stronger experience. While each involves a different strategy, common to both is the central place of novelty, which "is the essential element in all stimulation" (122). At its best, Scitovsky seems to argue, novelty would present us with changes sufficient to produce pleasurable sensations, whose source is the *experience* of change itself. Thus, in his account, insatiability seems traceable to two behavioral dynamics: (1) the *ongoing* adjustments organisms are continually making in search of a satisfying balance of comforts and pleasures; and (2) a *reinforcement effect* ("reward") associated with pleasure that strengthens the original drive and thus the tendency toward a repetitive behavior pattern.

By contrast, in the psychoanalytic model, desire originates in the biological wellsprings of the organism. Freud located desire in the id: the primary, undifferentiated (sexual) energy he called "a seething cauldron of excitement," whose sole psychological function was the production of wishes (Hall and Lindzey 1968). Closely linked to fantasy, the aim of desire is pleasure, which Freud understood as the experience of the discharge of tension inherent in this bodily excitement. Whether or not we endorse the Freudian construction of desire as specifically somatic, in the psychoanalytic view it is axiomatic that desire emanates from the deepest, most primitive substratum of the human psyche. Desire exists in potentially infinite supply and is therefore in principle never completely sated or satiable. Desiring bodies and minds can never attain more than partial, temporary satisfaction.

To refine Veblen's original observation, both of these approaches refer to sources of what might be called *chronic marginal dissatisfaction,* marginal because dissatisfaction is never total but only partial, varying in relation to numerous situational factors. While powerful explanations, however, these psychological perspectives need to be put into social and cultural context. By attempting to harness and amplify desire, and by defining the commodity as the source of its fulfillment, consumer culture taps into a huge reservoir of potential urges. We see the preconditions of this in the emergence of industrial capitalism, which in elaborately disciplined fashion *excluded* desire from the workplace, thereby preparing society for its containment and management within the realm of leisured consumption (Kovel 1981, 83).

But an enlargement and perpetuation of desire is traceable to other features of the modern economy. In addition to its denial in the workplace, an expansion of desire in the realm of consumption can be attributed to a sweeping and dramatic enlargement of the object world. In his analysis of value and exchange in *The Philosophy of Money*, Simmel (1990) proposes that desire originates in a separation and distance between subject and object. In his words,

> We desire objects only if they are not immediately given to us for our use and enjoyment; that is, to the extent that they resist our desire. The content of our desire becomes an object as soon as it is opposed to us, not only in the sense of being impervious to us, but also in terms of its distance as something not-yet-enjoyed. (66)

From the standpoint of Simmel's essays on the tragedy of culture (Chapter One), the growing alienation of subject and object in capitalist modernity has major implications in this respect.

With increasing objectification, the separation of object from subject worsens, widening the desire-producing gap. The subject's alienation from the world of objects, inherent in the separation of production from consumption, generates desire for those objects, a desire intensified by the proliferation of commodities and the growth of a system of market exchange by means of which these objects multiply and present themselves in appealing form to the subject. By objectifying existence, the commodity *ipso facto* increases desire, simultaneously constituting itself as the only means of its satisfaction.

Yet Simmel's account hardly suffices to explain dramatically rising consumption levels in the economically advanced regions of the world, and especially symptoms in U.S. culture of a sense of seemingly inexhaustible desire for goods. Such an explanation would have to consider the cultural processes serving to promote consumption and the social and psychological conditions supporting these processes. One place to look is in particular cultural movements and formations. As we saw in Chapter One, Campbell examines the historical background of the formation of a consumerist ethic of pleasure seeking emanating from the Romantic Movement. Romanticism implicitly endorsed the pursuit of individual pleasure by asserting the self's capacity for control over the meanings of things through the power of imagination. Here, pleasure is to be located in the realm of imagination itself, in an illusory hedonism that can become a force in our subjective experience of the world. This argument explicitly links the pursuit and experience of pleasure to the imagination and fantasy. According to Campbell, Romanticism claimed that both desire and pleasure operate only in the realm of the imagination and are thus a function not of the characteristics of objects themselves but rather of the way the self *experiences* these objects. If Baudrillard argued that we consume not objects but signs, Campbell claims that what we really consume are our own fantasies. He states,

> modern hedonism tends to be covert and self-illusory; that is to say, individuals employ their imaginative and creative powers to construct mental images which they consume for the intrinsic pleasure they provide, a practice best described as day-dreaming or fantasizing. (1987, 78)[18]

According to this description, the insatiability of desire inheres in the nature of daydreaming, for as with desire, as Campbell notes "there are virtually no restrictions upon the faculty of imagination" (ibid., 76). In these terms, the inexhaustibility of desire can be directly attributed to the powers of imagination and its ability to produce pleasurable mental states. Campbell emphasizes that pleasure is a "quality of experience" (ibid., 90), in other words that pleasure derives not from the properties of commodities themselves but from how we *experience* the sensation of these properties. This is "self-illusioned" in the sense that the consumer creatively spins daydreams around the consumption of commodities, independently of what advertisers do, since daydreaming is "endemic to modern societies" (ibid., 91)

In this view, the real pleasures of consumption are a product of the imagination. "The illusion is always better than the reality; the promise more interesting than actuality" (ibid., 90). This is evidenced in the amount of time consumers spend enjoying the *images* of consumption found in advertising, fashion magazines, and other forms of entertainment as well as in *window-shopping*, whose pleasures are embodied in the imagined use of seen objects or in the imagined *anticipation* of buying. Clearly, all of this mental work and psychic investment is a prescription for a state of insatiability. In Campbell's account, this takes the form of "'longing,' something which differs from desiring in so far as it occurs without the presence of any real object" (ibid., 87)

But insatiability is fundamentally two-sided, involving not only a desire for new objects but also a chronic, vague sense of dissatisfaction with the objects already present in one's life. Thus, the peculiar back and forth in modern consumerism between growing tired of existing objects, on the one hand, and the enduring search for new gratifications, on the other. In Campbell's formulation,

> Longing and a permanent unfocused dissatisfaction are complementary features of that distinctive outlook generated by self-illusory hedonism, and both can be said to be inevitable consequences of the practice of day-dreaming. (ibid.)

What Campbell fails to adequately explain, however, is the source of this dissatisfaction. Certainly, dissatisfaction is not only a consequence but also one of the constituents of an active fantasy life. But understanding desire in relation to dissatisfaction complicates the problem of insatiability in ways calling for yet other explanations. Indeed, thinking of consumer culture as geared to the direct stimulation of desire through images of pleasure might tell us less than an examination of how this culture generates states of dissatisfaction. A focus on dissatisfaction suggests that we think of the *arousal* of desire and its *frustration* as two sides of the same coin, and that we look at the mechanisms of consumer culture that systematically frustrate the consumer in ways that lead to further purchases. Scitovsky's view of the individual as continually seeking equilibrium presupposes a *chronic state* of dissatisfaction, however variable in scope and intensity, which is presumably rooted in the human condition. But an alternative argument is that states of perpetual dissatisfaction are built into the system of consumer capitalism.

First of all, chronic dissatisfaction can be seen as a consequence of the effects of commodity aesthetics, stemming specifically from the gap between the commodity's illusory promise and what it actually delivers. Extending Haug's work, repeated disappointments could be expected to prolong and even strengthen desire. Campbell's contribution is to draw attention to the effect of our own fantasies in these disappointments. In a twist on Haug, it can be argued from Campbell's vantage point that if the desire for goods and services constitutes itself in the realm of imagination, the frustration and therefore perpetuation of desire originates in a discontinuity between the pleasures projected by commodities and the self's *own* daydreams and fantasies about what would constitute pleasure.

Before going further, Campbell's account is sufficiently important to an understanding of consumer desire for us to consider its limitations. First of all, his account tends to be overly ideationist and reductionist by narrowly locating the hedonist attitude and the propensity to daydream in the romantic ethic. Campbell overlooks the extent to which modern hedonism was shaped by new modes of representation of consumer products and ideals already beginning in the eighteenth and nineteenth centuries that were tied less to romanticism than the commercial hustle and bustle of the rising bourgeoisie.[19] Innovations in art and technology were already at this time contributing to the formation of a modern subjectivity focused on pleasure seeking through the powers of imagination and sensation. In particular, during the nineteenth century with the growing autonomy of the signifier, the new sphere of images was imparting novel capacities and means of indulgence in daydreaming and fantasy. But even if we grant Campbell the validity of his historical argument, the means of self-illusion have been powerfully extended and intensified through mass media in the twentieth century, especially in the practices of advertising. The world of daydreaming, thus, is hardly reducible to movements in ideas, but is also deeply implicated in the impact of new media. Finally, a more serious flaw is Campbell's severing of the self from the commodity, which is assigned a relatively insignificant place in the consumer's experience of pleasure. Indeed, since he explicitly regards daydreaming as endemic to modern life, Campbell's account could be construed as having little if anything to do with actual consumption. It may be the case that people spend a great deal of time consuming mere fantasies, but the key question must be the relationship of these fantasies to real commodities and consumption practices.

A second major source of consumer dissatisfaction is suggested by Marxian theory. Despite its concentration on the problem of need rather than desire, there is a dimension of Marxian thought that is germane to the question of consumer insatiability: the theme of alienation. The concept of alienation, a condition precipitated by the separation of production from consumption, has been rendered in images of an isolated individual rootless and powerless, a daily existence often devoid of meaning and purpose (especially at work), a boredom that breeds restlessness and a search for excitement. While this picture is often overdrawn, there is abundant evidence that the capitalist mode of production hollows out the institutions of work, family, neighborhood, and community, along with traditional cultural identifications, depriving the individual of anything in the way of a meaningful role and identity except as consumer. The specifically Marxist dimension of this argument is that the self, stripped of a sense of purpose, identity, and recognition in the realm of production, is driven to seek these values in the world of consumption. More broadly, a socially and psychologically fragile society, given over to the instrumentalities and tedium of production and bureaucracy—in other words, processes of rationalization[20]—depends heavily upon the meanings and fulfillments promised, and temporarily provided, by hedonistic consumption. The latent self-dissatisfaction inherent in alienation and loss of place and identity is made manifest by the endless stream of commercial messages telling consumers of unhappiness and imperfections (Berger 1972) that can be relieved only through the consumption of goods. Feeding this manipulated dependency on consumption is the constant exposure to artificial, unrealistic standards of happiness, beauty, and success that only intensify dissatisfaction with self.

Third, the psychological state of insatiability has its cultural counterpart in *novelty*, which presents itself as the obvious solution to dissatisfaction (Scitovsky 1992). One of the defining characteristics of modernity ("new" is often synonymous with "modern"), novelty has shaped the realm of consumer culture as much as it has the world of "serious" art. In an extension of his insights into imaginative hedonism, Campbell in a later statement (1995) appropriates the theme of "the new" to argue that it fits perfectly the consumer's inclinations towards daydreaming and longing. It is much easier for consumers to project imagined pleasures onto unfamiliar products and experiences than onto familiar ones, making the new preferable to the old. Campbell cites the work of John Urry (1990), who argues that the essential ingredient in the pleasures of tourism is the imagined anticipation of pleasure in the act of touring, the quintessential experience of discovering "the new" through the visual senses. In a shift from his earlier emphasis on fantasy, here Campbell suggests that tourism is the "paradigm case" for all modern consumption.[21] Like tourists, what all consumers consume is novelty itself. In this conception, to the extent that consumption is about pleasure, novelty—and thus insatiability—is a necessary condition for the reproduction of consumer culture. In this sense, to consume means to give expression to an enduring thirst for the unfamiliar.[22]

Novelty, of course, is more than a cultural precondition for the consumerist state of mind but is deeply ingrained in the socioeconomic system. The dramatic turnover of goods characterizing advanced capitalism means that novelty is an inevitable feature of an expansionist and profit-driven economy. In this sense, "insatiability" might be the wrong term for patterns of consumption that in fact represent an adaptation to a practical situation, namely, the consumer's need or wish to "keep up" with a constantly changing marketplace, a condition regulated by strategies of planned obsolescence on the one hand and the cultural subsystem of fashion on the other (Chapter Four). Thus, the phenomenon of novelty can be viewed as a function not only of a manipulative sales effort, but also of the change-based logic of capital. Rapid goods turnover *per se* speeds up the consumption process independently of any subjective or cultural conditions promoting higher rates of consumption at the level of object desire. In this respect, endless consumption should be viewed not only as a function of consumer dissatisfaction with old possessions, but also of the social and material logics of identity and personal life set in motion by an inherently dynamic economic system. The constant introduction of new products into the marketplace creates a set of expectations and practical problem-solving situations for consumers that articulate with but are quite different from the purely psychological factors governing desire.

Looking at the other side of the process, however, recurring desire for commodities is requisite to a speedy and reliable movement of these commodities, and so the system finds ways to motivate purchases on a purely subjective level. The seesaw of consumer desire and disappointment and the production of new economic goods mutually constitute each other in the form of a causal feedback loop. Psychologically based chronic marginal dissatisfaction drives the economy by exerting pressure to develop new products, while marketplace novelty in turn constitutes its *own* source of dissatisfaction with existing goods by seductively promising to replace them with better ones.

Perhaps the main consequence of novelty as a systemic feature of capitalism is that continual, rapid product turnover introduces a kind of chronic but manageable instability, in both the system and the individual. By holding out the prospect of satisfaction through future purchases while simultaneously creating dissatisfaction with the old products, new commodities perpetually undermine consumers' perceptions and definitions of their place in the system. In an extended essay on the problem of insatiability, William Leiss (1976) examines an important aspect of this destabilizing process by linking the workings of a goods-intensive economy to an ongoing confusion of consumer need.[23] According to Leiss, a rapidly changing marketplace requires consumers to continually reinterpret their needs, by implication placing a strain on definitions of self and status. Two consequences of a fast turnover of goods are worth noting here. First, Leiss argues that turnover creates a "shallowness of wants," so that paradoxically in a high-intensity consumption society, individuals become increasingly indifferent to each of their specific preferences while simultaneously consuming more in a frantic effort to stay abreast of the market. Second, product change and differentiation lead to a "fragmentation" of need that translates into a fragmentation of personality, so that the individual must work ever harder to sustain a coherent sense of self and identity in the rapidly changing stream of products, spending more time and effort on consumption (16–19). Ultimately, "the relation between needs and commodities in our society is so ambiguous" (26) that the determination of consumer satisfaction becomes "problematical" (27). By this account, insatiability (dissatisfaction) is an outcome of the inability of consumers to determine whether or not their wants are being truly satisfied.[24]

Finally, alongside the destabilizing consequences of marketplace novelty is a related state of confusion in the symbolic or cultural system. In Leiss's argument, a rapid-turnover economic system aggravates what he claims has always been a "double ambiguity" involving the material and symbolic "correlates" of the commodity. With proliferation and fragmentation in the characteristics of commodities, the indeterminacy of material need has its counterpart in the ambiguity of what commodities mean to consumers. In his words,

> The realm of needs becomes identical with the range of possible objects, while the nature of the object itself becomes largely a function of the psychological state of those who desire it. . . . Thus there arises the possibility for the extensive simulation of experience through the manipulation of messages about things. (93)

The tendency toward fragmentation both multiplies the meanings of objects and creates an enlarged realm of simulation constituted by images of those objects. Thus, disturbances in consumers' interpretations of their needs are amplified by the significatory and symbolic ambiguities surrounding the products. The initial drive to consume in response to the uncertainties of material differentiations in the commodity is thus intensified by its cultural differentiations at the level of semiotic and symbolic processes, that is, in the messages about commodities' *meanings*.

The dynamics of culture, of course, differ in significant ways from those of markets, and Leiss, while recognizing a new fluidity of meaning, falls short of explaining the sources of the cultural ambiguities surrounding commodities. Here, semiotics again becomes relevant. In Baudrillard's competing interpretation, the fundamentally "unlimited character" of consumption cannot be explained by a "theory of needs and satisfaction" but only in terms of "the social logic of differentiation" (61). Rejecting notions of want and desire (Leiss's "psychological states"), Baudrillard sees the insatiable character of consumption as a predictable outgrowth of the sign system, which is ceaselessly referential: "The sign or mark of distinction is always both a positive **and** a negative difference—this is why it refers on indefinitely to other signs and impels the consumer on to definitive dissatisfaction" (1998, 61–62, original emphasis). In Baudrillard's argument, what the consumer seeks is not product satisfaction but difference from others. Since the socially coded sign system makes available "an infinite range of difference" (Introduction, Ritzer, 7), the consumer is fated to pursue commodities indefinitely in search of a satisfyingly competitive position vis à vis other members of society (Chapter Four). If signs themselves are the objects of consumption, then consumption is inherently inexhaustible, since the sign system has no natural boundaries or limits.

Conclusive explanations of a problem as complex and vexing as consumer insatiability remain elusive. Chronic marginal dissatisfaction, as we have seen, is attributable to a host of factors, including both the nature of desire and the workings of the economic and cultural systems of capitalism. However troubling, insatiability thus seems an inevitable feature of the existing system and will therefore remain a fundamental aspect of consumer subjectivity.

At the same time, despite the multiple forces behind this tendency, insatiability is elastic, like demand itself. There is an unevenness to dissatisfaction that manifests itself in a variability of shopping and purchasing habits, the length of time a consumer holds on to a commodity, different types of lifestyle, and so forth. The logic of insatiability does not easily translate into constant discontent or frenzied buying. Not only are there natural limits on spending levels and an enthusiasm for consuming (income levels, practical considerations), but many contemporary consumers, perhaps an increasing number, are consciously putting the brake on their consumption practices, repudiating a life of material excess and endless buying by scaling back to more modest, ecologically minded lifestyles. Here as elsewhere in the study of consumption, we find that the dominant tendencies of the system coexist with countertendencies in the form of shifting attitudes and responses among consumers.

Consumer Culture and the Self: Hedonism and Narcissism

In the foregoing, the aestheticization of the commodity was situated at the center of a calculated promise of pleasure through goods consumption. In this respect, the theory of commodity aesthetics points to a process of rationalization in the motivational structures of consumer society. At the same time, ironically this theory portrays the commodity as an object of sensual and social pleasure insinuating itself as compensation for life's shortcomings and the "disenchantment of the world" (Weber 1958a, 155, "Science as a Vocation") accompanying the selfsame process of rationalization shaping modern society. It should be further noted that defining the commodity as an object of visual attraction is to locate it in the broad trend toward the privileging of vision in modern Western culture generally (Jay 1993; Levin 1993). Indeed, this conception provocatively suggests a continuity between commodities and the visual arts. Be that as it may, commodity aesthetics transforms consumption into a form of pleasure based upon a gratification of the visual senses and by extension, the physical senses in general.

What emerges from this discussion is yet another category of valuation, what could be called the commodity's "pleasure value." While consumers buy for a range of reasons, including basic material needs, pleasure value has increasingly come to shape consumption practices alongside the commodity's sign value. This represents an important shift *in emphasis* in the meaning and function of consumption from the much-discussed goals of emulative status seeking and social display toward consumption as an act of self-gratification. Although social meanings are an integral part of self-gratification, much consumer activity is now suffused with a *wish for pleasurable experience* in the acquisition, possession, and use of commodities. By implication, this means that consumption practices are increasingly motivated by a search for entertainment and fun.[25] While the concept of entertainment carries connotations of cheap thrills and theatrical amusement, the notion that commodities can entertain has slipped into our consciousness almost unnoticed. This in turn reflects a social and cultural shift towards the principle of performativity. The recent theoretical emphasis placed by academics on performativity is consistent with a changed discourse and consciousness that stresses the performative features not only of human behavior but of things themselves (see Chapter Five).

Determining the pleasure value of a commodity depends upon three major criteria. First, there is the *sensual appeal* of the commodity, which is the dominant tendency of the commodification process. Consumer culture's accentuation of the sensual pleasures is captured in the comments of Zygmunt Bauman:

> The excitement of a new and unprecedented sensation—not the greed of acquiring and possessing nor wealth in its material,

tangible sense—is the name of the consumer game. Consumers are first and foremost gatherers of sensations; they are collectors of things only in a secondary and derivative sense. (1999, 38)

While perhaps overdrawn, this statement alludes to a new consumer hedonism based on the physical senses. Focusing the pleasure principle on sensual and specifically, visual, enjoyment follows logically from the nature of material goods—as physical objects, commodities are first and foremost visual objects. Haug and others have accordingly emphasized "sensuous appearance" as the source of pleasure in acquiring or experiencing things in a commodity society. The pleasure principle, however, has triumphed in consumer culture also because of the inherently democratic character of sensory experience and the pleasures of the senses.

But visual appeal is only one criterion of pleasure value. Beyond aesthetically based sensations, the hedonistic impulse appears secondarily in the discrete pleasures associated with the *functions* or *functional effects* of commodities. One thinks of the pleasures (comforts, conveniences, joys, excitements, fun) found in home appliances, automobiles, hi-tech gadgets, vacation homes, recreational goods, and so forth. Advertisements for these and other products extend the promise of enjoyment beyond their purely sensual characteristics to their functional qualities, that is to say, what they actually "do." Unlike the effects of commodity aesthetics, the pleasures of functionality remain poorly understood when considering the attractions and positive reinforcements of commodities.

Finally, as indicated in the previous sections, pleasure resides perhaps even more securely in the experience of *novelty*, whether understood in Scitovsky's terms as a psychological/physiological change in the level of arousal or alternatively, as inherent in the subject's discovery and appropriation of new objects and fresh experiences. The mere "newness" of a commodity therefore is an important determinant of its capacity to gratify.

The pleasure value of commodities, then, while increasingly anchored in their sensual characteristics, has a number of dimensions. Moreover, as we have seen, consumer pleasure does not derive exclusively from the commodity *per se*. Overlapping the pleasures of objects and packaged experiences are those of fantasy and daydreaming, important constituents of self-image and the gratifications associated with the feelings and emotions. Though Campbell's (1987) theory of consumer pleasure as illusory hedonism brackets commodities themselves, to dwell exclusively on the characteristics and functions of commodities is to overlook the ways that an active mental and emotional life can nourish the pleasures of living in a consumer culture. Here, not only is pleasure tied to self-made illusions or imagined gratifications, but it accompanies the sense of power and freedom that can flow from an exercise of the imagination. Pleasures of this kind constitute a secondary elaboration of the hedonistic impulse and are a major target of the image-making processes of consumer culture. Through advertising images, in particular, consumer culture becomes a powerful medium of imaginary pleasure.

These observations once more raise the problem of meaning. To the extent that pleasure value replaces sign value, the importance of the "meaning" of a commodity (its semiotic or denotative import) diminishes relative to its "meaningfulness" (its symbolic or connotative import, its relationship to desire). For instance, one could argue that feelings of pleasure (or pride) in the size and appearance of one's home is less significant as a measure of social competitiveness than as an indication of satisfaction in one's accomplishments, wishes, and tastes in relation to self. Again, while the social and hedonistic meanings of consumption are never completely separable, the desires and pleasures of self have become just as significant as the commodity's social meanings.

All of this said, an understanding of the hedonistic core of consumer culture depends upon putting consumption in a broader context, namely the contradictions of modernity and the search for selfhood. The differentiating and pluralizing consequences of modernity have created the structural conditions for a thriving individualism, while at the same time paradoxically *undermining* the self. Modernity has thus turned the definition and development of self into a major "project" (Slater 1997, 85; Giddens 1991) while assigning consumer culture as its handmaid. But by addressing the needs of the self in largely artificial, shallow, and commercialized ways, consumer culture has simply reproduced the problem of what an "authentic" self is to base itself on, a problem only aggravated by the individualism of market society and the commodification of leisure time (Goldman 1983/84). As Don Slater argues, "consumer culture is part of a loss of self brought about by modernity rather than an efficient way of satisfying the needs of autonomous selves" (ibid., 83).

The rise of consumer culture can be read positively as a solution to the modern fragmentation of social structure and as a reflection of the heightened sense of personal freedom and expanded choice following the decline of traditional society. As a repository of pleasure and choice, with material abundance the consumer way of life has delivered on many of its promises. But as the Frankfurt School argued, while pretending to fill a void left by the alienating and rationalizing conditions of capitalist production and exchange, consumer culture only perpetuates aspects of the very dissatisfactions for which it claims itself a remedy. Consumer culture and consumerist ideology dispense the symbolic and other materials by means of which privatized and isolated individuals can construct promised selves and identities. But this turns into an endless task.

In taking its cues from the alienating and dehumanizing tendencies of modernity, consumer culture becomes a therapeutic culture (Lears 1983), promising compensation and recovery through self-fulfillment in consumption. By linking selfhood to pleasure and establishing a regime of pleasure-seeking consumption, the self is promised psychic remuneration for its losses. The putative satisfactions and fulfillments of self thus become the new building blocks of society and the basic rationale for private mass consumption as a way of life.

Importantly, the consumerist conception of selfhood is based upon an elusive but very real ambiguity, as reflected in the interchangeability of terms attached to "self." Celebrants and critics alike use the terminology of "self-gratification," "self-growth," "self-realization," "self-enhancement," "self-fulfillment," and so forth in characterizing consumer society and its penchant for catering to the needs and wishes of the self. The indiscriminate use of these terms, however, blurs a fundamental distinction between two kinds of self-project. For the first project, the term "self-gratification" seems most appropriate, carrying connotations of momentary pleasure involving enjoyments of the senses and the body (Featherstone et al. 1991; Lowe 1995), a carefully controlled search, however restless, for "immediate gratification." Some would simply call this project "having fun."[26] This sort of quest contrasts starkly with a second type of project for which "self-realization" is perhaps the most apt term. This concept implies a process of growth and development aimed at a future goal. Here, gratification is purposively delayed for a longer-term vision of what the self might become through effort and patience. This conception seems close to what Slater and others mean by an autonomous self, a self following its own path (rather than the soft, masqueraded coercions of consumerism), a self-determined self, if you will. In a more traditional discourse, this is the notion of "cultivation," as reflected in Simmel's (1968) essay expounding the "tragedy" of culture as a failure of the self to master the object world. The former project involves a search for instant gratification and strictly speaking, belongs to the category of hedonism. The latter project is constituted in emotional, mental, moral, intellectual, and other kinds of sustained effort that place the self in a developmental trajectory.

This distinction poses the central dilemma of the self in commodity society. It is clear that while consumer culture speaks rhetorically to both kinds of self-project, in practice it overwhelmingly endorses the pursuit of gratification for its own sake. Typically, the rhetoric of self-realization and self-fulfillment serves only as an alibi for the perpetuation of consumers' dependence on packaged and easily digested pleasures. Through a combination of distraction, amusement, and cajolery, the main tendency of consumer culture is to immerse the self in momentary gratifications.

It would be difficult to overestimate the significance of the self in modern Western society, and indeed the celebration and misfortunes of self are the very stuff of modern literature and theory. This is succinctly captured in Daniel Bell's comment that "modernism has thus been the seducer. Its power derived from the idolatry of the self" (1978, 19). What Bell does not sufficiently address, however, is the mutation of modernist self-worship into self-absorption, a state often characterized as pathological under the psychological rubric of "narcissism." Slater, who uses the more extreme formulation of "self-obsession," points out that narcissism is not "self-love" but rather a condition stemming from "an inadequate sense of the self and its boundaries" (1997, 92). Loss of self leads to a *preoccupation* with self and a correspondingly weakened connection with others. In this line of thought, by heightening and exploiting an obsession with self, consumer culture becomes both symptom and perpetrator of a widespread narcissistic condition (Lasch 1979; Giddens 1991, 200). In Slater's characterization, "The narcissist is driven by a desire for endless gratification, experience, and impulse, but with no possibility of any commitment" (1997, 93) Paralleling the narcissistic breakdown of the boundary between self and other is a disintegration of the distinction between private and public, and excesses especially of the private, all of which can be seen as a manifestation of the triumph of consumerism. For Christopher Lasch, this takes the form of an invasion of the private sphere by the forces of commercialism, inducing dependency on mass consumption (Chapter One) and intensifying the need for instant gratification of the ego.[27]

The clinical conception of narcissism attempts to interpret hedonistic consumerism in terms of its psychological roots and effects. This conception puts forth correlates between the workings of consumer culture and the narcissistic personality structure, arguing that by making self-gratification an end-in-itself, consumer culture sets the stage for a narcissistic orientation of self-glorification. As a corollary, in this view consumerism turns the self into a commodity (Davis 2003), converting humans into useable and saleable objects in formerly inconceivable ways. In the theory of narcissism, a fragile self perceives others and the world as objects of its own gratification, objects that can be approached like any commodity. In this view, the micro processes of personality formation bear a close relationship to the macro process of commodification. Worsening matters, the latter leads to an amorphous world of things, images, and sensations, breeding self-disorientation and confusion and thereby deepening self-crisis and aggressive, ego-centered defenses against the outside world.

Despite the many criticisms of Lasch's social/cultural conservatism, his psychoanalytic discourse makes a persuasive case for reading consumer culture as both cause and consequence of the figure of the narcissistic personality first theorized by Freud. Indeed, there seems to be a rough "fit" between the main features of narcissism as a clinical model of personality and consumerism as a way of life. However, a linking of narcissism and consumer culture encounters a number of problems. First, there is much evidence, impressionistic and otherwise, that self seeking is not the only consequence of consumer culture or a trait exclusive to it. Indeed, there exists an obvious social and interpersonal side to consumption that contradicts the main thrust of Lasch's analysis. Secondly, as we know, to find correlates is not the same as establishing cause and effect. But mainly, it is questionable whether a psychoanalytic account of the asocial tendencies of consumer society, especially in the technical language of Freud, is either necessary or helpful in describing and explaining self-seeking hedonism. Positing a homology between hedonistic consumerism and narcissistic behavior might provide suggestive insights into the socially and psychologically destructive aspects of consumer culture and its parasitical relationship to a fragile self. But regarding pleasure seeking per se, its furtive pursuit is better explained by forces already discussed: the degradation of work, the nature of desire and its insatiability, social fragmentation and isolation, and the motivational strategies of the culture industry. Since it is an established part of our vocabulary, the term "narcissism" remains a useful reference point for a troubling syndrome of our time. It thus seems appropriate to employ the term in a generic or conventional sense to characterize the more extreme forms of self-absorption and corrosive asocial tendencies of consumer culture. But as social and cultural diagnosis, the usefulness of the psychoanalytic meaning of narcissism, at least in its original Freudian version, remains problematic.

Conclusion: Pleasure, Self, Identity

This chapter has attempted to reshape the central concerns of commodity fetishism and cultural theory by exploring the internal relations of the consuming subject and commodified object. This has been done in a loosely phenomenological mode by examining the pertinent psychological and social-psychological processes shaping the perceptions and consciousness of consumers and by considering the variability in the meanings of commodities. Only cursory attention has been given to relevant aspects of the emotions and the unconscious, an important dimension of consumer subjectivity about which the psychoanalytic perspective still has much to offer.

The analysis began with an ontology of consumers and commodities that focused on the sensuous characteristics and experience of commodities and their operation in a matrix of signs and symbols. This analysis formed a backdrop for the problem of insatiability, perhaps the most theoretically intricate feature of consumer capitalism. The main goal of this discussion has been to think about the subjective impact of the commodity system on consumers and specifically, the nature of the grip that consumerism holds on them. For this purpose, commodities have been read primarily as objects promising self-enhancement and pleasure but carrying an array of complex and often contradictory meanings and effects.

The analytical strategy proposed here avoids many of the pitfalls of the agency/structure dualism and of system-based models such as political economy and semiotics, which tend to ignore how consumers actually perceive, define, experience, feel about, and respond to commodities as objects. An effort has been made toward some general assertions that acknowledge the boundaries and limits imposed by systems while focusing on the actual workings of commodity culture as they play themselves out in the psychic life of consumers. This has involved recontextualizing critical theory in more conventional but still critical readings of actors' relationships to commodities.

This analysis has been consistent with the position of cultural studies that one-dimensional readings of consumption as domination and manipulation tend to overlook the meaning-creating acts governing actual consumption practices. But it departs from cultural studies in a number of respects. Mainly, seeking sources of both conformity and creative change, my analysis traces meaning back inside the commodity itself. Unlike cultural studies' politicized emphasis on "resistance," a balance has been sought between subjects' compliance with the dominant codes and structures of consumerism on the one hand and the sources of potential breakdown of these identifications on the other. This has involved exploring the psychological dynamics along with the ambiguities of consumption in the context of a system of signs and symbols. Hence, the domination/resistance paradigm has been recast in new terms. The tensions between the dictates of the system and the desires of meaning-seeking subjects has been redefined as an opposition between the instrumental purposes of the sign system of consumer capitalism and the expressive meanings and values of an inherited, shared world of symbols. The semiotic/symbolic divide thus points to new ways of thinking about the dominating and manipulative aspects of consumer society versus its potentialities for creative human action and fulfillment. These ways of thinking, in turn, presuppose the importance of self, reading consumer culture in context of the larger modernist project of selfhood.

This chapter has argued that consumer culture represents a complicated mixture of hegemonic control on one side and the quest of social subjects for meaning, identity, and pleasurable satisfactions on the other. An important subtext of the argument against viewing consumers as pawns of the system has been that consumer culture is anything but one-dimensional *insofar* as and *in the specific sense* that it is shaped by meanings and pleasures that provide a degree of fulfillment and hope in an otherwise unrewarding and often bleak society. When society and self are made fragile by a lack of materially and emotionally supportive institutions, consumer culture, while in the last analysis superficial and hollow in its present form and therefore unable to genuinely redeem, at least offers provisional relief along with faint echoes of a more authentically pleasurable and meaningful existence. By feeding on a world of symbols, consumer culture supplies us with limited but often energizing and hopeful cultural resources for the development of a more satisfying way of life. There is in the world of consumption a potential for genuine self-fulfillment and selfhood, and in the absence of major societal transformation, even the most hedonistic forms of consumer culture can at minimum contribute something to self-renewal.

Questions of identity have been raised only peripherally in this chapter. In the theory of commodity aesthetics, identity is linked to the appearance of things, including both people and objects. "The look" becomes all-important, with style and fashion the conventionalized vehicle of both self- and social identity. Gratification of self through the commodity is the means by which the consumer both self-constructs an identity and acquires an identity in the eyes of others. Given the social foundations of self-recognition, at a deep level the desire for commodities is inseparable from the need for social recognition and acceptance. The types of pleasures that one chooses to indulge are now of at least equal significance to other indicators of social status. Sensual gratification converges with social and cultural fit in defining the subject's place in the consumption system. The bearing of social and cultural relations on identity processes will be the topic of the next chapter.

Lifestyle, Status, Identity

4 The Social Relations of Consumption

An appropriate reading of the place of consumption in the modern search for identity requires locating commodities and selves in their social context. In this regard, the distinguishing feature of modern consumption is the emergence of what has come to be called "lifestyle."[1] Through culturally inscribed codes and symbols, lifestyle patterns give expressive coherence to the social practices accompanying the rise of consumer culture and consumers' participation in the modern project of selfhood.

The concept of lifestyle is central to a mapping of contemporary consumption practices in general and issues of identity in particular. Regarding the latter, lifestyle functions as (1) a vehicle of self-identity by providing resources for definition of self, and (2) a determinant of social and cultural identity by providing outward indications of where one fits in the social and cultural scheme of things. In the latter respect, lifestyle performs important communicative functions by giving expression to consumers' cultural dispositions and tastes.

In turn, lifestyle consequently has close links to social status. By communicating information about cultural dispositions and tastes, lifestyle patterns provide markers of social status and class boundaries. Indeed, lifestyle and status are so closely intertwined that formulating the relationship between them is a key problem in the sociology of consumption. Lifestyle patterning and status positioning are thus the main features of the social relations of consumption that are the foundation for the formation of a consumer identity. The main purpose of this chapter is to examine these twin concepts and what they tell us about the shape of contemporary consumption and its implications for identity. Lifestyle and status phenomena, of course, do not occur in a vacuum and therefore need to be contextualized in the larger system of which they are a structural part. Specifically, lifestyle and status need to be looked at in relation to the workings of the consumer marketplace. The impact that consumption has on identity is shaped and conditioned by the dynamics of this marketplace in particular and of the capitalist economy in general. While consumer lifestyle has become the main determinant of status positioning, the latter in turn has become increasingly complex as a consequence of changing market dynamics. I argue that what is perhaps most significant about the market today is its contradictory tendencies towards the simultaneous elimination and redrawing of status differences. How this happens, the form it assumes, and its consequences will be explored in the following pages as a prelude to a fuller discussion of identity in Chapter Five.

Status, Lifestyle, Identity

The notion that commodities are extensions of the self (Belk 1988; Dittmar 1992; Landon 1974; Malhotra 1988) offers a basic point of view for establishing connections between identity and the products and experiences we consume. However, even when consumption seems exclusively about the self, sometimes occurring in isolation from others, its meanings are fundamentally social in nature (Dittmar 1992). As will be taken up in Chapter Five, we express and define ourselves, wittingly or not, through complex processes and networks of social interaction and communication. Our relationship to commodities is socially and culturally mediated by groups and social structures.

The concepts of lifestyle and status are indispensable for examining the social dynamics of consumption and indicating how these dynamics effect identity formation. Of the two, status is the more foundational concept in sociological approaches to consumption but at the same time the more problematic. Taken in its hierarchical or vertical meaning, status is usually linked to class and thought of as the social aspect or consequence of property relations, or the unequal distribution of economic resources and power relations generally (Turner 1988). However, the declining importance of production roles and the increased difficulties of measuring class membership have clouded and complicated this linkage. Developments, particularly since World War II have weakened ties between patterns of social behavior, increasingly shaped by consumption, and the familiar sociological indicators of class position, income and occupation.[2] Consumer culture now addresses individuals and groups more as members of categories and networks based on lifestyle attachments and other nonclass demographics than in terms of class identities. This suggests that status claims are now often predicated on forms of expressive behavior differentiating people along a horizontal axis of noneconomic criteria. To the extent this is the case, lifestyle patterns have become markers of *difference* rather than inequality, leaving the concept of status increasingly ambiguous.

While certainly debatable, the weakening of visible class boundaries, especially in the United States, seems to have rendered the concept of class a mere backdrop to other categories of identity. This change was registered most publicly in the emergence of the identity movements of the post-sixties era, which focused attention on the differences and divides of gender, race, ethnicity, sexual orientation, and other noneconomic identities. Not coincidentally, the ascendance of identity politics and the rise of a new consumer consciousness and culture that obscure older class divisions occurred at approximately the same time. Today, identity politics have been mainstreamed and commercialized, furthering the dissolution of class boundaries by consumer culture.[3] The corporate promotion of lifestyle along with new kinds of status anxieties engendered by media images of "the good life" have worked in conjunction with identity movements to undermine familiar and reliable demarcations of class, although without entirely abolishing perceptions, and certainly the realities, of class inequalities and loyalties.

However, while the rise of identity movements is part of the recent story of consumer culture, and partially explains the direction of identity formations in recent years, it is mainly consumer culture itself that has diluted the significance of class in favor of *other* identities organized mainly around lifestyle practices. While the experience of class has obviously not disappeared entirely, class differences are now strongly *mediated* and *subsumed* by the discourses and experiences of lifestyle. Insofar as many lifestyle practices still involve hierarchical comparison and competition, while not clearly corresponding to class lines, they continue to resonate class relations, often reproducing them in new forms and guises.

Now only a vague and uneven reflection of class difference, lifestyle is indisputably the central concept for understanding the relationship between consumption and identity. Complicating matters, however, the concept of lifestyle can have multiple meanings, corresponding to the multiple dimensions of identity formation through consumption. Unpacking the term discloses two major usages. First of all, lifestyle can broadly refer to observable ways that individuals or households spend their money and time. Certain types and quantities of goods, services, or entertainments are regularly consumed or not, depending on purchasing power and an element of choice, resulting in a material and social pattern of living (or survival). According to this meaning, everybody *by definition* has a lifestyle, whether they are lavishly spending millionaires, materially modest environmentalists,[4] or members of the homeless population. This generic definition has obvious practical applications but is imprecise and theoretically limited. While based on a basic criterion of differential patterns in the use of money and time, this definition is restricted chiefly to monetary factors and purchasing practices. It excludes the social practices of shopping and the use of particular goods, and it ignores the level of expressive or communicative display in the ways people consume.[5]

In contrast to the emphasis on spending patterns, the second definition places primary importance on patterns of *use* and more importantly, *style*. As Chaney (1996) puts it, lifestyle is "a style, a manner, a way of using certain goods, places, and times that is characteristic of a group" (5). What shapes a lifestyle, then, is not mere spending patterns, but the particular *ways* in which consumer goods and other material resources are deployed in everyday life settings. In this definition, it is not so much what is purchased or possessed by the consumer as it is how commodities enter into the consumer's life practices. *How* food is consumed, for example, is just as significant as the particular food items themselves. As the term signifies, the rise of lifestyle registers the growing importance of style in the consumption process as well as in modern culture generally. What distinguishes consumer culture as a particular historical form of consumption is its *stylization* (Lury 1996, 77–78), a process apparent both in consumer products (commodity aesthetics as discussed in Chapter Three) and practices. Indeed, "lifestyle" suggests that life itself becomes stylized, in a way that has an identifiable pattern and boundaries. Especially for the affluent, consumerist ideology insinuates that life can become a work of "art" in the sense that it can be turned into an expressive vehicle of aesthetic taste. In this meaning of the term, lifestyle implicates consumers in an *attitudinal* regime in which commodities are consciously approached in a distinctive way.

This second notion of lifestyle can be contrasted to Herbert Gans's important concept of taste culture. Gans defines taste cultures as consisting of values, cultural forms, and media expressing the "standards of taste and aesthetics" of various subgroups of society (Gans 1974, 10). As part of a critique intended to overcome the division between high and popular culture, Gans sees a strong relationship between taste cultures and class (ibid., 70), effectively reading the former as class subcultures. This conception comes close to Bourdieu's emphasis on the distinctive taste dispositions of members of different classes and class fractions (Chapter Two). The overlap between Chaney's characterization of lifestyle and Gans's concept is apparent, with two major exceptions. First of all, Gans's taste cultures refer mainly to cultural *content*, whereas lifestyle is primarily about *style*. Taste cultures were identifiable by particular goods, entertainments, leisure activities, and arts, and the values they expressed. However, most current definitions of lifestyle, Chaney's included, place emphasis on how such things are used, or the *execution* of taste. In contrast to taste culture, lifestyle might be characterized as built around *performance* more than mere possession. Second, in kinship with Bourdieu's distinctions, Gans's taste cultures are inseparable from the socioeconomic categories from which they emerge, whereas lifestyle is more directly related to the forms and dynamics of consumer culture. Finally, whereas for Gans the functions of taste cultures were to "entertain, inform, and beautify life, among other things" (ibid.), lifestyle is a more multifarious phenomenon involving identity, pleasure, escape, status, and novelty (Lury 1996, 46).

The material aspects of style, of course, gain important meaning in the context of the social functions of lifestyle. Emphasizing lifestyle as a strategy for counteracting the anonymity of modern life, Chaney focuses attention on how the differentiating effects of lifestyle practices distinguish and communicate status horizontally. In his view, lifestyle is significant mainly as a means of social representation:

> Lifestyle is a patterned way of using or understanding or appreciating the artefacts of material culture in order to negotiate the play of criteria of status in anonymous social contexts. Clearly the currency of lifestyles is the symbolic meaning of artefacts, that is, what they are seen to represent over and above their manifest identity. (ibid., 44)

This and similar characterizations invite comparison to the classic statement of Max Weber, which explicitly links lifestyle to status groups. Like Veblen (1934), Weber still saw an alignment between class and status, stating that "class distinctions are linked in the most varied ways with status distinctions" (Weber 1958a, 187). Nevertheless, he acknowledged a shift in weight from class relations to the status order, recognizing the communicative aspect of lifestyle and its growing significance. Weber remarks that

> The decisive role of a 'style of life' in status 'honor' means that status groups are the specific bearers of all 'conventions.' In whatever way it may be manifest, all 'stylization' of life either originates in status groups or is at least conserved by them. (ibid., 191)

In a subsequent quote, Weber came closer to current views of the nature and distinctiveness of status groups as varying independently of class structures, saying that in contrast to classes, "'status' groups are stratified according to the principles of their *consumption* of goods as represented by special 'styles of life'" (ibid., 193, original italics). At the same time, this quote makes clear that Weber is still referring to vertical status, claiming only that the basis of stratification in the status order is consumption rather than production.

Despite his acknowledgement of separate status formations, in Weber's writings the question of class still always hovers in the background, not unlike today. In line with Veblen's conception, Weber saw that status groups could be class-based, insofar as classes or fractions thereof formed into groups or communities (one thinks of occupationally based communities or interest groups, or occupants of similar income categories who share like-minded tastes in consumer goods). But he oscillated between thinking of status groups as economic in character (his mention of classes and consumption) and alluding to noneconomic entities, such as ethnic, kinship, and religious groups. Schematically, Weber's model is threefold: status groups can be formations based on (1) class membership, (2) consumption patterns, and (3) social and cultural affiliations and loyalties. Given the weakened correlation between lifestyle status and class position, a contemporary understanding of status in terms of lifestyle would depend primarily on (2) and secondarily on (3).

In another gap between past and present, whereas Weber seemed to regard status groups as complex formations, defined by their lifestyle characteristics only in some ultimate sense, recent theorists (Bocock 1993; Chaney 1996; Featherstone 1991; Lury 1996) have tended to *reduce* the dynamics of status to lifestyle groupings. Lifestyles are neither a mere aspect nor an example of status groups. Rather, for all practical purposes the two are nearly synonymous, lifestyle phenomena having infused the whole system of status relations. With the obscuring of class, status considerations now prevail, and status claims are brought forth in the form of lifestyle attachments. Without making explicit distinctions between vertical and horizontal status, however, these writers imply a move away from the notion of ranked status. Nonetheless, contrary to their approaches, we should expect to find class factors, especially income and education, still shaping and limiting lifestyle patterns (a consequence of what Weber called "life chances" (1958a, 181). Indeed, research continues to suggest rough correlations between income and educational levels on the one hand and lifestyle differences on the other.[6] Correlatively, this suggests that class meanings to some extent still find expression in the semiotic and symbolic content of lifestyle practices. For instance, yachting still resonates "upper class," casual yet stylish suburban living "middle class," and the Harley-Davidson motorcycle "lower class."

It is nevertheless true that as consumerism has turned consumption into an often-fervent and for some, obsessive, way of life—and a dominant social ideology shaping perception, cognition, and attitude—lifestyle has become a relatively autonomous and dominant social pattern, acquiring a life of its own. This is particularly the case for the affluent, whose growing disposable incomes have fueled unprecedented levels of consumer spending and a dramatic growth in middle- to upper-income lifestyle agendas. Indeed, like consumerism itself, lifestyle from the beginning was an outgrowth of conspicuous forms of wealth among members of the modern upper class. But with the extension of credit to wider sectors of the population, the lifestyle phenomenon has spread beyond the affluent, generating broader income markets governed by new social and cultural logics. The result is a proliferation of divisions and differences in the field of style and taste. Thus, lifestyle, with its seemingly endless variations, is now less attributable to conventional class categories than to a host of complex social and cultural influences involving new forms of financing, spending, and marketing and the demographics of gender, age, ethnicity, race, sexuality, and other social categories. New types of lifestyles have appeared in the form of highly specialized and hybrid products, services, and packaged experiences (tourism, extreme sports, wining and dining, environmentalism, wilderness adventures, home improvement regimes, high-tech entertainments, to mention only a few), reflecting a new kind of marketplace that is differentiated along nonclass lines.

In turning to its relationship to identity, the foregoing comments on lifestyle might be summarized in the following definition: lifestyle is an observable and complex pattern of expressive social and cultural practices based on the stylized use of commodities, settings, situations, and time—primarily but not exclusively within the sphere of leisure. Lifestyle is a pattern of individual or group behavior and activity that communicates taste preferences, customs, and habits through semiotic codes and sociocultural symbolism.

The first part of this definition highlights the *self* and *group* aspect of lifestyle, focusing on a particular cluster or configuration of consumption practices serving its members' needs and desires. The second part points to the communicative, external, or *relational* aspects of lifestyle, which locate subjects *positionally*, both horizontally and vertically, in relation to others with different lifestyles. This definition is consistent with Bourdieu's conception while keeping the unity and coherence of lifestyle patterns, more evident in French than American society, open to question. The first aspect can be a source of self-identity as it arises from within and in conjunction with social and cultural identity; the second aspect pertains exclusively to social identity, a sense of standing *vis-à-vis* others and of fitting into the larger society. Also, it is within the experience of the first aspect of lifestyle that consumption practices can impart a sense of cultural identity stemming from identifications with the meanings and pleasures associated with certain leisure and group activities. Although cultural identity tends to be ascribed through the self's relationship to ethnicity, language groups, religion, and the like, these traditional identifications are increasingly being expressed through lifestyle practices.

There is no question that with the modern breakdown of older and more stable social structures, social identity is increasingly tied to lifestyle membership. However, as suggested above, it is not always clear how this changes the concept of status. Today, identifications with given lifestyles *appear* to be much less a matter of social ranking than in the past. There is some evidence that spending and use patterns have become less emulative in Veblen's sense and more a means of locating and identifying individuals and groups in unfamiliar and rapidly changing social and cultural contexts and milieux.[7] Given conditions of social anonymity and impersonality, and a deeply ingrained egalitarianism on noneconomic issues, at least in the United States (Tocqueville 1945), the phenomenon of lifestyle tends to give precedence to the marking of *differences* as much as if not more than to inequalities (Bocock 1993, 80). Knowing how well one is doing in a competitive and putatively open class system would seem to be of no more concern than setting oneself apart as a member of a stylistically and socially distinct group or category (Patterson 2006, 51; Schor 1998, 58). Since consumption codes are highly unstable and equivocal and therefore less reliable than in the past (see next section), lines of socioeconomic hierarchy are often difficult to discern in lifestyle formations. Given an uneven distribution of economic and educational resources, lifestyle formations will always correspond roughly to class structure (Warde 1994). However, what these formations look like and what they *mean* to consumers is centered as much on taste preferences and sociocultural differences as on considerations of vertical status. *Inter alia* lifestyle is a means of carving out an identifiable social slot within an anonymous mass: lifestyle addresses consumers' needs for dissimilarity and boundaries. In this sense, lifestyle formations are commodity society's version of familiar, routine group processes. The other side of the need for differentiation is the wish for place, involving a need to feel a sense of acceptance and belonging as a participant with like-minded others in an active sharing of tastes and interests. Fulfillment of this need also involves the goal of "fitting in," finding a comfortable means of conforming. Lifestyle thus not only differentiates social subjects from one another but facilitates tangible and patterned *connection* to others. Lifestyle is a badge of membership in a group or subculture that creates new forms of attachment adapted to the system of commodities. Lifestyle gives shape to the process whereby use and possession of commodities establishes ties to physical place, to social context, and to other people.

The theme of belonging obviously raises questions of comparison between lifestyle and "community." Certainly one can find tendencies in certain lifestyles towards the tightly knit, face-to-face, and affective relations and commitments that we think of as defining community. But the highly configured and bounded character of lifestyles has led to contrasts with community, exemplified by Bellah and his coauthors (1985, 72), who refer to lifestyles as "enclaves." Also, since they are based on the specialized interests and desires of their individual members, lifestyles are seen by these authors as "segmental," both in the sense of involving only part of the person and in including "only those with a common lifestyle" (ibid.).[8] Giddens (1991, 83), too, has characterized lifestyles as segmental, but in a different and perhaps more illuminating sense. Citing the "multiple milieux of action" in modern society, Giddens observes that individuals' modes of action vary with context, resulting in the emergence of what he calls "lifestyle sectors," a "time-space slice" of an overall pattern of lifestyle activity. This notion calls our attention not only to its specialized and internally complex character but also to the adaptability of lifestyle to the multidimensional and mobile character of modern life.

But the need for social identity is no more important than modernity's emphasis on self-identity (Giddens 1991). Just as the rise of consumer society was in large measure a response to the modern project of the self, posing consumption as the vehicle and measure of self-creation, so has the expansion of consumer society in turn led to a heightened consciousness of self (Chaney 1996, 123). The growth in commodities, and the increasing imperative to define oneself through consumption, has intensified self-awareness in both public and private life. Thus, the strong links between lifestyle and the self, or as Giddens puts the matter, lifestyle's "inevitability for the individual agent" (1991, 81). In this regard, lifestyle can be thought of as giving "material form to a particular narrative of self-identity" (ibid.).

The centrality of self in the appeals of consumer culture in turn raises important questions about the role of choice. As alluded to above, lifestyle formations have both individual and group axes. While his formulations take account of both, Giddens highlights the element of choice and therefore tends to concentrate on the individual. In pointing out that lifestyle has little applicability to traditional cultures, he argues that it "implies choice within a plurality of possible options, and is 'adopted' rather than 'handed down.'" Lifestyle choices are "decisions not only about how to act but who to be" (ibid.). This is representative of the common view that, analogous to the situation of the "free" market, unencumbered individuals choose their lifestyles in accordance with their particular needs or wishes. But the group realities of lifestyle and the need to belong are inconsistent with this overly voluntarist picture. As a group phenomenon, lifestyle imposes limits and constraints on individual choice (Warde 1994, 69) by means of the norms and peer influences characterizing any group. In many respects, lifestyles are coherent social practices that operate as reference groups (Hewitt 1989; Shibutani 1955; Turner 1956), with all their pressures to conform. Moreover, like other modern institutions, lifestyles acquire a disembedded and abstract character (Giddens 1990, 1991), exerting wide influence through media and advertising and thereby exercising constraints beyond the level of local participation. In this sense, lifestyles often are not merely group memberships, based on direct social interaction, but highly elaborated cultural categories extending through media-based time and space, creating powerful models for millions of people.

Attempting to take into account both the individual and group axes of lifestyle phenomena thus poses a dilemma for theorizing identity. This is illustrated by the inconsistency in Bauman's extensive commentary on the centrality of modern consumerism to identity and self.

In *Freedom* (1988), he explicitly connects consumption and individual freedom, rather optimistically appraising consumer society in such remarks as "the remarkable freedom of the consumer world" (57) and "shifting the area of individual freedom from competition for wealth and power to symbolic rivalry creates an entirely new possibility for individual self-assertiveness" (58–59). This is followed in *Thinking Sociologically* (1990) by an account of consumption focused more on the theme of belonging, in which lifestyles (or "neotribes) become the dominant mode of social membership, what "we join in search of our identities" (156). These contradictions in Bauman's characterization of modern identity reveal a chronic tension between freely chosen identity and the demands of group life.

There is no easy way of distinguishing either motivations or outcomes in weighing the relative importance of lifestyle and its various functions for the individual. However, with respect to individual freedom and expression as opposed to the comforts and pressures of group life, in the context of the uncertainties and vulnerabilities of contemporary society, the relocation of personal freedom and choice to the realm of consumption might seem less significant than the *group* benefits of lifestyle membership. Posed as a matter of freedom versus belonging, and given other possibilities for identity, Warde's comments, in a critical assessment of Bauman's theory of consumerism, are suggestive: "the consumer chooses the group as much as, and probably more so than, the style: and membership of the group commands a certain path through the enormous number of commodities on sale. Belonging comes before identity" (Warde, 70). However, insofar as this boils down to the eternal tension between individual vs. group interest, it is perhaps the wrong way to pose the problem. The important insight in Warde's statement is that a conscious or intentional search for identity might not be the primary motivation for lifestyle pursuits. Instead, he asserts, people are really looking for a means of belonging from which an acquired lifestyle identity might follow. But in subjects' own minds it would seem difficult to separate the two, and indeed social psychology tells us that self-identity is dependent on participation in group life and that our sense and definition of self develops *through* interactions with others (Mead 1932; Jenkins 1996). By implication, stylistic or expressive identifications are, for many consumers, proxies for group identifications and supports.

Moreover, Warde's position overlooks the innumerable opportunities for individuals to engage in lifestyle pursuits outside of group boundaries and settings. The disembedding of lifestyle from physical settings and tangible social attachments means that consumers can stylistically configure their lives in highly individualistic and idiosyncratic ways through the various apparatuses of consumer culture. Shopping sites and electronic media provide abundant means and materials for consumers to construct lifestyles in isolation from the group. Just as media and advertising expand the power of lifestyles as reference groups, they simultaneously facilitate selective self-expression through direct and often finely tuned appeals to private consumers. Active identifications can thus take shape around lifestyle in the form of cultural categories and models that individuals encounter in the media and shopping malls.

Dynamics of the Consumer Marketplace

The foregoing has inquired into the relationships among class, status, lifestyle, and identity both from the standpoint of social actors and the social meanings and effects of consumption as a modern phenomenon. This picture, however, requires grounding in the social and economic changes shaping the contemporary system of consumption. Status and lifestyle along with processes of identity formation are part of the dynamics of consumer capitalism. Specifically, what stands between the consumer on the one hand and his/her lifestyle and status on the other is the operation of a market. The processes shaping consumer identity are largely an outgrowth of the social and cultural effects of the consumer marketplace. In turn, the workings of the market are a consequence of the mutually constituting effects of macroeconomic and sociocultural processes.

With an accumulation of studies focused on the social and cultural dimensions of consumption, the relationship between production and consumption has too often been artificially divided (Fine 1995, 127). Chapter One showed how leading theories of consumption have drawn heavily on ideas about the capitalist economy, including the influential argument that demand is driven by production. Galbraith (1958), Baran and Sweezy (1968), and others have maintained that levels and patterns of consumption are attributable to production output. These thinkers assert a direct link between consumption and production by way of an elaborate advertising and sales apparatus designed to motivate spending on things already produced or in the pipeline. As mentioned previously, the main weaknesses in this view stem from the problematic assumption of need creation and a more general lack of perspective on the noneconomic (cultural, psychological) factors shaping consumer subjectivity and desire. In effect, this paradigm explains consumption too readily as a unilateral outcome of production.

Nevertheless, since the object of consumption is *commodities*, it is imperative to maintain a focus on the economic marketplace, which is the foundation of the dynamics and overall shape of consumer behavior and lifestyle patterns. As implied by the discussion in Chapter Three of commodity aesthetics, the pursuit of novelty and resulting chronic marginal dissatisfaction are largely explainable in economic terms. At the same time, theorizing the relationship between economic production and consumption can avoid crude economic determinism by recognizing the influences of culture and psychology on consumer consciousness and practices.

In recent decades, changing production, distribution, and marketing practices have transformed the conditions under which we consume and the social and cultural factors influencing how we communicate through purchases and possessions. Among the range of factors that could be addressed on the production side of the economy, those presented in David Harvey's influential work on the "post-Fordist" regime of "flexible accumulation" (1989) are especially relevant. According to Harvey, the rigidities of so-called Fordist mass production together with growing global competition led in the 1970s to innovations in the U.S. economy that enabled producers to adapt more quickly to changes in consumer markets and to threats posed by foreign competitors. The flexibility of this new regime consisted of "an increasing capacity to manufacture a variety of goods cheaply in small batches" (ibid., 155). The new strategy had two pillars: (1) rapid product innovation, leading to an acceleration in turnover time, and (2) specialized products aimed at small market segments. The twofold effect of these changes was an overall speedup in trends and cycles in the marketplace and its increasing differentiation based on new methods of target marketing aimed at particular demographic and lifestyle categories.

These changes can be seen as setting the stage for a transformed consumer marketplace. Acceleration and segmentation in product marketing require a carefully managed system of fast-paced and highly specialized consumer demand. Accordingly, the design, advertising, and marketing functions of capitalism shifted into high gear, dramatically reshaping the consumer landscape and the dynamics of lifestyle formation.

The economic reasons for segmenting the market are readily apparent. Segmentation means smaller and more manageable production units and greater flexibility in production schedules. It also rationalizes the planning process, giving producers increased precision and control over the market by means of demographic mapping and prediction. More generally, a segmented market expands the overall selection of goods and services, instilling in consumers a greater sense of choice, strengthening the motivation to buy. By addressing the need for greater individuality, targeting lifestyle clusters *within* socioeconomic strata (Schor 1998, 11) increases the variety and volume of commodities in the marketplace generally, the overall effect of which is higher rates of consumption.

At the same time, it would be a mistake to reduce contemporary consumption patterns exclusively to these economic changes. Harvey's account of production methods as determinants of social and cultural conditions is overdrawn, and some research has cast doubt on his main thesis (Fine 1995). A more balanced interpretation would be that the regime of flexible production and new consumption patterns are mutually constitutive, not causally linked. For one thing, the economic sources of market segmentation need to be weighed against the social and cultural origins of lifestyle as a new vehicle of differentiated status and identity formation. In a view that implicitly disputes Harvey's economic narrative, Schor has argued that mass-produced goods are "too homogeneous, too common," therefore creating a need for more differentiated products capable of "conferring distinction" (1998, 58). To expand on Schor, market differentiation can be seen as a reaction to the homogenizing trends of fifties consumerism and as an antidote to the excessive standardization and conformity of mass production symbolized by suburbanization. Thus, the idea of target marketing is congruent with the emergence of divergent consumer lifestyles accompanying a growing desire and need for individual and social demarcation. In part, the turn toward target marketing in the seventies addressed a real need for greater self-expression initially evident in the sixties counterculture (Cross 2000, 176). These changes involved mutually reinforcing trends based upon a convergence of economic adaptations and sociocultural shifts. Individuation and personalization of style and taste in goods and services represent the corporate system's response to (1) the new cultural values of self-fulfillment and rebellion celebrated by the counterculture, and (2) the themes of difference and diversity driving the identity politics and social movements of the seventies. Just as much as the market was segmented for reasons of efficiency and cost-cutting, then, social and cultural change exerted pressure for economic change, opening up new marketing possibilities.

Speedup in the turnover of goods leads to yet another set of effects on the marketplace, further illustrating the confluence of economic forces and the internal workings of consumer culture and psychology. In Chapter Three, the practice of rapid-goods turnover was linked to the problem of consumer insatiability. The thirst for novelty inherent in consumerism is simultaneously quenched and re-stimulated by an economic system based on a steady flow of continually changing products. Oscillation between the satisfaction and frustration of want is endemic to a fluid market and a cause of growing instability and confusion in the marketplace (Leiss 1976), a situation resulting in a breakdown of the consumption codes, or, put differently, a condition of "undercoding" (Schor 1998, 42). A theory of novelty must recognize both economic innovation *and* sociocultural change as sources of insatiable buying. Material and nonmaterial factors interact in complex ways to create a highly mobile and diverse marketplace whose overall effect is rising levels of consumption.

The key principles governing this marketplace are *style* and *fashion*, the crucial links between product development and heightened consumer demand. Central to status formations, style and fashion have been the fodder of consumer culture from the beginning, especially in the realm of clothing (Davis 1992). In an economy geared to rapid change, however, these factors assume critical importance.

Style (Ewen 1988) is key to understanding the marketplace because it is the major prerequisite of market change and adaptability. As an object of perception, style exists as surface, as appearance, representing the most ephemeral aspects of commodities. The foundation of the design side of commodity aesthetics, style gives visual form and shape to products but is at the same time precisely what is most changeable about them. Style, in other words, is what makes product change and differentiation feasible, since these are executed most readily at the level of visual design. The excessive significance attached to surface qualities makes it possible to engage in endless product variation through changes in the mere appearance of commodities. One of the chief functions of consumer society's new "cultural intermediaries" (Bourdieu 1984) is "catering for and promoting a general interest in style itself" (Featherstone 1991, 91). At the sociocultural level, it is the "style" in "lifestyle" that is the basis of differentiation in consumption patterns and therefore variations in lifestyle-based identity. The celebration of style in consumer culture is thus the foundation of creativity and innovation required of a rapidly changing marketplace. Style supplies the cultural energy driving the economy, providing the material form for new kinds of lifestyle identifications.[9]

The vehicle of style is fashion, the dynamic process determining which style or variation thereof prevails at any given moment in the real and imagined life of consumer products. Fashion has always been the motor of consumer culture, moving people "to buy, dispose of, and buy again" (Leach 1993, 92). The handmaid of novelty, fashion is the means whereby consumer demand is regularly fed by a strategy of planned obsolescence. Always a marker of status and wealth, especially when lines of class grow vague (ibid., 91–92), fashion now has a special appeal to growing numbers of consumers using lifestyle to actively construct ("to fashion") a social and cultural identity. Fashion is what ties individual consumers to a collectivity, and the status order, providing both distinction and a sense of belonging. At the same time, as the culturally dynamic dimension of style, fashion provides a means of negotiating change in the status order.

The essential principles governing fashion in contemporary culture are presented in Simmel's classic essay "Fashion" (1957). Beginning with the idea that fashion is rooted in imitation, Simmel proceeds to outline its dual nature, saying that fashion simultaneously expresses a desire for both sameness and differentiation or dissimilarity. Fashion gives expression to opposing social tendencies toward the uniform and constant on the one hand and a need for demarcation on the other.

Fashion, then, is governed by the "two fundamental functions" of "union and segregation" (ibid., 297). In this respect, fashion is the cultural analogue of the contrary needs of group conformity and social distinction manifested in lifestyle. As Chaney observes, "The dynamics of change in different modes of fashion . . . mirrors broader processes of lifestyle formation" (1996, 49). The role of style and fashion in the type of economy described by Harvey cannot be overestimated. In terms of market segmentation, style is central to product diversification. Regarding market speedup, "the mobilization of fashion . . . provide(s) a means to accelerate the pace of consumption" (Harvey 1989, 285). Even in the absence of this acceleration, as Bauman reminds us, "market activity would soon grind to a halt" (2001, 155) without the incessant discarding and replacement of objects simply because they have gone out of fashion. An intensification in the circulation of goods requires fashion to work overtime, in speeded-up cycles. Fashion trends multiply as industry pours more resources into design and marketing, compressing the curves of the fashion cycle for the purpose of hastening purchases.[10]

This picture of intensified change and differentiation in the marketplace has led a generation of theorists to conclude that trends in consumer culture have effectively undermined not only class distinctions but social distinctions generally. Certainly, rapid turnover and segmentation lead to a fluid and volatile marketplace and corresponding disruptions in the semiotic/symbolic order, the general result of which is a confusion of rules and meanings governing spending and an ensuing destabilization of status. However, social distinctions find ways of reasserting themselves despite continual weakening. The consumer landscape is in reality shaped by a set of contradictory processes, reflecting opposing tendencies of breakdown in social distinctions and reaffirmation of boundaries.[11]

Exploring these contradictions begins with an updating of what Chapter One called the "paradox of affluence" (26). Beginning in the fifties, in the context of an expanding economy and weakening class lines, consumer goods assumed unprecedented importance as markers of status. But the expanding abundance accompanying these changes meant that goods acquisition could never prove anything more than relative success. What began as a problem of novelty inherent in growing abundance has become a conundrum of fluidity in the social and cultural codes governing consumption.

In today's marketplace, the lines of status undergo continual dissolution through the accelerated introduction of new products and styles. But just as predictably, these lines are quickly redrawn in an effort to maintain the boundaries of social status. This dialectic of blurring and redrawing is driven by two interrelated dynamics. First, increased output tends to create an oversupply of product, which in combination with rapid turnover leads to a condition of "inflation." Just as monetary oversupply causes devaluation of the currency, material abundance leads to a devaluation of goods. Corresponding to this material process is an incipient confusion in the meanings of goods resulting from product differentiation and sheer excess (Leiss 1976). Goods devaluation generally brings two results. While consumers develop an attitude of indifference and boredom, a loss of meaning also provokes a search for new boundaries and attachments. This in turn incites the introduction of new products that promise to re-establish the logic of difference and thus status underlying the commodity system. But this simply recreates the original problem of oversupply, and the cycle perpetuates itself (Dunn 1998; Featherstone 1991; Leiss 1976). Successive waves of new products erase previous markings of distinction and difference but replace the old consumption codes with new ones. Segmentation and excess thus constitute a back and forth rhythm of semiotic disarray and countermoves to redefine the lines of status.

The second dynamic involves a vertical movement of status markers. Here, the status system undergoes erosion through the familiar process of "marketing down" (Dittmar 1992, 96–97; Dunn 1998, 119), whereby cheap imitations of upper-class goods are disseminated to lower-income consumers. In this case, fashion violates the boundaries of status, setting off a new and defensive round of goods innovation among the higher strata. Simmel recognized this phenomenon of semiotic/symbolic migration followed by regrouping as a characteristic feature of the fashion system.

Just as soon as the lower classes begin to copy [the upper classes'] style, thereby crossing the line of demarcation the upper classes have drawn and the uniformity of their coherence, the upper classes turn away from this style and adopt a new one, which in turn differentiates them from the masses; and thus the game goes merrily on. (1971, 299)

Featherstone characterizes this interminable trickling down of status markers as producing "a paperchase effect in which those above will have to invest in new (informational) goods in order to re-establish the original social distance" (1991, 18). Largely a phenomenon of mass production, which homogenizes through widening distribution of the same or similar goods, marketing down has assumed new forms in the framework of target marketing as manufacturers find ways to leverage their appeals to downscale demographics through the deployment of styles associated with the affluent and wealthy classes. At the same time, vertical distance can be disrupted through the inverse dynamic of "marketing up" the styles of lower-income groups, as exemplified by designer jeans that reference working-class garb and, perhaps more perversely, extreme price markups for the "distressed" look imitative of the clothing of poor and carefree hippies.[12] When this happens, of course, there is no social incentive for a redrawing of boundaries.

A porous status system and an upscaling of style (another way of saying a downward marketing of "luxury") have heightened the need for visibility in marking the status meanings of commodities. Designer logos on clothing have given high profile to the phenomenon of branding (Klein 1999), which serves to reinstate status and lifestyle boundaries in a clothing industry suffering from fashion excess and stylistic free-for-all. Product branding becomes a necessary means of both marketing down and reasserting hierarchy as higher lifestyles are extended to lower-income consumers. Branding, then, assumes special importance in an increasingly ambiguous and fluid status order.

A volatile consumer marketplace thus intensifies two opposing tendencies evident from the beginnings of consumer culture. On one level, the marketplace is a powerful democratizing influence.[13] While the standardization inherent in mass production and marketing promotes a sense of equality in the way things look, by widening the demographic circle, rapid goods circulation and target marketing democratize by means of inclusion. A shift in emphasis to lifestyle *differences* implies increased spending rates among more groups and categories and therefore a growing dissemination of status symbols. In other words, more consumers get in on the game. The marketing-down strategy induces appearances and feelings of upward mobility by making it possible to acquire a semblance of prestigious status symbols, thereby enabling identifications with those higher up the ladder. At the same time, the display of lower-class styles among the affluent ("reverse" status symbols) strikes a note of egalitarianism, implying a degree of acceptance of ordinary people and an openness to their tastes, values, and lifestyles. All such tendencies towards the abolition of distinction thus create an *appearance* of democracy.[14]

On another level, the marketplace perpetuates and reinforces status divisions. Despite a dispersal of status symbols, market segmentation inevitably reflects differences in purchasing power, reproducing in increasingly subtle and differentiated ways a system of vertical differences. And for every trickle down of cheapened luxury items, there is a new fashion or product for the privileged rich. As Hondas begin to look like Mercedes, some models of the latter become even more luxurious and financially out of reach for those lacking private wealth. As low-priced Wal-Marts spread like an epidemic, upscale department stores and specialty shops reaffirm their presence and authority by increasingly extravagant and invidious means. Thus, the marketplace has it both ways, both creating the impression that more consumers are climbing the ladder through access to the material possessions and styles of the affluent while simultaneously perpetuating a system of hierarchical differences that enables the wealthy to retain their coveted positions and lifestyles.

The Diderot Effect

One of the most significant but least discussed topics involving market dynamics is the so-called "Diderot effect." In an essay titled "Regrets on Parting with My Old Dressing Gown," the French philosopher Denis Diderot (1713–1784) tells the story of what happened to his study after receiving the gift of a luxurious scarlet robe. As a direct consequence of the introduction of this new possession, Diderot found it necessary to gradually replace everything in his study. In the presence of the new robe, the belongings in his room began to look old, worn, and drab; in short, the old furnishings simply didn't "fit" the newly acquired object. The seeming unhappiness and melancholy this caused Diderot is less important than what the story tells us about how the material things comprising our domestic surroundings must "go together." Consumer goods exhibit a certain consistency, they complement each other with commonalities that follow a logic that is inescapable and independent of our will. What Diderot unexpectedly discovered was a pattern of consistency among all his furnishings that was disrupted by a new object. This perception of pattern is a familiar and common occurrence, a phenomenon that McCracken calls "products complements" (1990, 119).

What the Diderot effect reveals is that material goods tend to group together in interrelated unities based upon commonly shared elements. Diderot suffered the distress of having to redo his entire room because the new object, which he chose to keep, failed to conform to the underlying unity of the old items. While the unity itself and its significance are apparent, determining its nature and origins is rather more complex. The question thus arises, what is this unity and what is it based on?

McCracken (ibid.) makes the argument that the "Diderot unity" has to do mainly with cultural meaning. Reaffirming the central role of semiotic/symbolic codes of consumption, McCracken asserts a correspondence between consumer goods and cultural categories, a correspondence that he believes "helps determine which goods will go together" (ibid., 120). He gives the example of the Rolex watch and the BMW automobile, goods that he believes are "structural equivalents" in terms of how product categories become aligned with cultural categories, in this case involving social class. If goods are coded according to such cultural categories (which aside from class would include age, race, ethnicity, gender, and other factors), unities emerge across an array of products that have comparable exchange and sign values. Whereas exchange value coheres mostly around class categories, both types of value tend to intersect around the same or similar cultural meanings, and this coherence determines a certain consistency among many different kinds of products that are perceived as "going together" culturally. As McCracken argues, meaning gets into things through (1) "the advertising and fashion system," and (2) "innovative groups," the former attempting to match the meanings projected by the advertisement and its product, the latter initiating new patterns of consistency. Finally, he states that "non-linguistic" material goods do not communicate well in isolation. To function as cultural and social communicators products need "redundancy" (ibid., 121), which is attained by grouping numerous objects together. Consumer goods, then, cluster around their assigned cultural categories, which means that the complementarity of products is based upon a logic of cultural meaning. While this explanation of the Diderot unity accords with semiotic theory and Bourdieuian models of status distinction, it also reveals an important limitation of this body of work. An exclusive focus on the cultural and social status of objects misses the impact of visual meaning. While the perception of cultural meaning in a cluster of goods surely matters in the emergence of a "Gestalt," a strong alternative explanation would show how goods go together on the basis of their visual qualities. Diderot's old objects exhibited a completely different set of physical characteristics than his new robe. It is often the case that objects just don't "look right" together as a result of physical incongruities, whether related to their age (patina or lack thereof) or some other characteristic such as style, color, size, materials, and so forth. In many cases, such physical differences are related to cultural and social codes but just as often they are reducible to mere appearance. McCracken's account of the Diderot unity underestimates the significance of commodity culture in terms of the physical presence and appearance of the objects themselves. Properly understood, incongruities among objects are in large measure attributable to sheer material differences. It follows that as *physical objects*, consumer goods adhere to a kind of logic that is to some extent independent of their cultural and social coding.

Nonetheless, whether the focus is on the coding or the physical qualities of goods, there is no doubt about the efficacy of Diderot unities and their consequences for consumption. First of all, the principle furthers our understanding of the material bases of lifestyle formation and the nature of the patterned consistency of particular lifestyles. Certain goods, as well as styles, activities, and pleasures, tend to cluster in how people live and spend their leisure time. This is reflected in the marketing of lifestyle through advertising and fashion, as exemplified by television ads that package *sets* of lifestyle preferences in the framing of their products. For instance, in some ads SUV's are contextualized in a wilderness lifestyle complete with all the signifiers of the affluent outdoor recreational consumer, as signaled by clothing, personality, setting, environment, and other products. The internal consistency we observe in particular lifestyles thus reflects the relative coherence of the cultural and social codes governing consumption. In fact, there is a sense in which any particular lifestyle *is* a Diderot unity.

What is perhaps most interesting and consequential about the Diderot effect, however, is its relationship to the workings of the consumer-goods market. As a unity, a patterned consistency, the phenomenon carries great force, as demonstrated by Diderot's own apparently reluctant and drawn-out effort in replacing his furnishings. In today's consumer market, we find a number of possible manifestations of the Diderot effect. In their normal mode, Diderot unities act to preserve the continuity of our purchases, actually protecting us from disturbances that might accompany major changes in lifestyle or taste preferences. In this respect, the tendency toward goods consistency has a conservative impact on the market, insofar as our existing patterns or styles of material possessions serve as a barrier against innovative marketing efforts. Of course, this does not entirely preclude the buying of new products, since novelty continues to exert its power at the level of single purchases, but only serves to maintain the present general level and direction of spending. We would, however, expect the Diderot effect to have more force at the middle to higher ends of the market, since those at the lower status levels would be open to change in an upward direction and therefore more actively seeking to transform their lifestyles. The redrawing of status boundaries, which is mainly concentrated at the higher levels, involves new products and fashions, not fundamental change in lifestyle patterns. While not seriously discouraging the marketing of new products and fashions overall, Diderot unities serve to restrain the fashion cycle, especially in the trendy and exclusive regions of the market.

But the Diderot effect can work in just the opposite direction, in a "radical mode" (ibid., 125), as it did in Diderot's case. The introduction of a new commodity can precipitate an extended round of buying, resulting in a whole new set of complementary goods. In this case, the force of unity works against continuity in spending patterns, acting to transform a lifestyle or an aspect thereof into something substantially different. This poses the question, how can the same force of unity be capable of both preserving and destroying an existing consumption pattern? As McCracken points out, the "machinery of marketing works constantly to encourage 'departure purchases,'" purchases made outside of the normal pattern. Along with the familiar marketing ploys, rapid goods turnover and market segmentation obviously increase pressure toward departure purchases by accelerating the introduction of new products.

To summarize, the Diderot effect has significance for marketplace dynamics in a number of ways. First, it helps illuminate the process of lifestyle formation by drawing attention to the consistency factor in lifestyle patterns. Second, it suggests an important counterweight to the weakening of status boundaries accompanying a rapidly changing marketplace. The force of unity in goods selection constrains the tendency toward breakdown of the status system stemming from a confusion of consumption codes. Finally, in its radical mode, the Diderot effect sheds a different light on the problem of consumer insatiability. Much buying occurs not out of uncontrolled desires or a state of chronic marginal dissatisfaction, as previously discussed, but rather from a requirement inherent in the nature of material possessions themselves for complementary grouping. In part, spending is driven by the cultural and physical logic of commodities as members of interrelated sets of objects.

Inclusionary Consumer Marketing: Notes on IKEA Egalitarianism[15]

IKEA, the highly popular and successful Swedish company specializing in home furnishings and accessories, exemplifies many of the marketplace trends discussed above, most notably the enlarged and aggressive effort at marketing down. More broadly, the business and shopping culture of IKEA is a dramatic case of the democratizing tendencies of contemporary marketing practices. What most distinguishes IKEA is an enthusiasm for bringing upscale middle-class products to large numbers of people at affordable prices. A simple statement of this egalitarian mission is given prominent visibility on the IKEA Group Corporate website: "Our vision is to create a better everyday life for the many people."

This vision has been implemented through IKEA's sophisticated strategy of combining contemporary design with functionality and low prices. Design is made synonymous with middle-class taste and thereby becomes the vehicle by which visible signs of affluence are made accessible to people of modest means. Of special relevance is the fact that the IKEA emphasis on design gives expression to the centrality of style in the contemporary marketplace. IKEA products could be roughly described as interior European modernism done in Scandinavian style. But the company's genius consists in joining the attractions of design to practicality and affordability (lots of fiberboard) along with versatility. By this means, it captures a broad demographic of consumers who can buy into a trendy middle-class lifestyle while gaining the satisfaction of purchasing highly functional and practical products at minimal cost.

IKEA is a merchandizing pioneer in another important respect. The strategy of branding so essential to status and lifestyle marketing typically relies on the use of naming through labels and logos, most evident in the clothing industry. IKEA, however, has ingeniously engaged in what might be called product self-branding. All IKEA goods appear to have a distinct look that identifies them as IKEA products. Everything from sofas to cabinets to bathroom mirrors is done in a style reflecting a common aesthetic that is clearly part of the IKEA design philosophy. This means not only that brand identity is achieved directly through product design and style as opposed to artificial markers, but that IKEA products enable immediate purchase of a ready-made, top-to-bottom lifestyle for the home. This aspect of IKEA marketing and merchandizing exemplifies the extent to which lifestyle pattern has been reduced to product design as well as a "totalizing" use of style.

For many observers, the popularity of IKEA is nothing short of a sensation. According to a Business Week cover story of November 14, 2005, IKEA has become a "global cult brand." Indeed, the story quotes CEO Anders Dahlvig as saying that "awareness of our brand is much bigger than the size of our company." The magazine rightly links this claim to the fact that IKEA is not selling just furniture but more importantly, a lifestyle, one "that customers around the world embrace as a signal that they've arrived." The IKEA phenomenon epitomizes the development of lifestyle as the focal point of contemporary consumption, and the company carries out its packaging and marketing of lifestyle on an unprecedented scale. As the Business Week story comments, with some exaggeration, "Perhaps more than any other company in the world, IKEA has become a curator of people's lifestyles, if not their lives." Consumer culture has made atmospherics no less important than merchandizing, and in this realm, too, IKEA stands out. There is something stirring about the whimsical, eye-catching exterior of the IKEA blue and yellow stores, not to mention the extraordinary size and scale of the buildings and their imposing presence. The IKEA appearance is a unique combination of the practicable and carnivalesque. While "yuppies"[16] are in some evidence, many if not most of IKEA's shoppers would be categorized as lower middle or working class. Casual observation suggests that IKEA attracts a diverse population of mostly young working people or college-aged consumers from many walks of life, an indication that the chain's attempt to sell to "the many people" has indeed succeeded.

Whatever eagerness and loyalty IKEA generates among its customers undoubtedly is related to the experience of shopping in its alluring showrooms and buying its versatile-looking products, an experience of one-stop shopping with many extras thrown in. IKEA stores represent a visually impressive packaging of the "shopping experience." In addition to the gratifications promised by the merchandise, the store layouts are designed and managed to maximize the pleasures of shopping. Using innovative shopping styles and economies of scale, IKEA stores feature huge warehouse-like settings, resembling an upscale home furnishings version of Home Depot. What shoppers mostly find are modestly priced but stylish items mimicking what 20 or 30 years ago could have been found only in small to medium-sized stores for the already prosperous. The astonishing number of available items—"7,000, from kitchen cabinets to candlesticks" (Business Week, ibid.)—and the sheer volume and selection of merchandise both excites and overwhelms. This setting creates a feeling of immersion in a sea of commodities and a sense of infinite possibilities for home display, practical comfort, and entertainment through "mix and match" practices. As signs in the store say, "Something for Everyone."

One of the striking physical aspects of IKEA is its replication, whether intended or not, of the atmospherics of other large-scale public sites and their fusion into an overall experience of "bigness." Most immediate is the sense of being inside a warehouse. The gigantic factory-like spaces are filled with tons of items in bulk form. This especially describes the "Marketplace," the large downstairs area where customers find small, specialized items, pick up the larger ones on display on the showroom floor, and make purchases at the checkout stands. An atmosphere of workplace industrialism is evoked in the do-it-yourself selection and purchasing methods and assemble-at-home products. We could surmise that in addition to cost-cutting through self-service and economies of scale, this aspect of the IKEA experience appeals to working people who feel comfortable in these surroundings and enjoy being recognized as self-reliant.

At the same time, though, IKEA carefully routes consumers through its showrooms in an example of what might be called, at the risk of offending Weber, "soft rationalization." From entrance to exit, shoppers are carefully routed through the entire display of goods, guaranteeing exposure to every item in the store. In combination with the visual pleasures of furniture sets, special lighting effects, and the overall arrangement of merchandise, this can create feelings of manipulation and "gentle coercion" (Business Week, ibid.) not unlike those we associate with mass advertising. This aspect of IKEA shopping can result in an experience of being overly handled and controlled, making customers feel like they, too, have become products on an assembly line.

If there is an antidote to this assembly-line feel, it is perhaps the countervailing sense that while shopping at IKEA one might be in the presence of "culture." In fact, there is an aspect of IKEA shopping that is vaguely reminiscent of the experience of visiting a museum. In a special section devoted to wall hangings of inexpensive but nicely framed reproductions, one finds a simulacrum of an art museum outfitted with faux examples of European modernist painting. But the routing of shoppers by signs and arrows prominently placed throughout the huge shopping complex broadly re-enacts what happens in any museum. IKEA cleverly combines the help-yourself method of box store shopping with an experience of modish spectatorship not unlike what occurs inside places like the Metropolitan Museum of Art in New York City (there is even a café midway on the tour). The museum imaginary adds yet another dimension to the illusion of partaking of a stylish middle-class lifestyle by insinuating that shoppers are "cultured" enough to appreciate fine art reproductions. Yet, as one might expect, IKEA has its detractors. While some critics object to what they claim is the poor quality of IKEA products, others seem offended by the very concept of large-scale marketing of what they perceive as cheapened versions of "the real thing." At least one Internet story sounds an alarm at the chain's rapid encroachment on the marketplace and its colonization of lifestyle (the Onion, April 28, 2004, Issue 40–17). IKEA's dramatic success with affordable design in the form of cheaply constructed products undoubtedly stirs the passions of the status and style gatekeepers. Certainly, IKEA is enjoying huge profits by breaking all the rules. While such protestations originate from a variety of impulses, they clearly demonstrate the tendency to redraw the status boundaries in the face of market democratization.

The New Emulative Spending

Inherent in Western ideologies of economic individualism and "free market" capitalism, an ethos of competitiveness has over time become deeply ingrained in U.S. society and culture. An inescapable effect of this ideological trait has been a division of society into "winners" and "losers." As a social process, competition sorts society into the "successful" and "unsuccessful," creating social-structural inequalities and a binary opposition in the culture. A matter as touchy as social class itself, the paradigm of winning and losing has a subtle but pervasive presence in everyday life. The tensions it produces are effectively displaced and managed in the form of cultural metaphor, common in everyday speech but manifested most openly in the institution of organized sports. Widely accepted in occupational life, competitiveness has led a more shadowy existence in the realm of leisure pursuits, where it bears a certain stigma. While its signs are evident, expressions of competitive behavior in the leisure realm tend to be suppressed or talked about in highly coded and mediated ways. Nevertheless, given its cultural resonance, conditioned and instinctual proclivities for not "losing out" to others, and persistent changes in the marketplace, competitive feelings about status and pursuit of the good life seem unavoidable.

In this context, the democratizing features of consumerism assume special significance. Aside from its impact on chronic marginal dissatisfaction, if the consumer marketplace erases status distinctions only to reinstate them as quickly as possible, what does this imply for the consumerist promise of inclusion in the good life and for the status game as a whole? Obviously, consumerism plays both sides of the fence, since there is nothing inherently incompatible about sharing the good life, however unevenly, while perpetuating a system of status. Yet the persistence of status distinctions and even more, their fluidity, would suggest that consumer spending inevitably reflects and reproduces the competitiveness of occupational life. The "paperchase" effect, in particular, insinuates that competition thrives in the realm of consumption and is sometimes intense and unrelenting, at least within certain income and educational categories. Keeping in mind that whatever competition exists originates within the machinery of marketing itself, since it is sellers who are the real competitors, incessant changes in the marketplace would seem to press buyers into competitive forms of spending.

It is important to ask, however, whether the consumer status game is truly a competitive one, as it seemed to critics in the fifties (Chapter One), or whether the endless pursuit of consumer goods represents a process of emulation as originally claimed by Veblen. Competition means active struggle between "winners" and "losers," whereas emulation involves striving to *be* like others, seeking to achieve their position or identity. Though it might provoke an element of competition with peers, who are often in similar socioeconomic circumstances, the downward marketing of status symbols puts consumers in a position of emulating members of higher strata in hopes of sharing in more attractive lifestyles by means of imitation. Whether or not they feel competitive, or even succeed in the endeavor, is largely a subjective matter, not an observable or measurable feature of the social process of consumption. While it might be tempting to reduce the complex workings of consumer status to a game of competition, striving for the consumerist version of the "American dream" (in other words, upward mobility) is really more a matter of attempting to *become* somebody different, to acquire a new self and identity.

The social ambiguities of status buying generate the underlying dynamic that keeps the economic system moving ahead. A major consequence of status blurring, as Veblen and Galbraith understood, is that emulative spending in principle has no real endpoint (Chapter One) since the standards keep changing. Recalling Baudrillard's assertion that the object of consumption is signs, if consumers are seeking not just satisfaction but *difference* (Chapter Three), then a blurring of distinctions in what is already a seemingly infinite and complex universe of coded status differences only deepens the problem of knowing where one stands. As marketers know, this can result in a fierce but lucrative dynamic of emulative spending in an effort to stay in the game. But from the standpoint of consumers, this type of spending can be highly problematic. The volatility of this spending dynamic has become more or less endemic to the consumer marketplace, augmenting worries about where one fits in the status order. Increased material excess together with an unending stream of advertising and media images of the "good life" make consumerism seductive and addictive in ways that raise anxieties about being left out. Market volatility thus has psychological consequences, intensifying consumers' sense of having to "keep up" in a continually shifting marketplace, worsening fears of falling behind.

The resulting tendency to feel that one must run just to remain in place has been aggravated in recent years by a combination of economic and sociocultural change. As Schor points out, there appears to have been a dramatic rise in emulative spending[17] during the eighties and nineties. This appears to be a result of rapidly rising income levels for select groups (Frank and Cook 1995) and a corresponding upward shift in socioeconomic and lifestyle reference groups. What has emerged is a major upscaling of the lifestyle marketplace. As Schor convincingly argues, in addition to rising incomes among pace-setting groups, elevated standards can be traced to the declining influence of neighborhoods, the traditional context of social comparison (keeping up with the Joneses), and a corresponding shift in reference-group pressures to the workplace and mass media, particularly advertising (1998, 2000). Thus, increasing numbers of consumers of only modest means have experienced growing exposure to an "economically diverse set of people" (1998, 10). This is readily apparent in the case of television advertising and other mass media, where the images and messages of the sales pitches to higher-income groups reach a broad viewing audience. This leads to new social comparisons extending up the ladder in an example of what might be called "reference group stretch." In short, the lifestyles of the affluent, not to mention "the rich and famous,"[18] have emerged as the emulative standard for a majority of the population.[19]

The net effect of these changes has been rising aspirations and expectations across a wide swath of the middle and working classes as well as among the affluent themselves. The democratizing tendency inherent in marketing down has taken the form of celebrating an up-scaled version of the comforts and luxuries associated with upper layers of the middle class, establishing an increasingly expensive lifestyle as the norm for everyone.

As Schor notes, these changes have had socially perverse effects on those under the sway of the upscaled ideal. First of all, the upper-middle class—the new model of emulation—now often feels poor as its *own* standards and spending levels have soared to unprecedented heights. Expectations have climbed so steeply among members of this class that many with annual household incomes of over one hundred thousand dollars complain of not being able to make ends meet in the face of rising living expenses. Scholars and journalists have bemoaned the pressures placed on affluent families by aspirations for the best private schools and colleges for their children, trendy and expensive tastes in designer goods, the purchase of second homes, costly vacation travel, and other accoutrements of rising standards of success, comfort, and pleasure. In combination with the rising costs of living in urban and metropolitan areas of the country (concentrated on the East and West coasts), ascending lifestyle expectations have created a quality of life squeeze, with a majority of the population working more hours, spending less time with their families, and, ironically, never getting around to enjoying whatever new luxuries they might be acquiring. Nor is there time and energy, paradoxically, for the modern ideal of nurturing or fulfilling the self through consumption.

Second, among those with less spending power, given their chronic economic insecurities, the stresses of rising lifestyle standards can lead to yet more troubling symptoms of dissatisfaction, frustration, anxiety, and depression. For those lacking money, the raised bar of consumption is a prescription for a sense of failure even worse than before the upward push in expectations.

The negative effects stemming from inflated expectations points to a number of unsettling problems with our present system of consumption and consumer culture. As noted earlier, insatiability is built into the system. The normal level of chronic marginal dissatisfaction, however, is heightened with increased pressures to emulate lifestyles that can be bought only at the cost of soaring personal debt, not to mention anxiety and worry. The Diderot effect only worsens this problem by requiring multiple expenditures with every upward swing in personal or household lifestyle. More generally, a combination of collective material abundance *and* a higher standard of emulation set up millions of people for a stressful and unhappy life of consumption in pursuit of lifestyles that are unrealistically extravagant. Indeed, the search for self-fulfillment through materialistic forms of emulation would seem to be doomed. Higher levels of consumption, as Scitovsky (1992) argues, hold out the promise of greater personal pleasure only to disappoint with the boredom of satiation and mere comfort. In this regard, the promise of pleasure-driven consumption is a treacherous deception because its hedonism is ultimately self-defeating. While offering temporary stimulation and pleasure, aggressive consumption, especially at higher levels, leads to dissatisfaction followed by successive rounds of spending, and eventually more dissatisfaction (Veblen 1934).

Conclusion: Competition, Emulation and Belonging

A decline in the relative significance of class and its replacement by lifestyle has introduced complex challenges to the analysis of status and identity. These challenges are partly attributable to the historical shift of status attribution from class categories to lifestyle attachments. The meaning of status becomes murky once class identities are subsumed by other identities based on lifestyle patterns rooted in assorted social and cultural categories and groupings. By valorizing difference and group membership, lifestyle formations diminish the importance of vertical position in favor of status differentiations along more horizontal lines. This tendency has been furthered by the democratizing trends of the consumer marketplace. In this respect, lifestyle patterns respond to a search for membership in a group or community of likeminded consumers differentiated by style more than social rank. An overshadowing of vertical status is also attributable to the intermingling of the multiple functions of lifestyle, which promise consumers not only status but identity, group participation, cultural membership, a sense of belonging, hedonistic pleasure, escape, popularity, and self-fulfillment. Of these many putative functions, this chapter has drawn special attention to the importance of lifestyle attachments as a means for locating the self socially and for a sense of place and belonging in an otherwise anonymous society.

Yet, lifestyles clearly still reflect inequalities in income and education and therefore reproduce a vertical status system, in however novel and unpredictable ways. To the degree that they persist, lines of vertical status, as we have seen, are quite real, though complicated and blurred by continual shifts and upheavals in the consumer marketplace.

While it remains unclear how much of the status positioning intrinsic to consumption is competitive as opposed to emulative, there are good reasons to regard the latest trends in consumer spending as primarily emulative in nature. Given a need for social membership, emulation is a logical outcome of market upscaling. If, as argued in the preceding section, the recent steepening of the spending curve is less an expression of competition than emulation, this upscaling can be read as a dramatic example of peer pressure. While in many respects a reversion to the era of Veblen, today's emulation of the higher-ups is not so much a matter of competing with others in climbing the ladder as a manifestation of desire for conformity and acceptance, a wish to fit into changing social standards.

This is not to say that consumers don't have competitive *feelings* in pursuing the good life or that competition plays no part in consumption practices generally. The question is, how are these feelings manifested and what form does competition take in the arena of consumption? Technically, competition requires two or more parties struggling over a prized goal or object. Typically, situations of competition arise from scarcity, such as in the job market when, as often happens, thousands of applicants vie for a mere handful of jobs. It is not entirely clear what it means to say that consumer spending is competitive when there seem to be more than enough commodities to go around for those who can afford them. Rather, we find competition taking more limited forms, for instance when shoppers storm a store for a limited supply of the latest fad or to get first choice of the sale items on the first day of the holiday shopping season. Sales of limited-edition high-ticket items with strong snob appeal is another situation with potential for competition, in this case among the prestigious and wealthy few who, often suffering large egos, see themselves as trend setters. But neither competition nor competitive feelings could be a governing principle of consumption *per se*, unlike what we find in the world of production and jobs.

This raises some fundamental questions about the empirical study of consumption. First and most elementary, how would one design a questionnaire to "get at" motivational information? How conscious are consumers of their own motives? Second, how is an outside observer to read the meaning for consumers of given purchases or possessions in terms of vertical status claims? Given the psychology and social psychology of possession, what might appear to be status purchases might very well be tied to other impulses, needs, or desires. Multiple factors can influence a single purchase—besides peer pressure, there are questions of taste, product familiarity, disposable income, convenience, practicality, desire for high-quality goods, and so forth. Such factors can operate completely independently of socially competitive feelings or status claims. Finally, and this poses a conundrum, perhaps what is perceived as competitive *or* emulative spending is nothing more than the effects of an intractable signifying process, whereby commodities, and those who possess them, inevitably get "always already" defined by consumption codes, despite the multiple motivations and intents of consumers (Chapter Five).

The implication is that to the extent they still play a role in consumption practices, status-seeking meanings intermingle with other meanings of consumption and become relatively indistinguishable from the search for social membership and group experience, along with a wish to be popular and attractive. Status markings are merely one dimension of more complex social processes. What appears to be competitive behavior on the part of consumers might at bottom be an attempt to emulate out of an instinct to conform or for related reasons of recognition, acceptance, and belonging.

Finally, insofar as we might still find what appears to be competition or competitiveness in the realm of consumption, it now takes much less the form of either class *or* status competition. The strong differentiating tendencies of the marketplace, in combination with an intensified focus in consumer culture on the self, have engendered forms of competition more *individual* and *personal* in nature, often having to do with identifications involving family and friends. Acquisition and display of goods and styles now seem more related to self-expression, feelings of pride, and a search for self-esteem than a wish for social status. In keeping with the modern project of the self, and reflecting its narcissistic dimension, possession and display of goods and styles—"lifestyle performances"—are increasingly centered more on the self and its aggrandizement than on social standing.[20]

5 The Identity of Consumption

Since the beginning of modernity, the theme of identity has been a preoccupation of thinkers in disciplines ranging from philosophy to the social sciences to literature and the visual arts. In recent decades, the topic of identity has received an extraordinary amount of attention in academic discourse.[1] Initially a response to the identity politics of the seventies, identity has also been at the center of theoretical and political engagement with issues of social and cultural difference emerging from "globalization," manifested in a burgeoning "postcolonial" scholarship addressing questions of nationalism, race, and ethnicity. As a result of these developments, identity has been linked closely to culture, a linkage that has served as a theoretical framing device for a generation of scholars in cultural studies and cultural sociology. This sweeping interest in identity has, in many respects, shaped the wave of cultural analyses of consumption discussed in Chapter Two. There is consequently now a large body of ideas about new forms of identity based on consumption, along with a general consensus that consumption and consumer culture are now a focal point of identity formation in advanced societies. It has become almost axiomatic that worldly possessions and lifestyle practices, and the media and advertising images purveying them, play a major role in how we see ourselves and others.

The preceding chapters have recounted some of the changes underlying this transformation. The rise of consumer culture has paralleled a widespread decline in job security and the meaning of work; a waning of familial, neighborhood, religious and other traditional ties; and the decay of civil society. As a consequence, notwithstanding the persistence and revival of traditional forms of identity, often in *reaction* to these changes (Dunn 1998; Harvey 1989), material goods and lifestyles now exert an inescapable influence on our perceptions of self and other in everyday life.

The popularity of the identity theme, however, has had troubling unintended consequences. In consumption studies, the topic has become so common and formulaic that too many simplistic and questionable claims have gone unchallenged. Too often there has been a failure to acknowledge the complexity and elusiveness of identity and its multiple forms and manifestations across the social spectrum. Studies often neglect to define and contextualize identity, resorting instead to rhetorical formulations with faint overtones of political correctness. Moreover, many studies, mostly of a postmodern persuasion, are slanted toward a conception that subverts identity, seeing only fragmentation and instability where others have seen a "core" or integrated self-identity that is relatively coherent and stable. Certainly, identity is never singular but always constituted of a multiplicity of perceptions, attitudes, values, beliefs, performances, self-understandings, sensations, and so forth. But more often than not, people see themselves in ways that exhibit a certain internal consistency and continuity, unlike the picture of discontinuity and dispersal frequently drawn in fashionable "postmodernist" writings. For these and other reasons, the study of identity has given us more questions than answers.

By the same token, consumption is not just about identity but is itself a complex economic, material, social, and cultural practice serving multiple functions, both expressive and instrumental in character. Generally speaking, it remains unclear the *extent* to which consumption shapes or conditions identity formation and *how* this occurs.

As a consequence, theorizing identity in that intricate psychic and social space where consuming subjects and commodities meet calls for caution if not outright agnosticism. As shown in Chapter Three's treatment of the subjectivity of consumption, the processes by which the commodity becomes an object simultaneously of desire and dissatisfaction, and the relationship of the commodity to the modern project of selfhood, are fairly well understood. Locating identity formation in these processes, however, is a more challenging task. The interconnections between identity and consumption are complicated, uneven, and ambiguous. And the degree to which identity formation today actually rests on consumption as opposed to *other* practices and affiliations, for instance work (Gottdeiner 2000, 23), remains open to question.

With these issues in mind, this chapter attempts to theorize and take measure of the relationship between identity and consumption. Continuing the major themes of earlier chapters, attention will be directed mainly to personal identity, with social and cultural identity considered as separate but closely related dimensions. Finally, cutting across all three dimensions of identity is a fundamental distinction between how we see ourselves (self-identity) and how others see us.

Conceptions of Identity: Modern and Postmodern Discourses

From the vantage point of the contemporary West, identity would not seem to be a problem in what we call "traditional society." In these relatively small and integrated social units, identity is ascribed at birth by the group or community through the hierarchical relations of religion, kinship, tribe, village, gender, and age. This form of identity is based upon inherited, externally imposed systems of beliefs and values. Lacking individualism as we know it today, in these kinds of societies the individual is absorbed by the group (Durkheim 1961, 1964).

By contrast, modern Western societies transferred the task of defining identity from the group to the individual, making the external pressures of community less consequential than one's inner resources.[2] While ascription will never disappear entirely, modern society has defined identity as something to be achieved through individual effort, will, and self-interest.

Yet the modern search for self and identity was severely handicapped from the beginning. In addition to the burden it placed on the individual, given the social divisions of class and other lines of difference and conflict following the breakup of traditional social structures, modernity inherited a legacy of chronic tensions and contradictions.

The modern conception of a search for self and identity was always clouded by new forms of power and inequality of a largely class nature and an alienation caused by the ascendancy of the market and bureaucracy. Modernity has required individuals to negotiate multiple social, cultural, and economic divisions accompanying chronic change. Thus, modern identity has always been plural and dynamic while at the same time ridden with conflict and anxiety (Dunn 1998).

In modernity, identity, like self, has thus become a *problem, a goal, a project.* The main challenges of this project have been to reconcile divided and competing identifications within a single individual and to find an "authentic" self in the face of rootless anonymity. The ideal of a modern identity can perhaps only be best described as aiming for a "complex unity." This has meant that the self is definable in multiple ways, developing along diverse social and cultural axes, but nevertheless functions and acts as a unity as represented by a coherent, albeit developing, narrative. A product of social change, turmoil, and uncertainty, the modern self has been seen as internally divided, a container of multiple identities, but a self that nonetheless exhibits varying degrees of continuity and integration.[3] While often shaped by multiple cultural influences, modern identity has been tied to ever-shifting *social* contexts, relationships, and struggles.

This conception offers one approach to understanding the importance of lifestyle to identity formation. Lifestyle is an outgrowth of modernity and addresses its major tensions (Chaney 1996). One the one hand, lifestyle responds to the anonymous and fleeting character of modern life by locating the individual in a sociocultural or group formation providing definitions of self and other. On the other hand, as a manifestation of the dynamic and liberating side of modernity, lifestyle membership offers opportunities for creative self-expression reaching beyond identities formed from established social arrangements. Lifestyle is thus a primary means of achieving identity in a commodity-based society organized around ideologies of choice and personal fulfillment. Lifestyle facilitates both social membership and the expression of individuality, allowing the individual to retrieve a sense of group identity while remaining distinct from others (Chapter Four).

If modernity invented the problem of identity, the condition of postmodernity (Harvey 1989; Jameson 1984) seems to problematize the very idea of identity, generating a set of alternative discourses that undermine modern conceptions. Significantly, these discourses can be seen as rooted in a spreading consumerism. Despite the close relationship between a dominant variety of postmodern theory and identity politics,[4] the theme of the postmodern is deeply implicated in the post-World War II consolidation of mass culture and the triumph of image and style in the media, design, and marketing industries (Dunn 1998; Huyssen 1986). The emergence of a postmodern perspective on identity is inseparable from a broad intellectual and theoretical reorientation precipitated by changes in everyday culture and consciousness associated with the impact of these industries. This is reflected in the close links between postmodernism and the study of consumption as a cultural process (Featherstone 1991).

Postmodernism's ties to consumer culture are especially evident in two features of this movement's view of identity formation. First, in contrast to the modern conception, where an emphasis on achievement reflects the industrial ethos of work and production, the postmodern conception places strong emphasis on the element of choice, reflecting the transition to a consumption-based society. Here, the task-oriented regime of industrial capitalism is replaced by a regime of pleasure. Second, the postmodern conception of identity is an important outgrowth of the impact of the image-making apparatuses of consumer and media-based society on subjectivity and perceptions of self. Here, identity formation is assimilated to the effects of images.

In particular, the postmodern conception speaks to the supremacy of style and fashion and the explosion of consumer goods shaping affluent suburban life beginning in the fifties. This setting was a launch pad for the rise of lifestyle as a self-conscious form of new kinds of consumption and identity. Once definitions of self came to depend more exclusively on lifestyle choices in consumer goods, identity took on a more provisional and ambiguous character. While a modern reading sees lifestyle as anchoring identity, the postmodern reading destabilizes identity by emphasizing its dependence on ever-changing style and fashion. As we've seen, trends and cycles in the marketplace alternately define and *problematize* the signs and symbols through which consumption communicates. Postmodernists thus highlight the fluctuating and unstable phases of the marketplace. The complex but relatively stable identity linked to modernity gives way to a more *fragmented* identity reflective of the image-based intensities of mass media and a rapidly changing, highly differentiated marketplace.

Postmodernists, however, attach special significance to lifestyle. Lifestyle becomes a means of experimentation, of inventing and reinventing the self by playing with identity (Chaney 1996, 44). Identity is once again externalized, in the form of a growing dependence on commodities and images, whose proliferation makes it possible to fabricate identity through potentially endless stylistic makeovers and new forms of role playing. In the first instance, goods and images offer an eclectic diversity of seductive possibilities for bodily self-innovation. This is one source of the notion of hybrid identities. In the pure version of this model, one can self-consciously assemble a set of commodified traits—through hair styling, cosmetics, clothing, body art—that redefine the self. For all practical purposes, this conception reduces identity to a matter of appearance, or "the look." In the second instance, lifestyle is a context for inventing new roles and modes of living and acting, through forms of entertainment and other means. Whether based on bodily appearance or social behavior, in a postmodern reading, identity formation rests on an appropriation of image and style aimed at creating a *persona*.

A number of familiar postmodern themes emerge from this picture of self-invention, one of which is fluidity. In contemporary society, group boundaries are fluid insofar as people are able to move freely from one subculture to another, making identity susceptible to change (Bocock 1993, 80–81). This has given rise to the notion of a "nomadic" subject (Melucci 1996; Deleuze and Guattari 1983) that is constantly negotiating identity from a position of detachment and mobility (Dunn 1998). Given an endless stream of media images and representations, particularly in television and advertising, desire itself is in a constant state of flux (Bocock 1993, 93), a response to the ceaseless flow of messages urging consumers to buy new products. The fluidity theme also appears in Chaney's argument that the other side of modern anonymity is the possibility of infinitely negotiated meaning (ibid.). In a highly symbolic environment composed of strangers, meaning becomes contestable and dense. Postmodern theory valorizes this aspect of modernity. At bottom, however, the notion of fluidity stems from the instability of meaning inherent in a world of surfaces, which are by nature ephemeral, superficial, and infinitely manipulable. In such a world, novelty, the pursuit of which is the ir-reducible psychological ground of consumer culture (Chapter Three), becomes an end-in-itself.

In line with the new power of appearances, postmodern notions of identity also draw on the idea of performativity. In the larger body of postmodern thought, this term projects numerous meanings. But in the present context, the term suggests that identity is constituted not of fixed traits, innate or otherwise, but rather is enacted behaviorally. In the postmodern view, identity is constituted in and through perfor-mance and (in some theoretical versions) reducible to it. This is yet another formulation pointing to the exteriorization of identity in signs, objects, and images.[5] In its weaker version, the linking of identity and performance runs parallel to the privileging of style over substance. Performativity ties identity to the more superficial aspects of personal-ity, the collection of observed behavioral traits at the self's surface. But in its stronger version, an assimilation of identity to performance can mean a disappearance of self. If self is understood as consisting of a set of inward perceptions, meanings, feelings, and attachments, the notion of performativity threatens the erasure of self by locating identity in outward appearances. Consistent with the emphasis in consumer cul-ture on sensory experience, the notion of performance suggests that identity formation takes place within the boundaries of what is known only through the physical senses.

Why the metaphors of performance and performativity have come to occupy such an important place in the postmodern lexicon is a curi-osity in itself but beyond the scope of this discussion.[6] However, there are at least two possible ways to think of identity as performance. First, performativity implies that identity is executed through behavior or action, carrying connotations of role-playing or script enactment. Of course, "performance" is part of the vocabulary of theater or drama, carrying insinuations of "acting." The term also has associations with linguistic utterances or actions, implying a connection to the notion of textuality. Performativity is thus another postmodern gesture to the sovereignty of culture and specifically its constructed or enacted char-acter. But performativity has a subsidiary meaning reflecting the su-premacy of visual experience in consumer culture. Identity is made visible to the extent that it is expressed or manifested through material possessions. Thus, identity is enacted through ownership and use of commodities. In both meanings, as performance, identity formation is inseparable from "the spectacle" (Debord 1977) that has become paradigmatic of a society suffused with signs and images.

Finally, the overriding theme in theoretical postmodernism is the notion of a fragmented subject, and this is most apparent in the vocabulary of "difference" permeating postmodern discourse. Conventionally, we think of identity ("sameness" or "similarity") and difference as contrasting or opposing principles. If postmodernism admits only of difference, it would seem to subvert the very possibility of identity. But identity and difference are two interrelated conceptual frames of a single process and therefore mutually indispensable. To talk at all about identity in the sense of defining self and other is necessarily to deal with both identity *and* difference, since these are conceptually and philosophically mutually constitutive. In this respect, modern and postmodern conceptions are mutually interdependent.

The competing modern and postmodern images of identity represent a tension between two theoretical paradigms focused on *contrasting aspects* of posttraditional society. These images also represent divergent traditions in how we think about the relationship between identity and difference. A comprehensive reading of consumption and identity formation ideally would incorporate both images into a social-psychological framework reflecting the complex overlapping of sociocultural conditions projected by each. As we'll see later in the chapter, the actual dynamics and effects of consumption today support both conceptions.[7] But it is necessary first to develop the theoretical foundations for this discussion.

Accounting for Identity: Problems with Actually Existing Social Constructionism

Most academic work on identity, theoretical or otherwise, has drawn on the theory of social constructionism. Generally, this theory takes society to be the product of active social subjects whose practices and interactions are the source of emergent social structures and institutions (Berger and Luckman 1967; Blumer 1969; Mead 1934). The constructionist idea that social life is a product of human activity and social processes originated from a variety of sources (Dittmar 1992,

67) and is so broad in scope as to be considered a whole perspective rather than a single explanation. As a way of looking at social life, social constructionism has deservedly received attention from many kinds of theorists. With its emphasis on process, subjectivity, and agency, constructionism has served as an effective corrective to overly deterministic theories focused on institutional arrangements, the weight of culture, and other systemic forces generally thought of as constituting "objective social reality." As a general conception of society, constructionism points to promising solutions to the chronic agency/structure dualism and related dichotomies by restoring a sense of the genesis of social structures in the practices of social actors.

Unfortunately, despite or perhaps because of its explanatory breadth, constructionism in practice is plagued by ambiguities and misconceptions. Generally speaking, there is a "weak" version that balances the active and creative aspects of social life, emphasizing process, against its more deterministic phases, involving structure and cultural inheritances. This version bases itself on a "soft" notion of agency that acknowledges an institutional/societal complex within which social action occurs. By contrast, there is a "strong" or "pure" version from which the idea of sociocultural determinism has been largely eliminated. This version has strong polemical overtones, reflecting its reactive stance against the position of essentialism"[8] against which constructionism has been put forth as a more legitimate or "correct" theory. It is the strong version, which appears to have prevailed in the politically charged environment of cultural studies and the related fields of feminist, race, and queer theory, that is most vulnerable to criticism. Constructionism in this form has been largely rhetorical and emptied of its original meaning. In fact, the strong version often appears in the form of an obligatory gesture or mantra. While the rise of constructionism has served as an antidote to the overly deterministic tendencies of other traditions, the strong version has lacked theoretical sophistication. Unfortunately, this is not unrelated to pressures to produce academically and politically acceptable ways of theorizing identity and difference, specifically an expectation to valorize "practice."

In renditions of constructionism common today, identity seems to be understood as constructed through processes of social interaction and the active appropriation of symbolic materials lending meaning and definition to self and others. A sound conception as far as it goes, this nevertheless leaves out the other side of the equation, the "always already" existing structures of social reality within which these processes occur and that are the historical outcome of past human practices.

Strong constructionist readings usually fail to acknowledge these constraining influences, making little if any reference to the familiar array of external factors shaping and constraining identity formation (Jenkins 1996, 23), both structural and cultural. Class, race, gender, sexuality, nationality, age, and religion are perhaps the most relevant factors that *impart* and often *fix* major parts of our identities. Many of these identities are given by the circumstances of birth. Neglecting the influence of categorical and group memberships obviously produces inaccurate and misleading accounts of the actual formation and composition of identity.

By neglecting constraining factors, strong constructionism often slides into indefensible arguments that say identity is based exclusively on the creative intentions and choices of social subjects. In this regard, postmodernists in particular should be taken to task for exaggerating the self-conscious, inventive, and fluid aspects of identity construction while downplaying or ignoring its structural determinants.[9] The flat generalization that "people construct their identities" is an unsupported assertion of pure agency. One of the best-known works on social constructionism (Berger and Luckman 1967) implicitly disavows such one-sided and undialectical statements. In the authors' treatment of this time-worn problem (Chapter Three), the subjective and objective dimensions of society are *interrelated.*

> The objectivity of the institutional world, however massive it may appear to the individual, is a humanly produced, constructed objectivity. The process by which the externalized products of human activity attain the character of objectivity is objectivation. (ibid., 60)
>   The relationship between man (*sic*), the producer, and the social world, his (*sic*) product, is and remains a dialectical one. That is, . . . (they) . . . interact with each other. . . . Externalization and objectivation are moments in a continuing dialectical process. . . . *Society is a human product. Society is an objec-*

tive reality. Man (sic) *is a social product.* (ibid., 61, original italics)

In other words, constructionism is not an argument that social subjects act out of "free will" or are autonomous agents of their own identity. It is rather a more complex theory saying, following Marx, that what are perceived as objective social structures or realities do arise from human social practices but are subsequently constituted as external forces that constrain society's members.

Another criticism pertains to how the strong constructionist perspective has been applied specifically to theorizing identity and consumption. While the impact of consumption and consumerism on our lives is hard to overestimate, there appears in much of the literature a vague hypothesis that social actors consume for the *sole purpose* of defining themselves. While this is undoubtedly true for many, and likely more so for those with material and educational advantages, it seems dubious as a generalization. Since people consume for a multitude of reasons, linking the search for self-identity to consumption practices in such an unmediated manner is unwarranted. In actuality, it is difficult to ascertain the extent to which we consume consciously in order to acquire or shape a self-identity as opposed to attaining other satisfactions. This represents a theoretical conundrum. Clearly, evidence abounds that people increasingly get defined through their possessions. But knowing the extent to which self-identity is something intentionally sought and achieved through consumption *or* merely an inevitable and perhaps unintended *consequence* of consumption is another matter.

A related problem is the difficulty posed by discrepancies between what possessions and their uses mean to their *owners* and what they might mean to *others* or society-at-large. As elaborated in Part One, we know that commodities and their social use communicate through semiotic codes. Lifestyles acquire meaning within a system of signs that at any given moment are relatively consequential. Since commodities are also signs (Baudrillard 1981), and to the extent that consumption patterns flow in and out of lines of class distinction (Bourdieu 1984), mere possession and use involves a grid of meanings that operate independently of subjects' intentions and desires. This suggests that even when actors consciously seek self-identity through what they consume, this identity is already traversed by consumption codes. In this respect, the modernist conception of lifestyle as providing social integration offers a more socially astute set of insights than the postmodernist argument of creative self-invention. To the degree they reflect consumption codes, lifestyles are badges of group membership that place limits on processes of individuation and self-creation. Within this context, the meanings attached to given commodities by individuals come up against semiotic boundaries. Under these conditions, the extent to which self-identity is "constructed" by social subjects is really a matter of debate.

To illustrate, I might wish to buy a BMW automobile for its reputation as a passenger vehicle setting high standards of design, engineering, comfort, and performance or perhaps to validate my self-image as someone who is "savvy" about cars, or for some other practical, personal, or emotional reasons. But mere possession of the automobile can culturally "type" me as affluent or trendy, as belonging to the professional-managerial class, and so forth. As commodity/sign the car sends a prestige message, constituting a status claim and a social placement, independently of my intentions or personal definitions of the purchase. The vehicle projects an image, set of meanings, and identity that have acquired a life of their own and that can overshadow the particular motivations of its owner.

Such meaning gaps have been a source of insights in the field of cultural studies but have also posed as-yet-unresolved problems. The encoding and decoding processes of consumption and the ubiquity of contested meanings have been theoretically analyzed at length by British scholars, involving numerous studies illustrating how subcultural groups develop "resistant" meanings through which to oppose the "dominant" meanings of media and other institutions (Chapter Two). The contributions of these early studies, however, depended largely on the notion of an oppositional *group* identity. Another strain of cultural studies emphasizing the "active" consumer as social or individual subject, modeled after Fiske's work (1987, 1989a, 1989b), has been less convincing. The many arguments given for the importance of style and lifestyle in resisting the inroads of capitalist consumerism ultimately beg the question of who or what finally controls the meanings of style, problematizing any easy translation of "active" into "resistant" (see Chapter Three, footnote 2). This is probably less a problem in the case of the United Kingdom than in the United States, where we find stronger individual identities and more amorphous group formations. At the same time, however, given the reach and power of the consumer culture industries in the United States and the extent to which material goods have become the focus of everyday life, perceptions and definitions of identity as shaped by consumption would seem to give advantage to the dominant codes.

From the perspective of U.S. society, certainly, questions about consumption and identity are far more complicated than those posed in the British cultural studies tradition. Keeping in mind the close links between meaning and identity, this requires some elaboration. Chaney's work can be taken as an example of the nature of the differences between the two countries. From the standpoint of the United States, his work exemplifies the limitations of analyses that reduce the problem of meaning to an alleged subversion of power by subgroups. Two of the three themes he focuses on in his account of "the practices of everyday life" are (1) that "meaning is inherently political because it is contested," and (2) that "meaning is inscribed in our uses of objects, activities, and places" (1996, 74). The first proposition unnecessarily (and crudely) restricts our understanding of lifestyle consumption, conflating it with political struggle. The second tells only one side of the story since meaning is likewise inscribed in the commodity at the point of production and through its circulation and reproduction within a cultural system. A claim that "meaning is . . . something accomplished in engagement, . . . made in the politics of social practice" (ibid., 73), while perhaps true to a point, negates the whole thrust of the theories of Baudrillard and Bourdieu, who despite their structuralist biases make compelling arguments that cultural signs have observable systemic effects.

This calls for a revised version of cultural studies that is less doctrinaire and more theoretically reflexive, one that holds opposing tendencies in tension while acknowledging the complexities of both human subjectivity and social processes. Divergences between the meanings of active consumers ("actors") and the commercially and culturally coded meanings of commodities (the "system") is a legacy of possibility for change that points beyond familiar British cultural-studies approaches to a different kind of theorizing.

A final criticism of recent constructionist-oriented writings revolves around the question of the extent to which identity is a product of *consumption*, whether understood as constructed by actors or determined by cultural codes, as opposed to *other* factors. On the one hand, consumption can be an opportunity for forming *new* identities, becoming who we want to be, whether on our own terms or those of consumption codes, and in this sense identity formation is constituted in and through the act of consumption itself. On the other hand, consumption practices are frequently an expression of *pre-existing* identities, so that the commodities in our lives function as signs or symbols of who we already are or think we are, or how we want others to see us. For instance, the food we eat, the clothing we wear, and our recreational activities often merely serve to solidify or further define and elaborate existing identities.[10] Insofar as this is the case, consumption patterns simply reflect already-observable differences among individuals and groups and can be read as expressions either of established self-conceptions or of how one expects or wishes to be seen by others. Strong constructionist arguments tend to miss the ways that consumption functions as an expression or validation of existing identities as opposed to a source of new ones.

The persistence of other, mostly ascribed identities complicates the question of whether the consumer way of life actually broadens individuals' options for identity and lifestyle or remains merely an ideal or imagined condition. The answer would certainly vary according to class location. The reality of pre-existing identities forces attention to a host of structural and cultural factors antedating the individual's contact with lifestyle options based on consumer goods and that often supercede the latter's appeal and impact. Class is but one identity among others that continues to shape, limit, or mediate lifestyle influences. The language of choice often characterizing the constructionist approach to consumption is problematic given the constraints of economic background and situation, not to mention the effects of gender, race, ethnicity, religion, and age.[11] At minimum, it needs to be acknowledged that lifestyle choices are conditioned and situationally bounded by antecedent, often more-enduring identities of which these choices are frequently only amplifications or modifications.[12]

Accounting for Identity: Meadian Constructionism

In ordinary language, identity is about knowing who a person is as distinct from others, as commonly represented by one's name, physical appearance, residential address, and so forth. Social thinkers, by contrast, usually think of identity in terms of *what* a person is, giving identity a describable content that locates one in the social/cultural world. Here, definitions or interpretations of persons are represented by analytical categories such as social roles, linguistic constructions, cultural beliefs, personality and body types, biographical narratives, and the like. In theoretical terms, identity is a social psychological formation of structural and cultural elements shaped by a variety of definitional processes both subjective and social in nature. Among the multiple sources of identity, the circumstances of birth, biography, history, social relations, and material environment are of obvious importance. Thus, identity is always a composite that emerges from an intersection of numerous factors, both enduring and changing.

As the previous section suggested, identity can be approached either as a form of self-definition or as a social attribution based on the perceptions and definitions of others. A full account of the formation of identity through consumption would combine both viewpoints. However, this is complicated by the constructionist theory that self and identity are constituted in social interaction and thus *interconnected* with the actions and communications of others. If the self is taken to be social in nature, self-definition is never strictly individual or private but shaped by social relationships. With regard to the meaning of a given *act* of consumption, self-identity should be kept analytically separate from socially conferred definitions. But at the level of identity *formation*, processes of self-definition are intertwined with socially shared meanings rooted in contacts with others.

Theorizing identity thus ultimately entails coming to terms with the *social* processes and meanings shaping the relationship between subjects and commodities. This presents a twofold task. First, a theoretical foundation needs to be laid for approaching identity formation as a social psychological process; and second, the resulting conception of identity needs to be articulated in the context of consumption. This involves examining the triadic relationship among self, other, and material object (Dittmar 1992, 9).

The theory best suited to this task is the variety of social constructionism found in the work of the social philosopher George Herbert Mead. Mead's work provides a way of linking identity and consumption by explaining the relationship between subjects and material possessions in terms of a social and symbolic theory of self. Regarded by many as the original social constructionist, Mead's theory redresses many of the shortcomings of contemporary constructionists by focusing on the social determinants of self. Mead's main insight is that the self is an emergent entity constituted by social relations. Mead saw the social production of self, furthermore, as conditioned on the linguistic and symbolic capacities of the subject and the subject's use of socially shared language.

Mead's approach to self/other relations leads to a distinctively dualistic conception of self-formation. While placing emphasis on the social, Mead regarded the self as having both individual *and* social aspects. The former aspect arises from (1) the subjective spontaneity of the actor, which is the source of indeterminancy in society, and the latter from (2) objective social reality made up of normative and structural elements, which is the source of social determinancy. Thus, the self is comprised of both subjective and objective components or, given Mead's emphasis on the self as process, "phases." The term "I" was his designation for the subjective phase of self; for its objective phase, he used the term "Me." In its capacity as "I," the self is creative and innovative, a source of change; as "Me," the self is a product of social influences, representing the institutionalized structures that limit or constrain behavior in accordance with social norms and expectations. It is through a process whereby the actor engages in symbolically "taking the role of the other" that society becomes "internalized" in the individual, that the self arises as a social self. This is a process whereby we come to see ourselves through perceptions and inner symbolic representations of how others see us. The self thus arises and functions from within a constellation of social relations involving a whole matrix of perceptions, definitions, and meanings constructed through interactions with others and by participation in social institutions.[13]

Obviously, Mead would see self-identity as intertwined with social relations. Self-identity can form only in the context of society, through the same processes of communication and role taking, constituting the larger process of socialization through which we become social participants. Self-identity results from a combination of the creative, prelinguistic energies of the subject, its active side, and the effects of social structure, which provide social form to the self, its passive influences. The duality of Mead's self exemplifies the incorporation of the concepts of agency ("I") and structure ("Me") into a single model. This model takes into account both the active and generative aspects of identity formation and the limiting and constraining conditions of society and culture. Mead would say that self-identity is constructed by actors, but only in and through the structures that inhere in society as an organized entity. From the standpoint of individuals, self-identity is constructed but ultimately formed and defined only *through* an internalization of the elements of an external social reality. This analysis of self comes to fruition in Mead's notion of the "generalized other." This term designates the actively formed totality of integrated social roles and attitudes, real and imagined, that the "Me" represents within/to the self. Mead always emphasized the reflexive qualities of the self—the "I" draws forth and responds to the "Me," which means that one literally interacts with oneself by making an object of oneself. The "I" thus interacts with the "Me," the representation of "other" as constituted in the self as object. Although rooted in inherited culture, this is a highly symbolic process in its own right insofar as it transpires in the mind of the actor and within the boundaries of the self as a *sui generis* entity. The generalized other, thus, emerges as part of a process of self-definition and therefore varies from one unique self-configuration to another. At the same time, the generalized other encompasses a *social* definition of self insofar as it constitutes a symbolic representation or mirroring within oneself of the attitudes, beliefs, and perspectives of other members of society.[14] Thus, in Mead's eyes the self is both subject and object, or phrased differently, a simultaneously individual and social subject.

Mead's fertile ideas provide a general framework for explaining how identity is produced through consumers' involvement with material goods. Applying this version of constructionism to consumption, Dittmar shows how Mead's concept of the generalized other can be used to theorize the link between identity and material possessions (1992, 84). Material objects symbolize "personal qualities and attributes," and the objects with which individuals surround themselves are viewed and responded to by others in these terms. "By simultaneously taking the perspectives of self and these others, individuals come to understand the meanings of their own possessions as parts of their identity" (ibid., 86). Internalizing the perspectives and responses of others, directly in social interaction and through institutionalized representations such as advertising and the media, the individual develops a sense of the meanings of material possessions for the self as mediated through the generalized other. In other words, others are the reference point for ascertaining the meaning and significance of material goods for the self. In this fashion, possessions define and become a part of one's self-conception. Defining ourselves through the internalization of the responses of others *and* through our material goods thus merge into a single process. By this means, self-identity is "established, maintained, reproduced and transformed in our relations with our possessions" (ibid.). In what amounts to a homology between goods possession and socialization, Dittmar adds that "individuals can take the *perspective* of the objects they own to gain a view of themselves through the symbolic meanings of their possessions" (ibid., original italics).

Triadic links among self, other, and object of consumption are thus established by incorporating goods possession into the social and symbolic processes by which the individual constructs an identity through the internalizaton and integration of others' perspectives. Not only do we construct meaning and identity around our possessions in the same *way* that we form a generalized other, but our relationship to possessions becomes a *part* of the generalized other. We define ourselves through our material possessions only within a social framework based on how we define ourselves through the viewpoints of others.

The statement that commodities are extensions of the self can now be elaborated and appraised through the lens of Meadian theory. In the conventional view, commodities express the consumer's tastes, interests, personal qualities, and self-conception as well as communicate social meaning. They are vehicles of both self-identity and the social attribution of identity. From a Meadian perspective, however, commodities are a *source* of identity, not an expression of it. If self-identity originates by way of the meaningful responses of others, it is others' definitions that shape or determine how our material possessions affect self-definition. There is thus a double meaning involved in saying that we define ourselves through our material possessions. Objects are both expressions *and* determinants of identity. Following his emphasis on the internalization of objects, however, Mead himself would regard commodities as formative of self and identity rather than expressive of them.

We can also situate Mead with regard to the question of how meaning is to be theorized. Although Mead always spoke of "symbols," there is no reason to believe that his model is in any way inconsistent with semiotics since in both cases he sees meanings are assigned to objects through social-psychological processes. Whether in the form of signs or symbols, meanings are social in nature and internalized by social processes. Thus, the generalized other offers an account of how the meanings of socially defined commodities enter into our conceptions of self. At the same time, Mead's references to symbols underscore his view of self-formation as a creative and emergent process. Showing a greater interest in social structure than cultural phenomena, Mead did not develop a theory of symbols or discuss their differences from signs (Chapter Three). But he understood the richness and power of shared symbols and our dependence on them as a means for acquiring a sense of membership in a collectivity.

The main weakness in this account, of course, is the absence of the psychological dimension of identity formation. Specifically, the weakness of Mead's theory of self, and social constructionism in general, is the lack of a theory of identification. Mead and other constructionists fail to address the internal psychological mechanisms that would explain why and how actors identify with particular social and physical objects as opposed to others and with what effects on self-conception. A theory of identification would contribute important insights into the rootedness of identity formation in desire and illuminate the nature of our attraction and attachment to objects (Chapter Three).

While this might be a task for depth psychology, the concept of identification is extremely useful to constructionist theory. Exclusive reliance on the term "identity" overstates the static or fixed character of self-definition, whereas the processual term "identification" introduces a dynamic, fluid, and temporal dimension to identity formation. In principle, the notion of identification is entirely consistent with Mead's emphasis on process. Simply put, we *have* identities but we *make* identifications. Reflecting the difference between modern and postmodern constructs, "identity" suggests stability and integration whereas "identification" connotes instability and change. From a postmodern stance, Diana Fuss argues that while "identification inhabits, organizes, instantiates identity," it also calls identity "into question," "keeps identity at a distance," undermining its function as a fixed or stable reference point. In her phrasing, "it is precisely identity that becomes problematic in and through the work of identification" (1995, 2).

However, while the contrast between identity and identification resonates an important difference between modern and postmodern interpretations, it would be a mistake to reify the distinction. A theory of identity formation needs to recognize *both* its stable and more fluid and shifting aspects. While Mead located the self in the social process, he nonetheless posited a set of normative reference points and meanings as its foundation. The concept of identification emphasizes the dynamic aspects of his theory by redefining identity as the recurring, continuous, or persistent moments of an ongoing process of identification within which, in Fuss's conception, identity disappears only to reappear, and so on indefinitely. Mead would regard "identification" as occurring in the emergent phase of self-development and "identity" as an endpoint of this process in the generalized other, a resolution or integration of multiplicity corresponding to the ideal of a modern identity based on social structure and cultural beliefs. In the postmodern conception, however, identification trumps identity in a commodity- and image-based world of shifting and unstable reference points.

Codified and Individuated Modes of Identity Formation: A General Consumption Schema

This brief background of constructionism and different theorizations of identity provides basic reference points for a general sketch of the interconnections between consumption and identity formation. Previous chapters have thematized the tension between (1) consumption as commodification, linked to exchange value, consumerism, and semiotic codes, and (2) consumption as meaningful and self-expressive activity, involving use value, creativity, symbolization, and a search for self-fulfillment and belonging. This tension has been cast in the analytical language of system and actor, understood as the mutually constituting sides of the consumption process. In reaching some general conclusions about consumption and identity, I propose a corresponding distinction between what I call "codified" and "individuated" modes of identity formation. The former refers to identities and identifications reflective and reproductive of the commodity/sign form linked to exchange value and corresponding issues of social status. The latter points to consumption practices in which identity forms around self-directed desires and practices linked to use value and relatively autonomous of semiotic codes and consumerist ideology.

Insofar as it involves questions of knowing "what" a person is, identity in the age of modern individualism has been based largely on a process of *typing*, involving placing persons in various socially and culturally defined categories. To the extent that we define ourselves and make distinctions among others through discourses that recognize different types of people, identity formation in consumer society is a process of constructing and developing types of identities based on our relationship to commodities. Most tangibly, this means our relationship to material possessions, their uses, and their differentiation in the marketplace. However, as previously indicated, commodification reaches far beyond material goods to include services and, increasingly, the consumption of images, events, representations, and so forth. Consumption today is often less about objects than experiences. Although material and economic development in the West has made individual and group identities most immediately dependent on a system of material objects, consumers are no longer defined exclusively in terms of their material possessions but also seen in terms of these other elements of their lifestyles.

Broadly speaking, codified and individuated modes of consumption-based identity formation could be thought of as involving different types of consumers. In the most fundamental sense, we would consider someone who defines self and other exclusively through consumption to be a different type than one for whom consumption in general seemed relatively unimportant in relation to identity. But for those for whom consumption makes a difference, most likely the majority of the population, identifications made *within* each mode will type a person, in the commodity/sign mode mainly on the basis of image appropriation and in the other mode through self-based definitions and practices of a more individualizing and putatively authentic nature.

The discussion thus far has drawn attention to the distinction between self-identity, or how one perceives and defines self, and socially attributed identity, or how one is perceived and defined by others. Self-definition and other-definition are the two major facets of identity formation, together providing an overall analytical frame for outlining specific connections between consumption and identity.

Identity formation can be conceptualized in three major dimensions. First, there is what we can call *personal* identity, which refers to a unique configuration of personal traits. This is represented by outward identifying characteristics that are both physical (the body, clothing) and behavioral (personality). These embodiments of identity are objects of self-stylization as well as others' perceptions and definitions. Another component of personal identity can be a part of self-definition but is predicated more on the perceptions and judgments of others, namely "character," or how we assess a person's moral or ethical worth.

Second, and this has been the focus of much of the foregoing discussion, there is what we can call *social* identity. Referring to the social aspects of self-identity and other's attributions, this dimension is central to Mead's theory. Including both ascribed and achieved statuses, this dimension could be further broken down into three parts. One basis of social identity is placement in a category, such as gender or race. A second basis is group membership, which often emerges from categorical memberships, as when social categories become bases of group formation. A third, somewhat overlapping basis of social identity are the social roles one occupies, which can be institutional in nature (parent, student, employee) or group-based (leader, follower, hanger-on).

Third, people in varying degrees and forms share in a *cultural* identity. This still often entails identifications with a cultural tradition or heritage, but just as likely includes identifications with an array of contemporary forms of "popular," "mass," or "elite" culture. Internally complex and overlapping in complicated ways with the other two types, this identity category is the most resistant to measurement and generalization. Indeed, the cultural saturation characterizing our times is arguably the primary source of a problematization of identity. Cultural identity has typically been part of one's "core" identity, comprised mostly of ascribed statuses (ethnicity, race, nation, religion, family). But this picture is now complicated in numerous ways. First, identifications with these categories often change and thus, to some extent

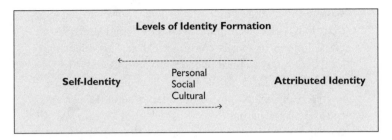

FIG 5.1   Levels of identity firmation

these have become achieved identities. Second, the rise of consumer culture introduces an expanded field of possibilities for identifications with material possessions and related consumption experiences along with their signifying and expressive characteristics. Third, the correlative shift in cultural expression to lifestyle practices means a proliferation of more fluid identities tied to the rapidly changing marketplace. Despite the continued constraints of class and other factors, therefore, cultural identity has increasingly become a matter of choice. Given these tendencies, cultural identifications have become the most complicated dimension of identity, whether self-defined or socially attributed.

Self-identity and attributed identity intersect at all three levels. Since our self-conceptions are constructed largely according to how we read others' responses (Cooley 1964), the personal, social, and cultural dimensions of self-identity are formed from definitions constructed in ongoing social interactions. At the same time, attributed identity is always at least partially based on the presentation of self, which while not necessarily identical is largely consistent with a person's self-image. The three aspects of identity are thus formed in a complex dynamic between self and other. This scheme can serve as a template for considering the possible forms of consumer identity and its two major modes (Fig. 5.1).

Codified Mode

1. Consumer Role. At its most basic level, the formation of identity in a codified mode means a tendency for people to

acquire the identity of *consumer*. This involves strong identifications with consumption as an activity and a corresponding definition of self as consumer. At its most elementary
level, this is a structural phenomenon insofar as social relations take the form of commodity exchange, converting all
members of society into consumers. In addition, corporate
culture cajoles us into seeing ourselves as consumers. Advertising and marketing encourage the development of
self-images based on how we spend and our material possessions. In both respects, consumption operates as a strong
metaphor giving shape and meaning to everyday life. When
this happens, daily activity, as Bauman observes, can be
transformed into "a kind of shopping" in which behavioral
traits cultivated in the shopping mall carry over to other
realms (2000, 73). Shopping becomes a model for everyday
living as the ideology and discourse of consumerism seep
into a whole range of institutional practices. Hospital pa-
tients, the insured, museum-goers, and even students are
redefined as "consumers," and the paying occupants of these
and other roles in public places come to see themselves accordingly. This has led defenders of the notion of a "public
sphere" to lament the substitution of the label "consumer"
for "citizen," a change that they consider a depoliticization
of society.

2. Self-Commodification. Second, in a perhaps more extreme
   and troubling manifestation of the impact of the commodity/
   sign form, consumerism can lead to a *commodification of
   self* (Davis 2003) in the sense that commodities set the terms
   under which we think about and construct our identities.
   This can take two interrelated forms.

On one level, in an instance of its "postmodern moment," consumer culture promotes the externalization of identity in images,
whereby consumers identify with what they see in media and advertising as well as at shopping sites. Many consumers strive to *model* themselves after the images of beauty, success, celebrity, and fame purveyed
in the mass media and shopping malls. Seeking identity through
image-based imitation means increased attention to external features

of the self, most notably the body and personality. Hence, this mode of identification is especially relevant to the formation of personal identity, though it has obvious relevance for social and cultural identity. This is a consequence of the excessive emphasis on appearance inherent in the triumph of style and more generally the reduction of consumer identity to the markings and messages of sign systems. The market strengthens this tendency by guaranteeing a constant stream of products and services promising to improve one's looks (Bauman 2001, 88). Extending Baudrillard's argument that the real object of consumption is the sign or code governing consumption, the valorization of physical appearance in the form of images suggests more generally that *appearances* or *persona* are the true objects of consumption and therefore identification.

One of the specific ways this occurs is through *stylistic identifications*. Style becomes a major reference point for definition of self, as manifested in identifications with dress, behavioral, and living styles. As styles change, identities change with them. Identifications of this kind support the postmodern notion of self and identity as fluid and eclectic.

Another specific form of self-commodification is *brand identifications*. The branding of products supplies a means for concretizing identifications with commodities since this practice provides consumers with status conferring names with which they can identify. Brand names come to represent preferred traits, qualities, values, and tastes, associated with certain manufacturers and retailers, that consumers can make a part of their self-definitions and self-presentations. Further, brand names can become insignias of membership in a lifestyle or group, thus serving an important function at the level of social or cultural identity.[15]

Identifications of this kind are *semiotic* in character and situate the consumer within the commodity/sign system. In this respect, identity is strongly influenced by the status meanings associated with the exchange value of commodities, with their connotations of class hierarchy. More generally, by identifying with the images and messages of advertising and the media, consumers enact the dominant code. To this extent, acts of consumption are closely tied to the dominant structures and meanings of commodity society, reflecting and reproducing *consumerism*. In its extreme form, these kinds of identifications are premised on a belief that consumption is more than just a means of signifying status but is an end-in-itself, serving to justify its own existence.

On a second level, the self gets commodified in the sense of being *treated* like a commodity. In the world of jobs and work, for instance, people are required to "sell" themselves—their skills, talents, personalities, accomplishments—to prospective employers. This can be generalized to all social relations insofar as people feel pressured to "produce" selves that can be "marketed" for appearance, personality, and other traits and qualities highly valued in a capitalist society. But treating the self as a commodity can be an aspect of consumption itself. Buying and displaying the right goods, cultivating the right lifestyle, is a form of selling the self to others whose approval is sought by people using consumption to acquire status and self-esteem. Here, an attempt is made to construct an identity according to criteria by which we judge all commodities. In effect, consumer culture conditions us to perceive the self as yet another product, transforming the modern project of self into the manufacture of a saleable persona.

Individuated Mode

The reach of consumer culture and the power of consumerism make it difficult to identify modes of identity formation that are not in some way, to some degree, influenced by the commodity/sign form.[16] This does not mean, however, that identity formation collapses entirely into the structures of commodity society or that the latter's effects are not counterbalanced or diluted by forms of consumption that to some extent escape the prevailing signifying codes. To delineate "non-coded" forms and aspects of identity formation through consumption, I've chosen the term "individuated mode." This terminology is meant to convey the capacity of individual consumers to exercise degrees of sovereignty and autonomy, creating their own definitions of commodities' meanings and uses. In this mode, consumers pursue a variety of options in distancing themselves from modes of consumption in which their identities are determined by "the code" or where strong identifications are made with consumerism as a way of life.

We can begin postulating distance between consumers and the commodity/sign form by thinking of consumption as an activity that merely extends or elaborates upon already existing identities. This presupposes the modern conception of identity, which points to integration, continuity, and sameness, involving identities that are ascribed or achieved within established institutional and cultural frameworks. Such identities are altered or reconfigured but not fundamentally changed through consumption practices. In this model, consumption becomes a material means of expressing a "core" identity made from identifications not directly related to possessions or commercially marketed lifestyles. Here, consumption plays only a modest role in identity formation and is limited to expressive elaborations of pre-existing identities (Halter 2000).

In a more direct way, identity formation in the individuated mode is defined by possessions and practices entering consumers' lives less as commercially coded products than as objects and experiences of personal significance expressive of one's individuality. Here, identification processes are less oriented to objects and consumption experiences as commodity/signs, with their preassigned meanings and effects, than to their individualizing qualities. In this sense, commodities serve the purpose of self-recognition, reflecting *meaningfully* back on consumers (Chapter Three) as they see something of themselves, actual or potential, in these objects. In this mode, consumers bring to consumption their own frames of reference and meaning. Also in this mode, consumption identifies in ways that are *mediated* or *subsumed* by self-identity and personality as well as the personal and social context in which consumption occurs. While this entails an individualizing or "tailoring" of the meanings and uses of commodities to persons and situations, the appropriation of commodities *as objects* can also serve as a means of defining oneself as a certain type of individual. As possessions, different kinds of objects and their specific traits function to type us *symbolically* in relation to established webs of social and cultural meaning. While semiotic codes play a part in the process of typing, they do not in this respect exhaust the meanings of either objects or consumption experiences in general, nor do they monopolize the choices consumers make in appropriating objects that they believe speak to them or give expression and shape to their self-concept.

Expressive and Instrumental

Within both codified and individuated modes of consumption, we can distinguish two elementary attitudes. On the one hand, consumers can identify with the specifically *expressive* aspects of consumption, focusing on the aesthetic properties of an object or an experience. As Chapter Three showed, commodities are aestheticized as part of the process of semiotic coding. However, most objects have aesthetic properties in their own right apart from their commercially codified characteristics. On the other hand, consumers can take an interest in their possessions' specifically *instrumental* qualities, valuing them as utilitarian as opposed to expressive objects. In this case, the practical uses or benefits of an object, coded or otherwise, become a source of meaning and satisfaction for those who might be inclined to see themselves as, say, "practical" or "industrious." Depending on the object in question, codified and individuated identifications alike occur along *both* of these dimensions simultaneously in varying proportions.

Major Dimensions of Identity Formation

All of these considerations suggest that there are multiple possibilities for identifying with one's consumption practices in general and with

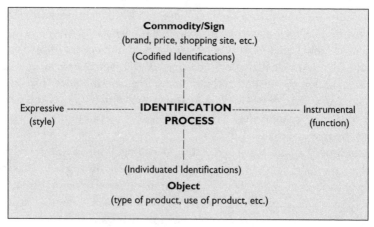

FIG 5.2   Matrix for consumer identification structuring

material possessions in particular. Following the distinction between codified and individuated modes of consumption, we can draw a parallel contrast between material possessions as commodities/signs and possessions as objects of personal meaning. Traversing this contrast is the difference between the expressive and instrumental values of one's possessions. Combining these two kinds of distinctions yields a fourfold matrix within which processes of consumer identification get structured (Fig. 5.2).

Lifestyle Practices

Distinctions between codified and individuated modes of identity formation become most apparent in the realm of lifestyle. In reconsidering lifestyle in this framework, we are looking at identity less in terms of roles and objects than from the standpoint of everyday social practices. As we've seen, consumption has increasingly coalesced into lifestyle patterns encompassing a range of consumption-related meanings and expressions within everyday life contexts.

There are at least two levels at which the commodity/sign can be either embraced or evaded in the pursuit of lifestyle. First, lifestyles can to varying degrees be packaged and marketed like the products they depend on (for example, the wilderness recreation industry, commercially organized tourism, or gated communities) and thus bought (or "bought into") like any commodity. To this extent, lifestyles represent commodified possessions that communicate status and other meanings on a par with purchased goods. At the same time, consumers can and do construct their *own* lifestyles reflective of their particular preferences and resources, typing themselves in relatively distinct and personal ways. Wilderness experience, touring, and community living can provide sources of identity without being commercially packaged for this purpose. Second, while all lifestyles are defined to a greater or lesser extent by consumption codes, observable differences can be found in the degree and kind of adherence to these codes. For instance, one can live a suburban lifestyle in compliance with fashionable middle class standards—high-tech gas grills, neat lawns, three-car garages, designer furnishings, and so forth—typing oneself as successful in the status game. But one can also assemble a lifestyle outside the code, perhaps filling domestic space with an eclectic collection of out-of-fashion, low cost, previously owned items that are comfortable, unique, functional, and personally meaningful, typing oneself as creative, budget-minded, and/or individualistic. In lifestyle pursuits, then, identity formation can lean in the direction of the codes or it can take more individualized and even esoteric and idiosyncratic directions.

The transformation of consumption into lifestyle patterns has become so pervasive that in most respects it is no longer appropriate (if it ever was) to talk about identity in terms of *particular* possessions or consumption practices such as shopping or displaying. As a broad pattern, embracing ensembles or sets of goods and practices, lifestyle now suffuses personal and social life in a more or less totalizing way. While social relations have hardly disappeared, they have been increasingly inflected or subsumed by lifestyle behaviors. Although some might beg to differ, the degree to which the phenomenon of lifestyle is "ideological" or "real" is not the point since the outcome remains the same. Sources of identity formation have shifted significantly from social roles and relationships to consumer spending and living patterns. In this respect, lifestyle has become a dominant sociocultural fact.

As a consequence, in consumer society identity has indeed become more complex and even unstable than various modernist definitions would allow. The differentiating effects of social structure characteristic of modernity have been largely superceded by lifestyle phenomena, whose cultural permutations and combinations provide seemingly endless options for the identification of self and other. By its nature, lifestyle gives consumers access to a potentially enormous range of expressive possibilities, however conditioned by socioeconomic resources. Most important, lifestyle is malleable; it can be molded and patterned to fit individual preferences, despite the obvious limitations imposed by the commodity/sign form, class position, and other constraints.

Acknowledging the force of lifestyle, however, does not *ipso facto* underwrite the postmodernist conception of identity as fluid and constituted only in performance. While strong tendencies in this direction are discernible in consumer culture, the rise of lifestyle does not destabilize so much as *complicate* identity formation. In this regard, the postmodern emphasis on hybridity resonates in this analysis more than notions of fluidity. The expanded and differentiated consumer marketplace has created heterogeneous forms of culture that are novel and unpredictable. As cultural democratization undermines the hierarchical structures and attitudes of modernity, identities are formed increasingly out of unpredictable mixes of disparate cultural influences. In contemporary consumer culture, the socially based complexities of modern identity tend to give way to the culturally based complexities of a postmodern identity shaped by a dynamic marketplace, material excess, and an increasingly globalized media system. At the same time, this is not to say that identity loses all coherence. Modern notions of integration and continuity still have a basis in the social and psychological realities of identity and identity formation despite the intrusions of commodity culture.

Conclusion: Reconsidering Consumption and Identity

The field of consumption poses special problems for theorizing identity formation and its dynamics, and the place of consumption in identity processes resists easy generalization. Not only is identity itself an elusive concept, but consumption constitutes a multifarious set of practices and meanings. In short, there are many different ways to consume and consumers can attach a variety of meanings to consumption.

One the one hand, impressionistic evidence suggests that social subjects turn to consumption as a means of self-definition, increasingly from a position of default given a lack of viable alternatives. Consumer lifestyles are now the most visible and compelling indicators of social placement and cultural preference. On the other hand, it would be a mistake to exaggerate the role of consumption or the impact of consumerism as an ideology or world-view in shaping or determining how one sees oneself or is seen by others. This is particularly true in light of the array of individual and collective *reactions* to modernity and materialism by those in the West wishing to revive traditional loyalties and attachments, exemplified by a reclaiming of ethnicity, religion, and family as well as an assortment of other cultural and social trends of an anti- or premodern character (Dunn 1998; Harvey 1989).

What this chapter has argued, however, is that despite the obvious and inevitable relationship between our identities and consumption practices, past efforts to link identity and consumption have not adequately faced these complexities. This is due largely to (1) the relatively primitive state of our theories of identity and identity formation, 2) faulty understandings and/or applications of the theory of social constructionism, and 3) lack of a theory of identification adequate to the goals of the constructionist program. At the same time, the impact of consumption and consumer culture on identity formation is inherently complex and therefore difficult to chart.

My analysis of the relationship between consumption and identity addresses these problems in a programmatic way. A general outline of study begins with the distinctions between self-identity and socially attributed identity; personal, social, and cultural levels of identity; and, most importantly but elusively, codified and individuated modes of identity formation through consumption and lifestyle practices. While many see the very notion of "lifestyle" as an ideological prop for consumer capitalism, the idea of lifestyle leads a double life as both ideology *and* a representation of the form our social and cultural existence actually takes in consumer society. As intimated in Chapter Four, identities and identifications have converged on lifestyle practices as a basis of social and cultural membership. The present chapter has expanded on this argument by showing that lifestyle identifications serve not only as means of social and cultural placement as dictated by the semiotic codes of status, but also as vehicles of self-expression and -fulfillment. This further suggests that we need to move beyond the subjective dynamics between commodities and consumers examined in Chapter Three to the ways identities are shaped by consumers' lifestyle patterns and practices.

Lifestyles, however, are inseparable from the larger social and cultural contexts from which they grow and that still compete with consumption-based identities. Whether in their role as consumers or not, social subjects have *multiple* identities that originate from a variety of sources. Theorists and researchers need to be wary of overestimating the significance of consumption and consumerism for identity formation relative to other, often enduring forms of identification, such as occupation, kinship, gender, and ethnicity. Identifications with one's material possessions and lifestyle intermingle in complicated ways with other, sometimes stronger identifications, which consumption only serves to materialize, elaborate, and certify. The intrusions of consumer culture have arguably weakened the hold of traditional and conventional affiliations, strengthening the role of consumption in definitions of self and other. Despite these changes, however, the extent to which people consume—or need to—for the purpose of constructing an identity remains ambiguous at best and therefore in need of more careful examination.

Assessing the place of consumption in our lives depends upon a fundamental distinction between those aspects of it that reflect and reproduce the commodity/sign form and those bearing potentials for the fulfillment of individualized needs and tastes. As objects, as opposed to commodities, material possessions can be vehicles of meaning and gratification at a distance from consumerism. Here, the theoretical tension between system and actor can be seen in the diverse and concrete ways that people consume on the basis of their personal tastes and passions.[17] Conceptualizing and measuring the difference between codified and individuated identifications remains a challenge. But this distinction is essential for getting beyond the artificial oppositions that have shaped past discussions of identity and consumption and that fuel perennial debates about the oppressive versus liberatory features of consumer capitalism. While reflecting the underlying contrast between exchange and use value, the distinction between codified and individuated consumption modes grounds this contrast in everyday life and the possible meanings that can be attached to consumption practices by social subjects and theorists alike. Finally, this distinction draws attention to the variable meanings of use value and a need to further unpack this concept. Forming a general framework of analysis, these distinctions provide an important guide for future thinking and research on different kinds of consumption and their impact on self and identity formation.

Conclusion

The legacy of critical thought informing this study remains an important source of ideas in controversies and debates about high-consumption society. The traditions of commodity critique, cultural studies, and social criticism of status seeking and hedonism are still relevant to the study of consumer society, consumer culture, and consumerism. On balance, however, these bodies of thought have given undue weight to structural forces, be they materialist, cultural, or ideological in nature. This is particularly true of theories under the sway of structuralism, poststructuralism, and semiotics, all of which underprivilege the role of subjectivity. At the same time, those varieties of cultural studies and social theory reacting to the disappearing subject have only inverted the mistakes of the structuralisms by adopting a version of social constructionism in which agency appears without any structural or cultural antecedents.

Appraising the contributions and limitations of these various approaches has been a primary concern of this book. While pointing to the excessive voluntarism of many constructionist writings, I have criticized structuralist formulations for overstating the impact of systemic forces. Restraining the pendulum, I suggest, requires a subjective mode of analysis that incorporates and synthesizes salient points of earlier theories from the standpoint of consumers as actors. In this analytical mode, it would be possible to acknowledge both structural and cultural constraints *and* the meaningful and experiential dimensions of consumption as practiced by individual and social subjects. Accordingly, the task of theoretically identifying consumption has entailed outlining fundamental linkages between subjective processes and the structure and functioning of consumer capitalism as a social and cultural system.

In emphasizing subjectivity, my goal has been twofold: (1) to rehabilitate the relevant aspects of critical theory, both materialist and cultural, by refocusing it on individual and social subjects' everyday relationship to consumption; and (2) to redress the totalizing tendencies of critical work, whether of the pessimistic or optimistic variety, with a grounded and more prudent assessment of the meanings and dynamics of consumption in the lives of consumers. My strategy has been to reconsider the claims of critical theory in the context of the modern project of self, redrawing the critique of consumerism around problems of selfhood and identity. A key point of departure has been the blind spots of British cultural studies. I have argued that to take the viewpoints or meanings of subjects seriously requires attending to the social-psychological dynamics of consumption at the level of individuals and their personal concerns, contextualizing these in social relations, the dynamics of the marketplace, and the larger cultural and historical forces shaping these meanings. My intent in questioning aspects of critical theories of consumption has been to broaden and balance them with alternative readings more appreciative of the subjective and material interests of actors. By contextualizing the consumer way of life in the project of selfhood and identity, relevant features of Marxism, the Frankfurt School, and British cultural studies have been recast to better reflect both historical trajectories and contemporary conditions. Finally, I have attempted to show that a stronger focus on the subjective standpoints and motivations of actors depends upon bridging theoretical traditions that have normally been kept separate.

The topic of consumption raises a range of theoretical issues encountered in the study of human behavior and social processes generally, most notably its chronic dichotomies. Critiques of consumption confront the "agency/structure" problem in a particularly profound way, since these critiques ultimately revolve around questions of the domination or control of social subjects. As I have argued, the language of agency and structure poses obstacles not only to theoretical clarity but to an accurate and grounded critical model of consumer culture and consumerism. The terms "actor" and "system" more accurately represent both the nature of the theoretical problem and what is at stake in critical controversies over consumption. My critique of consumption critiques has been premised on the importance of theorizing the *tensions* inherent in the actor/system relationship rather than evading or falsely overcoming them by adopting particular positions on either side. Theoretical synthesis and interdisciplinary progress depend upon a more skillful handling of these tensions and a deeper understanding of their rootedness in the subject/object dualism of Western thought.

This is another way of saying that my mode of analysis aims to avoid the familiar reductionisms and determinisms that force a choice between the perspective of system or actor. I have interrogated both the ("objective") structural conditions facilitating and constraining consumption practices within an organized system and the ("subjective") actions and meanings of individual/social subjects and their creativity and practical intent, as rooted in underlying human needs and desires. Consumers have been read as both (1) systemic *agents* acting out of largely unconscious forces shaped by the productive and reproductive needs of capitalism, and (2) human *actors* seeking to satisfy their needs and wants in meaningful ways. The fundamental axiom has been that consumption involves both (1) internal and external conditions and constraints whose effects often reach beyond subjects' awareness and control, *as well as* (2) intentional, meaning-seeking acts on the part of these same subjects.

The most complex part of my discussion has pertained to questions of identity, which few would dispute have been central to the topic of modernity. Individual and collective anxieties about identity have shaped U.S. culture and political discourse for generations. Identity politics have shaped much of academic theory for the last thirty years. Today, identity anxieties have been aggravated and transformed in a multitude of ways by "globalization." And in the new digital age, where electronic and virtual technology undermines our ability to know or certify the identities of others, identity politics compete with anxieties of a more individual and private nature. These recent examples show that since identity problems change over time, they need to be kept in historical context.

Much of the difficulty in studying identity, however, lies with the very concept. Not unlike subjectivity itself, identity is an amorphous and intangible phenomenon. In my own theoretical construction, identity has its stable and unstable aspects: on the one hand it is durable, on the other hand it appears as a sequence of moments in ongoing processes of identification. My modest treatment of this theme has attempted to elucidate consumer subjectivity and to provide a sketch of the foundations of a theory of consumption and identity. I intend my conclusions to convey the complex and conditioned character of the relationship between the two, challenging commonly accepted views about material possessions and identity formation.

My treatment of the related themes of self and selfhood has also been programmatic. Interpreting consumer culture against the backdrop of the modern project of self serves to provide historical context. However, the concept of self has also been a means of framing the subjectivity of consumption in social psychological terms and of grounding the experience and meanings of consumption in everyday life. A theory of consumer subjectivity would need to more fully engage the idea of self, showing its place in the dynamics of consumption, consumer culture, and consumerism.

The self can succumb to commodification, but being reflexive is simultaneously a bulwark against commodification. For this reason, the concept of self is essential to moving beyond older debates to a plane of discussion closer to the daily realities and experiences of consumers. Indeed, an understanding of the self has been the missing link in controversies over the manipulations and oppressions of hegemonic mass culture. As the mediating connection between system and actor, the concept of self is a powerful tool in theorizing the dynamic tensions between the two, providing strategic answers to questions about who and what controls the meanings and effects of consumption and what these look like on the ground. On another level, it is important to consider the emergence of new *types* of self and selfhood in commodity society. My discussion has alluded to the rise of a desiring self, an expressive self, a bodily self, a possessive self, and a stylized self. An evolving consumer culture thus structures the self in new ways, and this needs further attention in theorizing consumption's subjective aspects.

Another reason for connecting the project of self to the rise of consumer culture has been to highlight the larger forces of individualism and privatization behind the growth and commodification of material culture. The notion that objects are extensions of the self is deeply strengthened by modern individualism. Additionally, the increasingly privatized character of consumption has solidified a set of social and cultural attitudes supporting a belief in consumption as a means of self-fulfillment. While these historical trends are unquestionably a manifestation in part of the propagandistic sales effort of capitalism, concerns for the self in modern society are real and legitimate. Moreover, it is important to acknowledge that consumerism not only feeds off the capitalist profit motive, but draws strength also from the larger ethos of individualism shaping modernity.

At the same time, Chapter Three drew attention to numerous ambiguities surrounding the consumerist conception of selfhood, pointing out that among the many ways the self is represented in consumer culture, a basic divide is apparent between notions of self-gratification and self-realization. Given this distinction between two kinds of "self-fulfillment," the question immediately arises, what does self-realization mean in a society built on commodity relations, and what are the conditions of its possibility? Are we to take self-fulfillment through consumption to mean instant gratification or rather a developmental process in which consumption might be only a means to an end rather than an end-in-itself as claimed by consumerist ideology?

These questions reraise the contrast between consumption and consumerism and the kinds of meaning and identity it might be possible to construct through consumption practices devoid of consumerist ideology. Paralleling the discussion in Chapters One and Two of the differences between signs and symbols, Chapter Five posed the related problem of distinguishing between "commodities" and "objects." Since in a market society most objects *are* commodities, the distinction is analytical and relative to a host of subjective and objective factors. But this much seems clear: as objects that are bought and sold, and therefore defined by exchange value, commodities project a range of meanings pertaining mainly to the money economy, involving prices and the system of social status tied to them. As signs, commodities constitute a sociocultural system forming a ground of desire, anxiety, and emulation driving the status games discussed in Chapter Four. Commodities as such are constituents of a *consumerist* lifestyle as opposed to a lifestyle that is constructed *through consumption*. Thus, the commodity/sign offers a ready-made, code-based social identity. By contrast, objects as such elicit meanings of a different order based on their physical characteristics and use value. Objects occupy a realm of cultural, social, and personal meaning that both traverses and undermines the status system based on semiotic codes. Objects impart a sense of *meaningfulness* to their owners and users. Commodities are transformed into objects by virtue of their *specificity*, their ability as particular items to speak to an individual user (Miller 1991, 190). Holding potential for self-recognition, objects are constituents of a self-fashioned lifestyle created by consumers themselves and giving expression to their individuality. Whereas commodities carry prefabricated meaning and identity, by contrast objects offer the possibility of contributing to the construction of an authentic selfhood by reflecting and feeding back into the personal and cultural identities and traits of those who possess and use them.

I argue that consumption theory needs to devote more attention to this distinction. At stake is nothing less than the problem of overcoming the abstract and alienated universe of commodities so powerfully described by Marx and especially Simmel (Miller 1991) as well as the obsessions and discontents engendered by consumer culture and consumerist ideology, the focus of social criticism dating back to Veblen. If debates over the oppressive versus liberatory features of modernity have shifted from the sphere of production to that of consumption, it is imperative to interrogate the realm of material goods (and services, entertainments) in terms of its potential for the attainment of genuine selfhood, that is to say, of transforming commodities back into meaningful objects and experiences.

A promising step in this direction is the theoretical work of Miller, who argues, perhaps too facilely, that a negative valuation of goods, characteristic of the commodity fetishism tradition, be replaced by a positive valuation, based on the specificity of goods' relationship to an individual person or group, and a differentiation of such goods from all other goods in the marketplace. This involves a process of "recontextualization," in which goods are invested with personal meaning and value. In Miller's view, consumption can become a practice in which the "object is transformed by its intimate association with a particular individual or social group" (ibid., 191). Thus, consumption becomes a form of reappropriation and, *contra* the main thrust of critical theory, culture reacquires a positive meaning through the subjective work of the consumer.

Miller is suggesting that we envision a consumer culture that is transformed by investing in its products a different kind of personal, social, and cultural significance. This would involve restoring prominence to the use values of commodities in ways that make them available to consumers as *meaningful objects*, not merely objects with meaning, and it implies new kinds of relationships to objects that could overcome the ruptures thematized by commodity fetishism theory. This envisioning also presupposes a new understanding that culture in high-consumption capitalism is firmly rooted in a life with objects, and is in this sense irretrievably a *material* culture but one that might be rich in symbolism and thus evocative meaning (Jaeger and Selznick 1964). More importantly, imagining a different kind of consumer culture necessitates a rethinking of the subject/object dualism in the context of the social world of objects, in which material culture is assigned a special status and function in the formation of both self and social relations.

However, while Miller's argument for regarding commodities as potentially meaningful objects is properly contextualized in Simmel's theory of objectification and the "tragedy" of culture, his argument lacks a substantive account of the actual processes involved in turning commodities into meaningful objects and the construction of selfhood through their reappropriation. Miller rightly advocates a discourse of subject/object relations, but without offering a conceptual framework for talking about transformation from a state of commodification to a culture of meaningful objects and consumption experiences.

My analysis of the subjectivity of consumption has proposed both a social-psychological discourse centered on the self and a companion discourse of symbolization based on a distinction, both conceptual and historical, between signs and symbols. Regarding the former, it now seems appropriate to replace structuralist and poststructuralist notions of the subject with a conception based on social and self processes. This can be done without disavowing the insights and conceptual advances of structuralist approaches, which illuminate the workings of the social and cultural system governing consumption. But a social-psychological discourse brings us much closer to the meanings and consequences of consumer culture for the subjects who both reproduce and change it. Such a picture, in turn, provides a framework for analyzing how commodities can be reappropriated as objects of personal significance for the self and as a basis for new kinds of social relations. In this respect, the groundbreaking writings of Simmel on the problem of objecthood and self-realization remain a rich, untapped source of thinking about the modern project of self and its relationship to consumer society.

With regard to the theme of symbolization, my argument for a revisionist critical theory of consumption has been staked on the contrast between signs and symbols and the historical trend in capitalism towards a semiosis of culture. My implicit point of departure has been Baudrillard's striking proposition that *"this semiological reduction of the symbolic properly constitutes the ideological process"* (1981, 98, original italics), a statement representing a dramatic shift away from orthodox Marxism of a kind not sufficiently appreciated in consumption studies. As Mike Gane comments in characterizing this theoretical break, for Baudrillard "it was not use-value that should have been contrasted with exchange-value, but symbolic exchange that should have been contrasted with commodity exchange" (Baudrillard 1993, Introduction, x). By alluding to the symbolic as a normative basis of critique, Baudrillard established the destruction of symbolic exchange by sign systems as a framework for critically analyzing the culture of commodity fetishism. At the same time, in later writings Baudrillard talks about "the irruption of the symbolic within the semiotic" (Gane, Introduction, xii). Such an irruption would supposedly originate in human nature, which represents an "excess" (a borrowing from Georges Bataille) in the form of "energy, fantasies, drives, needs, and so on" (Kellner 1989, 42), a human nature that contradicts rationalizing capitalist modernity and thus revolts against it. Hence, the author of a theory of semiotic domination finds some hope in an anthropological conception of a lost world of symbolic relations associated with primitive forms of exchange. But by posing the symbolic as the unregulated and unconditioned energies of mind and body, the unsocialized substratum of human nature, Baudrillard's conception turns out to be not only crude but only vaguely related to symbols themselves.

However inspired by Baudrillard, my analysis has instead focused attention on a systematic comparison of signs and symbols and their *intermixture* in consumer culture, reading this intermixture as the very "stuff," the content, the material through which consumer subjectivity is both formed and animated by the commodity/sign. The historical shift from symbol to sign systems offers a way of rereading as well as qualifying pessimistic theories of modernity, especially Weber's treatment of rationalization, by recontextualizing them in the potentially opposing tendencies of consumer culture. I have attempted to show that critiques of consumerism would gain theoretically by translating the old language of manipulation and domination into a new language of signification *versus* symbolization. This distinction provides a new approach to the subjugating and liberating dimensions of consumer culture by holding them in tension, opening the concept of consumer culture to a range of possibilities.

My use of the semiotic perspective has also involved reframing it. While theories of signification claim to disclose the workings of language and culture-in-general, these theories have largely failed to develop a reflexive understanding of their own relationship to consumer culture. Semiotics has yet to be fully understood as the cultural strategy of consumer capitalism. At the same time, I have pointed to the process of symbolization as a means of creating meaning outside the commodity/sign system and therefore as a source of transformative possibilities for changing the culture of consumption. As a locus of the creative features of self, symbolization is the main line of defense against the dominating and oppressive features of capitalist modernity as well as a source of cultural and social renewal.

Finally, a theory of signs and symbols adequate to an understanding of the problems and prospects of consumption would need to address the aesthetic dimension of commodity society. Its ties to the sales effort notwithstanding, the massive transfer of aesthetic values from specialized institutions such as museums and art galleries back into daily life represents an unprecedented democratization of access to these values. Beholden to commodities and signs, the aesthetic has nevertheless been made available to large numbers of people, establishing itself as a criterion of use and pleasure value. The "strain toward the aesthetic" (Jaeger and Selznick 1964) inherent in culture everywhere reflects what appears to be a universal need for sensory meaning and enjoyment. That the aesthetic dimension contains liberatory potentials was an article of faith among key members of the Frankfurt School, particularly Adorno and Marcuse. While presently in the service of the commodity/sign, the aesthetic impulse inheres in processes of symbolization, shaping symbolic experience and meaning, as seen in its purest form in the realm of art. As John Dewey (1958) taught us, however, there are ways of thinking about the aesthetic that make it an essential part of our experience as living creatures and that bring it into the arena of everyday social life unencumbered by the dictates of a code. Accordingly, the aesthetic dimension has enormous relevance for the potential in objects and acts of consumption for genuine selfhood, identity, and connectedness to others.

Notes

Chapter 1: The Triumph of the Commodity: Theoretical Lineages

1. It is instructive that the word "consume" has always carried connotations of wasting or expending. Webster's Third New International Dictionary gives as its first definition, "to destroy or do away with completely" and its second, "to spend wastefully: squandor." Far from what economists have meant by the term, these meanings come closer to what some critics have said of modern consumerism.

2. Bourdieu is perhaps an exception to this rule, although the commodity as such is relatively absent from this work, which is more concerned with the class-differentiated symbolic meanings of objects.

3. See Marx (1973), p. 89, footnote 9.

4. See Frisby (1990) and Plotke (1975) for informative discussions.

5. Weber makes the argument that Marx's theory of alienation in the workplace was merely a limited case of a more general phenomena of rationalization occurring in noneconomic institutions such as the government and military, as if this constituted a critique of Marx's attribution of dehumanization to capitalist exploitation. Lukacs turns the tables on Weber by speaking of "the *capitalist* process of rationalization based on *private economic* calculation" (Lukacs 1971, 102, my emphasis). Thus, Lukacs rereads Weber's rationalization theme back into the context of capitalism and commodification. He uses Weberian *language* and Weber's totalization of the rationalization idea to make the argument that rationalization is at bottom an economic process based upon the production and exchange of commodities and the turning of labor into a commodity, all of

which in turn give society as a whole the structure of the commodity form. Calculation, the core of rationalization, presupposes social relations of *exchange*. Lukacs also seems to be arguing that reification has its origins in the commodity form only in the most general sense (the commodity penetrates the larger society), but that in a more specific sense, reification arises from the commodification of *labor*—the worker comes to see the social world *generally* as a structure of commodities because he himself, or rather his labor power, has already been transformed into a commodity. Finally, Lukacs also seems to suggest that the problematic subject-object split of modernity originates in commodification insofar as the worker comes to experience himself as both subject and object as a direct consequence of having his labor power (his "only possession" [ibid., 92]) commodified, turned into an object.

6. My rendering of the Frankfurt School will omit the work of Walter Benjamin, whose monumental *The Arcades Project* (1999) represents a uniquely ambitious and complex investigation into the culture of nineteenth-century capitalism. Benjamin is a brilliant and provocative figure in the theoretical literature on commodity society. However, given the complex and arcane character of his thought and method, it would be virtually impossible to do justice to his work in a brief summary. For a penetrating and inspiring treatment of this difficult thinker, see Buck-Morss (1989). See also the essay by Tiedemann, "Dialectics at a Standstill: Approaches to the *Passagen-Werk*," in *The Arcades Project*, pp. 929–945.

7. Much of the following discussion is based on Dunn 1986b.

8. In his revision of Galbraith's main argument in *The Affluent Society*, Hirsch (1976) uses this same term but with a different meaning than the one intended here.

9. In at least one interpretation, Lasch's efforts to link hedonism and narcissism suggests a Sade-like connection between the pursuit of pleasure and aggressive, predatory behavior patterns. See Gabriel and Lang (1995).

10. Campbell raises a number of pertinent questions about the place of fantasy, daydreaming, and longing in consumption, issues to be discussed in Chapter Three.

11. It is a poorly kept secret that professional marketing, sales, packaging, and especially advertising strategists know all about the commercial uses of Freud's theory of the id and the unconscious.

12. For the classic statement on Marx's theory of need, see Heller (1974).

Chapter 2: Culturalizing Consumption

1. The term has even acquired popularity in the vocabulary of the professional-managerial strata of specialists in business, government, and other bureaucratic organizations, who now speak of the "culture" of a firm, workplace, political party, and so forth.

2. The term "linguistic turn" is usually associated with the groundbreaking philosophical work of Ludwig Wittgenstein.

3. Semiotics is the study of signs or sign systems. This field was pioneered by the French theorist Ferdinand de Saussure (1966), who used the term "semiology," and the American pragmatist Charles Pierce (1931), whose preferred term "semiotics" has been widely adopted. For a useful discussion of these thinkers and their differences, and lineages of semiotic theory, see Gottdiener (1995). Structuralism is a varied body of work most closely connected to the anthropologist Claude Levi-Strauss (1963). Poststructuralism is a loose aggregrate of ideas focusing on the instabilities of language, discourse, and meaning. For general discussions see Coward and Ellis (1977) and Kurzweil (1980).

4. Anthropology has typically defined culture as "a way of life." For definitions, see Kroeber and Kluckhohn (1963).

5. Following Gottdiener (1995, 10), I use this term to mean the process of producing and consuming signs. As I argue later, images and information come to us increasingly in the form of signs.

6. This process is accompanied by a weakening of the earlier separation of production from consumption brought about by new modes of consumer participation. Consumers now enjoy increasing access to the means of cultural production, including photography, video, computer, Internet, talk shows, and a range of "alternative" mass media.

7. See the *Mirror of Production* (1975).

8. As derived mainly from Pierce as opposed to Saussure, in semiotic theory a "sign" is comprised of three components: to simplify, a "signifier" (image, sound), a "signified" (concept, idea), and a "referent" (object, event in real world).

9. "One cannot fully understand cultural practices unless 'culture,' in the restricted, normative sense of ordinary usage, is brought back into 'culture' in the anthropological sense" (Bourdieu 1984, 1).

10. The corpus of Bourdieu's work has been anchored in the concept of "habitus," a concept he deploys as a strategy for overcoming the subject/object dichotomy or "agency"/"structure" problem. For definitions and discussion, see Bourdieu 1977 and Swartz 1997.

11. Symbolic power is "a legitimating power that elicits the consent of both the dominant and the dominated" (Swartz 1997, 89). Compare Gramsci's notion of "hegemony" (Gramsci 1973).

12. According to Swartz, "Field struggle centers around particular forms of capital: economic, cultural, scientific, or religious. . . . In other words, *fields are arenas of struggle for legitimation*" (1997, 122–23, original emphasis).

13. While there is creative tension throughout Bourdieu's writings between the "subjective" and "objective" poles of social reality, and while his concept of habitus was designed to overcome this chronic opposition, in *Distinction,* and many would argue throughout most of his work, the objective

pole tends to prevail in the form of a distinctively structuralist mode of expla-nation (and this despite his attacks on structuralism).

14. The weight of evidence would seem to support Weber.

15. The applicability of Bourdieu's theory to the United States has been a topic of extensive debate. For an overview of the literature and a reformula-tion supporting Bourdieu's relevance, see Holt (1998).

16. Interestingly, the index of *Distinction*—an extremely lengthy text—lists only fifteen references to the term.

17. For overviews, see Blundell et al. (1993); Grossberg et al. (1992); Long (1997); Morley and Chen (1996); Nelson and Gaonkar (1996); and Storey (1996).

Chapter 3: The Subjectivity of Consumption

1. Marx (1959, 320).

2. In theoretical sociology, these competing images and models of so-cial life have been represented by symbolic interactionism ("individual," "process") and structural-functionalism ("society," "structure"), respectively (see Dunn 1972). By contrast, Marxian theory has always implicitly incorpo-rated key elements of both theories within an historical framework that ac-knowledges the importance of process *and* structure from a conflict perspective.

3. The most extensive treatment can be found in the work of Giddens, who has been a leading writer on this issue (1979, 1984).

4. These would include the early Talcott Parsons, symbolic interaction-ism, phenomenology, hermeneutics, ethnomethodology, language theory, communication theory, and related developments. For a discussion, see Gid-dens (1984).

5. See Giddens' ambitious structuration theory (1979, 1984) and Bour-dieu's concept of "habitus" (1977). See also Archer (1988), who makes a case for a "culture and agency" problem, which she rightly believes parallels and needs connection to the "structure and agency" problem.

6. I believe this is even the case with Giddens' important work on "struc-turation." Despite the appeal of his proposal to substitute "duality" for "dual-ism," his formulations and end point remain fundamentally structural in nature.

7. I intend to use these terms in a non-Parsonsian fashion. See Talcott Parsons (1951).

8. This statement endorses the validity and importance of symbolic inter-actionism (Blumer 1969) without rigidly adopting its position.

9. See George Ritzer (1993/1996).

10. Taking his cues from Veblen, Douglas and Isherwood, and Baudril-lard, Appadurai (1986), stresses the sociality components of commodity "needs" even more strongly than Haug or Berger.

11. For an overview of theory and findings, see Gitlin (1978) and Lembo (2000). For a more general critique of the Frankfurt School, see Kellner (1983).

12. I use the terms "active" and "resistant" only to mark familiar reference points to cultural studies. In fact, there has always been something misplaced in using these terms in talking about spaces of opposition. Certainly, one can be active in one's own oppression. As Slater points out: "Being active in one's consumption . . . does not mean being free (textually or socially) let alone oppositional" (1997, 171).

13. For relevant passages, see Weber (1958a, 1958b) and Durkheim (1951, 1961, 1964).

14. Historically, the eroticization of commodities has for familiar reasons been the work of men. Haug's comments (1986 19) on the essentially erotic appeal of commodity aesthetics are common to critical theories of consumer culture and entirely consistent with the folklore of advertisers and designers, particularly those in the Freudian camp of these industries.

15. See Simmel's discussion of the development of objects from utilitarian to aesthetic value, which he argues is "a process of objectification" defined by the increasing distance of subject and object (1990, 73–75). Simmel is referring here to the breakdown of the preindustrial/capitalist unity of subject and object, user and used, resulting from socioeconomic development. As the world fills with objects that are separated from their original utilitarian purposes and use contexts, they become autonomous, losing their utilitarian value and assuming greater importance in terms of their appearance, as objects of visual perception.

16. The vocabulary of "true" and "false" belongs to a discourse of logic and verification, not a discourse of needs. When used in relation to the concept of need, these categories become rhetorical devices leading to problematic value judgments. The determination of need is a function of time, place, culture, individuals, and material circumstances. Marcuse's distinction provides no criteria for determining where need begins and ends. Beyond the level of basic physical and psychological survival, the notion of need becomes amorphous. On the problem of needs, see Leiss (1976).

17. Unfortunately, Haug's treatment of commodity aesthetics suffers from his continued reliance on "need."

18. Campbell engages in a roundabout criticism of Baudrillard by critiquing Veblen's narrow conception of consumption as an activity driven by emulation of others. The meanings of consumption, Campbell rightly argues, cannot be reduced to emulative spending and, by implication, to the commodity/sign system.

19. Modern modes of representation (including "bourgeois" art) were very much responsible for transforming much of the Romantic worldview and sensibility into individual subjective states within the everyday context of consumer goods and social relations, especially in the nineteenth century. See Clark (1984).

20. See Weber (1958a, 1958b).

21. While Campbell's claim is a departure from his previous statement that consumers consume "fantasies," nothing is to prevent one from holding both positions.

22. Campbell's view is entirely consistent with Scitovsky's argument while providing a cultural dimension missing from the latter.

23. Leiss, too, employs the term "need" where "want" would be more appropriate. The interchangeable use of "need," "want," and "desire" weakens his argument.

24. By emphasizing the fragmenting effects of high-intensity consumption, Leiss offers what could be regarded as a postmodern view of commodity society. Self and identity are destabilized in the flood of novelty, the speedy pace of consumption, and whirlwind media images.

25. Indeed, with the rise of the service and entertainment industries there is increasing overlap of all three categories, with the category of entertainment assuming dominance. Not only do we consume ever-greater quantities of entertainment, but the latter has become the chief aspect or quality of all consuming activities, whether they be shopping, purchasing, using, or displaying. Facing unsatisfactory psychic (and monetary) rewards at work, the average consumer now has high expectations "to be entertained" away from the job. The blending of consumption and entertainment has two aspects: (1) the commodification of entertainment itself, such as in the mass media and other technologies, and 2) the weaving of entertainment into conventional forms of consumption, as exemplified in the amusement park/circus atmosphere of the shopping mall. Even the serious business of television advertising has been transformed into a highly sophisticated form of entertainment in a desperate effort to attract and hold audience attention.

26. In the fifties, Martha Wolfenstein (1955) detected a shift in child-training literature that she claims foreshadowed the rise of a "fun morality" in post-war American culture. In her view, play becomes "obligatory" as if it were a "duty," thus retaining remnants of an earlier Puritanism and its suspicion of unrestrained and unregulated pleasure. Just as the serious world of work has been infused with amusements, the world of leisure and play is now a serious endeavor in its own right.

27. In the *Fall of Public Man* (1992), Richard Sennett diagnoses the problem of narcissism differently as a displacement of a public by a private self.

Chapter 4: The Social Relations of Consumption

1. For a discussion of different approaches to lifestyle, see Holt (1997).

2. For instance, stratification research reviewed by DiMaggio (2001, 542–544) suggests that taste, a key element in lifestyle, shows a higher correlation with educational attainment than income or occupation. (It is not clear whether or not this research takes into account variations in type of education

and educational institution.) At the same time, other studies continue to show strong correlations between levels of education and income, suggesting that despite appearances, on some level consumption tastes are still at least indirectly structured by economic class variables. See Day and Newburger (2000). For an interesting attempt to disentangle the antecedents of consumption patterns based on Bourdieu's concept of cultural capital, see Holt (1998).

3. For example, see Halter (2000) on the "marketing of ethnicity."

4. These would be part of a category of scaled-down consumers that Juliet Schor (1998) calls "downshifters."

5. This narrow definition has its mirror opposite in the mistaken notion that lifestyle is a whole "way of life" or "living pattern," which wrongly equates it with "culture" in general.

6. However, as suggested in Chapter Two, impressionistic and research evidence do indicate much weaker and different kinds of correlations between class and lifestyle in the United States than in France and most other European countries. See Bourdieu (1984) and his critics, discussed and assessed in Holt (1998).

7. If we nonetheless feel more than ever before surrounded by conspicuous consumption, it is because previous lines of hierarchical competition are now increasingly effaced by *signs* (not realities) of spreading material abundance.

8. The authors of *Habit of the Heart*, who are concerned with the fate of community and character in the face of what the cover jacket of the book refers to as "fierce individualism," mainly see in the emergence of lifestyle a "narcissism of similarity" (1985, 72), a criticism that needs further questioning.

9. A striking development in mass circulation print media, especially newspapers, in recent years is the proliferation of "Style" and "Lifestyle" features, an innovation that speaks for itself. The contents of these features are an amalgam of articles and images falling outside conventional journalistic codes and formats. The seeming lack of a common theme in these sections is a curiosity in itself. Many newspapers have simply merged the old "Society Page" format, which is about social status, with fashion, shopping, home improvement, and entertainment features. The overall outcome, however, is dubious. While ostensibly addressing readers interested in lifestyle trends, these features are often hodgepodges of trivia, a padding that substitutes for serious journalistic writing.

10. For a broader statement on the cultural, social, and psychological functions of fashion, see Sapir (1937).

11. As I've argued elsewhere, "The logic of the commodity in this respect is inherently self-contradictory insofar as it both constructs *and* abolishes social distinctions" (Dunn 1998, 116).

12. Both of these disruptions of semiotic/symbolic status boundaries have reached their furthest extreme in the United States but are increasingly

commonplace in all Western industrialized countries as well as advanced parts of the developing world. This development would seem to lengthen the shadow already cast over Bourdieu's neat classificatory scheme of distinction.

13. Bauman argues that the market is an inherently democratizing force insofar as it recognizes no ranks, but only the power to spend: "All vehicles of inequality are denied but those of the price tag" (2001, 160). The market resists ascribed inequalities in favor of universal access—for those who can afford the price.

14. Naturally, I am talking about "democracy" outside the polling booth and workplace, but the democratizing character of consumer society is not without political implications. An appearance of spreading affluence, the faux upward mobility of mimicking the rich, the paltry celebration of blue-collar traditions in clothing and other commodities—all conspire to instill feelings of inclusiveness and equality in what is in reality a grossly unequal society. A common critical implication is that consumerism breeds passive acceptance of the status quo. In this respect, consumerism is a potent and perhaps insidious stabilizing force given the dramatic gaps between rich and poor, and the powerful and powerless. Consumerism, in Baudrillard's words, constitutes

> An equality before the Object and other *manifest* signs of social success and happiness. This is the *democracy of social standing*, the democracy of the TV, the car, and the stereo . . . which, beyond contradictions and social inequalities, corresponds to the formal democracy enshrined in the Constitution. Both of these, the one serving as a alibi for the other, combine in a general democratic ideology which conceals the *absence* of democracy and the nonexistence of equality. (1998, 50, original italics).

15. The following remarks are based primarily on personal field observations of an IKEA store in the San Francisco Bay Area and secondarily on other sources.

16. A popular acronym for "young, urban professionals," the mostly white and upwardly mobile new professional-managerial groups of the seventies who created the "latte" lifestyle so celebrated and satirized by the mass media.

17. Schor herself considers this a form of "competitive spending," which, as I've argued, is problematic.

18. "Lifestyles of The Rich and Famous" was the title of a popular television show in the eighties and nineties featuring voyeuristic images of extremely wealthy and extravagantly spending members of the upper class. This was only the most unabashed and indulgent of numerous television programs from this period, fictional and otherwise, portraying the luxuries (and hazards) of life in the upper class.

19. Schor argues that "the group that defines material success, luxury, and comfort for nearly every category below it" is "the upper middle class," which she defines as the upper 20 percent of the population, excluding the top few percent of the super-rich (ibid., 13). While for many reasons it's plausible to assume that media advertising has concentrated on this lifestyle range, making it the dominant ideal, "lifestyle television" has not hesitated to draw upon enchanting images from the lives of the *very* rich and privileged, stretching the audience's perception of the possible even more unrealistically than Schor suggests.

20. Peter Lunt notes a recent shift in research on consumption from an emphasis on the status meanings of goods toward "the way that goods provide opportunities for self-expression and personal development" (1995, 249).

Chapter 5: The Identity of Consumption

1. Some reasons for this state of affairs are discussed in my *Identity Crises* (1998).

2. The growing significance placed on the individual's inner life was a chief feature of Romanticism. For discussion of this and later variants of modern identity, see Baumeister (1986).

3. For a clear and concise example of how modern identity has been theorized, see Hewitt's model of identity. He lists four conditions of identity formation: continuity, integration, identification, and differentiation (1989).

4. I refer mainly to the postmodernist strains in feminist, queer, and race theory.

5. An obvious parallel could be drawn here to David Riesman's (1950) theory of a shift from an "inner-directed" to an "other-directed" personality type, or more generally from an emphasis on "character" to "personality." However, in Riesman's other-directed type, "personality" is a product of novel situational dependencies on social relations, specifically a growth in peer group pressures, not signs and images.

6. A discourse of performativity presupposes that human behavior and social practices are formally and perhaps substantively no different from the practices of fiction, theater, television and other forms of entertainment. Also, the postmodern rhetoric of performance can be read as a way of rehabilitating notions of action and agency following their eclipse in structuralist and post-structuralist theory, without losing the element of textuality or cultural script. For additional comments, see Dunn (1998, 236, footnote 12). Also, contexts for the emergence of this idea can be found in the work of Goffman (1959, 1967) and Butler (1990).

7. For a lengthy treatment of modern and postmodern constructs of consumption, see Firat and Dholakia (1998).

8. This is the belief that identity is innate. "Essentialism is classically defined as a belief in true essence—that which is most irreducible,

unchanging, and therefore constitutive of a given person or thing" (Fuss 1989, 2).

9. This mistake exemplifies the uncritical nature of a certain type of postmodernist thinking. The vogue in understanding identity as constructed and the correlative postmodernist emphasis on fluidity and hybridity play right into "free market" ideology, which assumes unconstrained choice in a vast and unfettered marketplace. While containing a kernel of truth, this perception denies the presence of a system that draws boundaries around and sets limits on identity formation. Furthermore, this view involves a strong class bias. It presupposes an educated, middle- or upper-middle-class subject with the material and symbolic resources to act in ways that fit the formulaic postmodernist image of society and culture. It excludes the large subpopulation of working and lower class subjects, whose consumption habits are not only different from those higher up the ladder but obviously constricted by material circumstances. Holt adds:

> One might speculate that postmodern theorists are embedded so deeply in the HCC ("Higher Cultural Capital"—RD) habitus that they are unable to muster the requisite sociological reflexivity to note that the ability to playfully aestheticize a wide range of consumption objects is esteemed, and so has become naturalized, in their social circles, but not in those of lower social classes. (1998, 22)

10. This is common in the case of one's cultural identity, the classic examples being ethnicity and nationality. See Halter (2000).

11. Statements about actors "choosing" lifestyle, and the idea of consumer choice generally, reverberate an age-old problem. Lurking in the tensions between voluntarism and the determinist implications of structure is the familiar philosophical bogeyman of "free will" versus "determinism." In social theory, the notion of choice will always remain problematic given all we know about structure, culture, socialization, social control, and the distribution of resources.

12. For example, see Stayman and Deshpande (1989).

13. For further elucidation of these ideas, see Blumer (1969), Dunn (1998), Mead (1934), and Wiley (1994).

14. Mead was vague regarding the internal process whereby we actually incorporate and integrate the viewpoints or attitudes of others into our self-conception. In a subtheory of the Meadian conception of a social self, Charles Horton Cooley (1964) invoked the notion of the "looking-glass" self. According to Cooley, our sense or conception of self is based on how we *imagine* others see us (184). Others function as a mirror for how we see ourselves. For a general statement of the psychology of this process, see Wicklund and Gollwitzer (1982). In a creative coupling of the psychology of Karl Lewin to the social psychology of Mead, the authors argue that self-definition is based

upon an assemblage and display of symbols that are recognized by others. Self-identity is constituted out of symbolic claims that are validated by the community.

15. There is a considerable body of research on the branding phenomenon. For example, see Fournier (1998) and Muniz and O'Guinn (2001).

16. Individual and collective efforts to escape the commercial marketplace are a subject unto itself with a history at least as old as modernity. In the contemporary West, examples of such efforts appear to be on the increase as more consumers become dissatisfied with commercialism and corporate culture. However, these efforts are mostly episodic in nature, taking the form of festivals and other carnivalesque practices that are group-based and temporal. For an interesting case study, see Kozinets (2002).

17. Collecting is an activity that epitomizes this type of consumption. See Belk (1995).

References

Adorno, T.W. 1941a. The Radio Symphony. In *Radio Research*, ed. Paul Lazarsfeld and Frank Stanton, 110–139. New York: Duell, Sloan, and Pierce.

———. 1941b. On Popular Music. *Studies in Philosophy and Social Science* 1 (1): 17–48.

———. 1945. A Social Critique of Radio Music. *Kenyon Review* 7 (2): 208–217.

———. 1957. Television and the Patterns of Mass Culture. In *Mass Culture: The Popular Arts in America*, ed. Bernard Rosenberg and David Manning White, 474–488. Glencoe, IL: The Free Press.

———. 1976. Popular Music. In *Introduction to the Sociology of Music*, 21–38. New York: Seabury Press.

———. 1978. On the Fetish-Character in Music and the Regression of Listening. In *The Essential Frankfurt School Reader*, ed. Andrew Arato and Eike Gebhardt, 270–299. New York: Urizen Books.

——— and Max Horkheimer. 1972. The Culture Industry: Enlightenment as Mass Deception. In *Dialectic of Enlightenment*, 120–167. New York: Seabury Press.

Appadurai, Arjun, ed. 1986. *The Social Life of Things: Commodities in Cultural Perspective*. New York: Cambridge University Press.

Archer, Margaret S. 1988. *Culture and Agency: The Place of Culture in Social Theory*. Cambridge: Cambridge University Press.

Baran, Paul and Paul Sweezy. 1966. *Monopoly Capital*. New York: Monthly Review Press.

Barthes, Roland. 1957. *Mythologies*. New York: Hill and Wang.

———. 1964. *Elements of Semiology*. New York: Hill and Wang.

Baudrillard, Jean. 1975. *The Mirror of Production*. St. Louis: Telos Press.

———. 1981. *For a Critique of the Political Economy of the Sign*. St. Louis: Telos Press

———. 1988. *Jean Baudrillard: Selected Writings*, ed. Mark Poster. Stanford: Stanford University Press.

———. 1993. *Symbolic Exchange and Death*. London: Sage Publications.

———. 1998. *The Consumer Society*. London: Sage Publications.

Bauman, Zygmunt. 1988. *Freedom*. Minneapolis: University of Minnesota Press.

———. 1992. *Intimations of Postmodernity*. London: Routledge.

———. 1999. The Self in Consumer Society. *The Hedgehog Review* (Fall 1999): 35–40.

——— and Tim May. 2001. *Thinking Sociologically*, 2nd ed. Malden, MA: Blackwell Publishing.

Baumeister, Roy. 1986. *Identity: Cultural Change and the Struggle for Self*. New York: Oxford University Press.

Belk, Russell W. 1988. Possessions and the Extended Self. *Journal of Consumer Research* 15 (September): 139–68.

———. 1995. *Collecting in a Consumer Society*. London: Routledge.

Belk, Russell, Guliz Ger, and Soren Askegaard. 2000. The Missing Streetcar Named Desire. In *The Why of Consumption: Contemporary Perspectives on Consumer Motives, Goals, and Desires*, ed. S. Ratneshwar, David Glen Mick, and Cynthia Huffman, 98–119. London: Routledge.

Bell, Daniel. 1978. *The Cultural Contradictions of Capitalism*. New York: Basic Books.

Bellah, Robert N., Richard Madsen, William M. Sullivan, Ann Swidler, and Steven Tipton. 1985. *Habits of the Heart: Individualism and Commitment in American Life*. Berkeley: University of California Press.

Benjamin, Walter. 1999. *The Arcades Project*. Cambridge, MA: Belknap/Harvard University Press.

Berger, John. 1972. *Ways of Seeing*. Hammondsworth, Middlesex: Pelican.

Berger, Peter L. and Thomas Luckman. 1967. *The Social Construction of Reality: A Treatise in the Sociology of Knowledge*. Garden City: Anchor Books.

Blumer, Herbert. 1969. *Symbolic Interactionism: Perspective and Method*. Englewood Cliffs: Prentice Hall.

Blundell, Valda, John Shepherd, and Ian Taylor, ed. 1993. *Relocating Cultural Studies: Developments in Theory and Research*. London: Routledge.

Bocock, Robert. 1993. *Consumption*. London: Routledge.

Butler, Judith. 1990. *Gender Trouble: Feminism and the Subversion of Identity*. New York: Routledge.

Bourdieu, Pierre. 1977. *Outline of a Theory of Practice*. Cambridge: Cambridge University Press.

———. 1984. *Distinction: A Social Critique of the Judgement of Taste*. Cambridge, MA: Harvard University Press.

———. 1991. *Language and Symbolic Power*, ed. John B. Thompson. Cambridge, MA: Harvard University Press.

Brake, Mike. 1980. *The Sociology of Youth Culture and Youth Subcultures*. London: Routledge and Kegan Paul.

Buck-Morss, Susan. 1989. *The Dialectics of Seeing: Walter Benjamin and the Arcades Project*. Cambridge, MA: MIT Press.

Campbell, Colin. 1987. *The Romantic Ethic and the Spirit of Modern Consumerism*. Oxford: Basil Blackwell.

———. 1995. The Sociology of Consumption. In *Acknowledging Consumption: A Review of New Studies*, ed. Daniel Miller, 96–126. London: Routledge.

Chaney, David. 1996. *Lifestyles*. London: Routledge.

Clark, T.J. 1984. *The Painting of Modern Life: Paris in the Art of Manet and his Followers*. Princeton, NJ: Princeton University Press.

Clarke, John. 1991. *New Times and Old Enemies: Essays on Cultural Studies and America*. London: Harper-Collins.

Cooley, Charles Horton. 1964. *Human Nature and the Social Order*. New York: Schocken.

Coward, Rosalind and John Ellis. 1977. *Language and Materialism: Developments in Semiology and the Theory of the Subject*. London: Routledge and Kegan Paul.

Cross, Gary. 2000. *An All-Consuming Century: Why Commercialism Won in Modern America*. New York: Columbia University Press.

Davis, Fred. 1992. *Fashion, Culture, and Identity*. Chicago: University of Chicago Press.

Davis, Joseph. 2003. The Commodification of Self. *The Hedgehog Review* 5 (2): 41–49.

Day, Jennifer Cheeseman and Eric C. Newburger. 2002. The Big Payoff: Educational Attainment and Synthetic Estimates of Work-Life Earnings. *Current Population Reports, United States Bureau of the Census* (March).

Debord, Guy. 1977. *Society of the Spectacle*. Detroit: Black and Red.

Deleuze, Gilles and Felix Guattari. 1983. *Anti-Oedipus: Capitalism and Schizophrenia*. Minneapolis: University of Minnesota Press.

Dewey, John. 1958. *Art As Experience*. New York: Capricorn Books.

DiMaggio, Paul. 2001. Social Stratification, Lifestyle, Social Cognition, and Social Participation. In *Social Stratification: Class, Race, and Gender in Sociological Perspective*, ed. David B. Grusky, 542–44. Boulder, CO: Westview Press.

Dittmar, Helga. 1992. *The Social Psychology of Material Possessions*. New York: St. Martins.

Douglas, Mary and Baron Isherwood. 1996. *The World of Goods: Towards an Anthropology of Consumption*. London: Routledge.

Duesenberry, James S. 1949. *Income, Saving and the Theory of Consumer Behavior*. Cambridge, MA: Harvard University Press.

Dunn, Robert G. 1972. On the Compatibility of Symbolic Interactionism and Structural-Functionalism in Contemporary Sociology: A Study of Theoretical Models. Unpublished PhD dissertation, UC Berkeley.

———. 1986a. Television, Consumption, and the Commodity Form. *Theory, Culture, and Society* 3 (1): 49–64.

———. 1986b. Mass Media and Society: The Legacy of T. W. Adorno and the Frankfurt School. *California Sociologist* 9 (1–2): 109–143.

———. 1998. *Identity Crises: A Social Critique of Postmodernity*. Minneapolis: University of Minnesota Press.

Durkheim, Emile. 1951. *Suicide*. Glencoe, IL: The Free Press.

———. 1961. *The Elementary Forms of the Religious Life*. New York: Collier Books.

———. 1964. *The Division of Labor in Society*. New York: The Free Press.

Ewen, Stuart. 1976. *Captains of Consciousness: Advertising and the Social Roots of Consumer Culture*. New York: McGraw-Hill.

———. 1988. *All Consuming Images: The Politics of Style in Contemporary Culture*. New York: Basic Books.

Ewen, Stuart and Elizabeth Ewen. 1982. *Channels of Desire: Mass Images and the Shaping of American Consciousness*. New York: McGraw-Hill.

Featherstone, Mike. 1991. *Consumer Culture and Postmodernism*. London: Sage.

Featherstone, Mike, Mike Hepworth, and Brian S. Turner, ed. 1991. *The Body: Social Process and Cultural Theory*. London: Sage.

Feuerbach, Ludwig. 1957. *The Essence of Christianity*. New York: Frederick Ungar Publishing Company.

Fine, Ben. 1995. From Political Economy to Consumption. In *Acknowledging Consumption: A Review of New Studies*, ed. Daniel Miller, 127–163. London: Routledge.

Firat, A. Fuat, and Nikhilesh Dholakia. 1998. *Consuming People: From Political Economy to Theaters of Consumption*. London: Routledge.

Fiske, John. 1987. *Television Culture*. London: Methuen.

———. 1989a. *Reading the Popular*. London: Routledge.

———. 1989b. *Understanding the Popular*. London: Routledge.

Fournier, Susan. 1998. Consumers and Their Brands: Developing Relationship Theory in Consumer Research. *Journal of Consumer Research* 24 (4) (March): 343–373.

Fox, Richard Wightman, and T. J. Jackson Lears, eds. 1983. *The Culture of Consumption*. New York: Pantheon.

Frank, Robert, and Philip J. Cook. 1995. *The Winner-Take-All Society.* New York: Free Press.

Frisby, David. 1988. *Fragments of Modernity.* Cambridge, MA: The MIT Press.

————. 1990. Preface to the Second Edition, xv-xlii, and Introduction to the Translation, 1–49. In *The Philosophy of Money,* by Georg Simmel. London: Routledge.

Fuss, Diana. 1989. *Essentially Speaking: Feminism, Nature, and Difference.* New York: Routledge.

————. 1995. *Identification Papers.* New York: Routledge.

Gabriel, Yiannis, and Tim Lang. 1995. *The Unmanageable Consumer: Contemporary Consumption and Its Fragmentations.* London: Sage.

Galbraith, John Kenneth. 1958. *The Affluent Society.* New York: Mentor.

Gans, Herbert J. 1974. *Popular Culture and High Culture: An Analysis and Evaluation of Taste.* New York: Basic Books.

Gerth, H.H. and C. Wright Mills, eds. 1958. *From Max Weber: Essays in Sociology.* New York: Galaxy.

Giddens, Anthony. 1979. *Central Problems in Social Theory: Action, Structure, and Contradiction in Social Analysis.* Berkeley: University of California Press.

————. 1984. *The Constitution of Society: Outline of the Theory of Structuration.* Berkeley: University of California Press.

————. 1991. *Modernity and Self-Identity: Self and Society in the Late Modern Age.* Stanford: Stanford University Press.

Gitlin, Todd. 1978. Media Sociology. *Theory and Society* 6 (2), 205–254.

Goffman, Erving. 1959. *The Presentation of Self in Everyday Life.* New York: Doubleday & Company.

————. 1967. *Interaction Ritual: Essays on Face-to-Face Behavior.* Garden City, NJ: Doubleday Anchor.

Goldman, Robert. 1983/1984. "We Make Weekends": Leisure and the Commodity Form. *Social Text* 8 (Winter): 84–103.

Gottdiener, Mark. 1995. *Postmodern Semiotics: Material Culture and the Forms of Postmodern Life.* Oxford: Blackwell.

————. 2000. *New Forms of Consumption: Consumers, Culture, and Commodification.* Lanham: Rowman and Littlefield.

Gramsci, Antonio. 1973. *Prison Notebooks.* New York: International Publishers.

Grossberg, Lawrence, Cary Nelson, and Paula Treichler, ed. 1992. *Cultural Studies.* New York: Routledge.

Habermas, Jurgen. 1983. Modernity—An Incomplete Project. In *The Anti-Aesthetic: Essays on Postmodern Culture,* ed. Hal Foster, 3–15. Port Townsend, WA: Bay Press.

————. 1984. *The Theory of Communicative Action,* vol. 1, *Reason and the Rationalization of Society.* Boston: Beacon Press.

Hall, Calvin S. and Gardner Lindzey. 1968. The Relevance of Freudian Psychology and Related Viewpoints for the Social Sciences. In *The Handbook of Social Psychology*, vol. 1, ed. Lindzey and Elliot Aronson, 245–318. Reading, MA: Addison-Wesley.

Hall, Stuart. 1980. Encoding/Decoding. In *Culture, Media, Language*, ed. Stuart Hall, Dorothy Hobson, Andrew Lowe, and Paul Willis, 128–138. London: Hutchinson.

———. 1990. The Emergence of Cultural Studies and the Crisis of the Humanities. *October*, 53: 11–90.

———. 1996. Cultural Studies: Two Paradigms. In *What is Cultural Studies? A Reader*, ed. John Storey, 31–48. London: Arnold.

Hall, Stuart and Tony Jefferson, eds. 1976. *Resistance Through Rituals: Youth Subcultures in Post-War Britain*. London: Unwin Hyman.

Halter, Marilyn. 2000. *Shopping for Identity: The Marketing of Ethnicity*. New York: Schocken Books.

Harvey, David. 1989. *The Condition of Postmodernity*. Oxford: Basil Blackwell.

Haug, W.F. 1986. *Critique of Commodity Aesthetics: Appearance, Sexuality and Advertising in Capitalist Society*. Minneapolis: University of Minnesota.

———. 1987. *Commodity Aesthetics, Ideology, and Culture*. New York: International General.

Hebdige, Dick. 1979. *Subculture: The Meaning of Style*. London: Methuen.

Heller, Agnes. 1974. *The Theory of Need in Marx*. London: Allison and Busby.

Hewitt, John. 1989. *Dilemmas of the American Self*. Philadelphia: Temple University Press.

Hirsch, Fred. 1976. *Social Limits to Growth*. Cambridge, MA: Harvard University Press.

Hoggart, Richard. 1957. *The Uses of Literacy: Changing Patterns in English Mass Culture*. Boston: Beacon.

Holt, Douglas B. 1997. Poststructuralist Lifestyle Analysis: Conceptualizing the Social Patterning of Consumption in Postmodernity. *Journal of Consumer Research* 23 (March): 326–50.

———. 1998. Does Cultural Capital Structure American Consumption? *Journal of Consumer Research* 25 (June): 1–25.

Huyssen, Andreas. 1986. *After the Great Divide: Modernism, Mass Culture, Postmodernism*. Bloomington, IN: Indiana University Press.

Jaeger, Gertrude and Philip Selznick. 1964. A Normative Theory of Culture. *American Sociological Review* 29: 653–669.

Jameson, Fredric. 1979. Reification and Utopia in Mass Culture. *Social Text* 1: 130–148.

———. 1984. Postmodernism, or the Cultural Logic of Late Capitalism. *New Left Review* 146: 53–92.

Jay, Martin. 1993. *Downcast Eyes: The Denigration of Vision in Twentieth-Century French Thought*. Berkeley: University of California Press.

Jenkins, Richard. 1996. *Social Identity*. London and New York: Routledge

Joas, Hans. 1996. *The Creativity of Action*. Chicago: The University of Chicago Press.

Kellner, Douglas. 1983. Critical Theory, Commodities, and the Consumer Society. *Theory, Culture, and Society* 1 (3): 66–83.

———. 1989. *Jean Baudrillard: From Marxism to Postmodernism and Beyond*. Stanford: Stanford University Press.

Klein, Naomi. 1999. *No Logo*. New York: Picador USA.

Kovel, Joel. 1981. *The Age of Desire: Case Histories of a Radical Psychoanalyst*. New York: Pantheon Books.

Kozinets, Robert V. 2002. Can Consumers Escape the Market? Emancipatory Illuminations from Burning Man. *Journal of Consumer Research* 29: 20–38.

Kroeber, A.L. and Clyde Kluckhohn. 1963. *Culture: A Critical Review of Concepts and Definitions*. New York: Vintage.

Kurzweil, Edith. 1980. *The Age of Structuralism: Levi-Strauss to Foucault*. New York: Columbia University Press.

Landon, E. Laird, Jr. 1974. Self-concept, Ideal Self-concept, and Consumer Purchase Intentions. *Journal of Consumer Research* 1 (2) (September): 44–51.

Lasch, Christopher. 1979. *The Culture of Narcissism*. New York: W.W. Norton and Company.

———. 1984. *The Minimal Self*. New York: W.W. Norton and Company.

Lash, Scott. 1990. *The Sociology of Postmodernism*. London: Routledge.

Leach, William. 1993. *Land of Desire: Merchants, Power, and the Rise of a New American Culture*. New York: Pantheon.

Lears, T.J. Jackson. 1983. From Salvation to Self-Realization: Advertising and the Therapeutic Roots of the Consumer Culture, 1880–1930. In *The Culture of Consumption: Critical Essays in American History 1880–1980*, ed. Richard Wightman Fox and T. J. Jackson Lears, 33–8. New York: Pantheon Books.

Lefebvre, Henri. 1984. *Everyday Life in the Modern World*. New Brunswick: Transaction Books.

Leiss, William. 1976. *The Limits to Satisfaction: An Essay on the Problem of Needs and Commodities*. Toronto: University of Toronto Press.

Lembo, Ron. 2000. *Thinking Through Television*. Cambridge: Cambridge University Press.

Lembo, Ronald and Kenneth H. Tucker, Jr. 1990. Culture, Television, and Opposition: Rethinking Cultural Studies. *Critical Studies in Mass Communication* 7: 97–116.

Levin, David Michael, ed. 1993. *Modernity and the Hegemony of Vision.* Berkeley: University of California Press.

Long, Elizabeth, ed. 1997. *From Sociology to Cultural Studies: New Perspectives.* Malden, MA: Blackwell.

Lowe, Donald M. 1995. *The Body in Late-Capitalist USA.* Durham: Duke University Press.

Lukacs, Georg. 1971. *History and Class Consciousness.* Cambridge, MA: The MIT Press.

Lunt, Peter. 1995. Psychological Approaches to Consumption. In *Acknowledging Consumption: A Review of New Studies,* ed. Daniel Miller, 238–263. London: Routledge.

Lury, Celia. 1996. *Consumer Culture.* New Brunswick, NJ: Rutgers University Press.

Malhotra, Naresh K. 1988. Self-concept and Product Choice: An Integrated Perspective. *Journal of Economic Psychology* 9: 1–28.

Marcuse, Herbert. 1964. *One-Dimensional Man.* Boston: Beacon Press.

Marx, Karl. 1906. *Capital.* New York: The Modern Library.

———. 1959. The Eighteenth Brumaire of Louis Bonaparte. In *Marx & Engels: Basic Writings on Politics and Philosophy,* ed. Lewis Feuer. Garden City, NY: Doubleday & Company.

———. 1973. *Grundrisse,* trans. Martin Nicolaus. New York: Vintage Books.

McCracken, Grant. 1988. *Culture and Consumption: New Approaches to the Symbolic Character of Consumer Goods and Activities.* Bloomington, IN: Indiana University Press.

McKendrick, Neil, John Brewer, and J.H. Plumb. 1982. *The Birth of a Consumer Society: The Commercialization of 18th Century England.* London: Europa Publications.

Mead, George Herbert. 1932. *The Philosophy of the Present.* Chicago: University of Chicago Press.

———. 1934. *Mind, Self and Society.* Chicago: University of Chicago Press.

Melluci, Alberto. 1996. *The Playing Self: Person and Meaning in the Planetary Society.* Cambridge: Cambridge University Press.

Miller, Daniel. 1991. *Material Culture and Mass Consumption.* Oxford: Blackwell.

Mills, C. Wright. 1956. *White Collar.* New York: Galaxy.

Morley, David. 1980. *The 'Nationwide' Audience.* London: British Film Institute.

———. 1986. *Family Television: Cultural Power and Domestic Leisure.* London: Comedia.

———. 1992. *Television Audiences and Cultural Studies.* London: Routledge.

Morley, David and Kuan-Hsing Chen, ed. 1996. *Stuart Hall: Critical Dialogues in Cultural Studies.* London: Routledge.

Mukerji, Chandra. 1983. *From Graven Images: Patterns of Modern Materialism.* New York: Columbia University Press.

Muniz, Jr., Albert M. and Thomas C. O'Guinn. 2002. Brand Community. *Journal of Consumer Research* 27 (4) (March): 412–432.

Nelson, Cary. 1996. Always Already Cultural Studies: Academic Conferences and a Manifesto. In *What is Cultural Studies? A Reader*, ed. John Storey. 273–286 London: Arnold.

———and Dilip Parameshwar Gaonkar, ed. 1996. *Disciplinarity and Dissent in Cultural Studies.* New York: Routledge.

Packard, Vance. 1957. *The Hidden Persuaders.* New York: Pocket Books.

———. 1959. *The Status Seekers.* New York: Pocket Books.

Parsons, Talcott. 1951. *The Social System.* Glencoe, IL: Free Press.

Patterson, Mark. 2006. *Consumption and Everyday Life.* London: Routledge.

Plotke, David. 1975. Marxism, Sociology and Crisis: Lukacs' Critique of Weber. *Berkeley Journal of Sociology* 20: 181–230.

Pusey, Michael. 1987. *Jurgen Habermas.* London: Tavistock Publications.

Riesman, David, with Nathan Glazer and Ruel Denney. 1950. *The Lonely Crowd: A Study of the Changing American Character.* New Haven, CT: Yale University Press.

Rifkin, Jeremy. 2000. *The Age of Access: The New Culture of Hypercapitalism Where All of Life is a Paid-For Experience.* New York: Jeremy P. Tarcher/Putnam.

Ritzer, George. 1993/1996. *The McDonaldization of Society.* Thousand Oaks, CA: Pine Forge Press.

Sapir, Edward. 1934. Fashion. *The Encyclopedia of the Social Sciences.* The Bobbs-Merrill Reprint Series in the Social Science, S-246, 139–144. New York: The MacMillan Co.

Schor, Juliet. 1998. *The Overspent American: Why We Want What We Don't Need.* New York: Harper Perennial.

———. 2000. *Do Americans Shop Too Much?* Boston: Beacon Press.

Scitovsky, Tibor. 1992. *The Joyless Economy: An Enquiry into Human Satisfaction and Consumer Dissatisfaction.* New York: Oxford University Press.

Sennett, Richard. 1992. *The Fall of Public Man.* New York: W. W. Norton & Company.

Shibutani, Tamotsu. 1955. Reference Groups as Perspectives. *American Journal of Sociology* 60: 562–569.

Simmel, Georg 1968. *Georg Simmel: The Conflict in Modern Culture and Other Essays*, trans. K. Peter Etzkorn. New York: Teachers College Press.

———. 1971. Fashion (1904). In *Georg Simmel on Individuality and Social Forms*, ed. Donald N. Levine, 294–323. Chicago: University of Chicago Press.

————. 1990. *The Philosophy of Money*, trans. Tom Bottomore and David Frisby. London: Routledge.

Slater, Don. 1997. *Consumer Culture and Modernity*. Cambridge: Polity Press.

Stayman, Douglas M. and Rohit Deshpande. 1998. Situational Ethnicity and Consumer Behavior. *Journal of Consumer Culture* 16 (3): 361–371.

Storey, John, ed. 1996. *What is Cultural Studies? A Reader*. London: Arnold.

Swartz, David. 1997. *Culture and Power: The Sociology of Pierre Bourdieu*. Chicago: The University of Chicago Press.

Thompson, E.P. 1966. *The Making of the English Working Class*. New York: Vintage.

Tocqueville, Alexis de. 1945. *Democracy in America*, vol. 2. New York: Vintage.

Turner, Bryan S. 1988. *Status*. Minneapolis: University of Minnesota Press.

Turner, Ralph H. 1956. Role-Taking, Role-Standpoint and Reference Group Behavior. *American Journal of Sociology* 61: 316–328.

Urry, John. 1990. *The Tourist Gaze*. London: Sage.

Veblen, Thorstein. 1934. *The Theory of the Leisure Class*. New York: Modern Library.

Warde, Alan. 1994. Consumers, Identity, and Belonging. In *The Authority of the Consumer*, ed. Russell Keat, Nigel Whiteley, and Nicholas Abercrombie, 58–74. London: Routledge.

Weber, Max. 1958a. *From Max Weber: Essays in Sociology*, ed. H.H. Gerth and C. Wright Mills. New York: Oxford University Press.

————. 1958b. *The Protestant Ethic and the Spirit of Capitalism*. New York: Charles Scribner's Sons.

Weingartner, Rudolph H. 1962. *Experience and Culture: The Philosophy of Georg Simmel*. Middletown, CT: Wesleyan University Press.

White, Leslie. 1949. *The Science of Culture*. New York: Farrar, Straus, and Giroux.

Wicklund, Robert A. and Peter M. Gollwitzer. 1982. *Symbolic Self-Completion*. Hillsdale, NJ: Lawrence Erlbaum.

Wiley, Norbert. 1994. *The Semiotic Self*. Chicago: University of Chicago Press.

Williams, Raymond. 1960. *Culture and Society: 1780–1950*. Garden City, NJ: Anchor Books.

Williams, Rosalind H. 1982. *Dreamworlds: Mass Consumption in Late 19th Century France*. Berkeley: University of California Press.

Willis, Paul. 1977. *Learning to Labor: How Working Class Kids Get Working Class Jobs*. New York: Columbia University Press.

————. 1978. *Profane Culture*. London: Routledge and Kegan Paul.

————. 1990. *Common Culture: Symbolic Work at Play in the Everyday Cultures of the Young*. Boulder, CO: Westview.

Willis, Susan. 1991. *A Primer for Daily Life*. London: Routledge.

Wolfenstein, Martha. 1955. Fun Morality: An Analysis of Recent American Child-Training Literature. In *Childhood in Contemporary Cultures*, ed. Margaret Mead and Martha Wolfenstein, 168–178. Chicago: University of Chicago Press

Index

Robert G. Dunn is Professor Emeritus, Department of Sociology, California State University, East Bay, and author of *Identity Crises: A Social Critique of Postmodernity*.